Scara

HAMPTON COURT

a history

The King's Staircase from Pyne's *History of the Royal Residences*
Courtesy of the British Museum

HAMPTON COURT
a history

by

PHILIP LINDSAY

Fellow of the Society of Antiquaries of Scotland
Fellow of the Royal Archæological Institute of Great Britain & Ireland

with
illustrations
by
Denis Duffield

MERIDIAN BOOKS ☉ LONDON
1948

FIRST PUBLISHED, JANUARY, 1948

REPRINTED, DECEMBER, 1948

Printed and Bound
in Great Britain by
Co-operative Wholesale Society Ltd.
at their
Printing Works, Longsight, Manchester
and Published by Meridian Books Ltd.
in conjunction with Good Books Ltd.

CONTENTS

ILLUSTRATIONS

ILLUSTRATIONS
By Denis Duffield

PRELUDE

A GREAT queen gave this house to us. But to call Hampton Court a house is to be, I fear, inaccurate. Rather is it a manor, a palace; yet I prefer to call it house, or even home, because it has been indeed the home of kings where crowns could be put by and dignity kicked off with tight shoes for the comfort of spiritual relaxation and of embroidered slippers cool to gouty feet. Here is not the crenellated grandeur of Windsor with its tubby motte and cold grey walls and its windy walks of which poor Fanny Burney moaned maliciously, if truthfully, nor the dank unfriendliness of the Tower of London. Hampton Court was a playground for kings and queens. St. James's Palace remained too tucked away, too over-peered by curious cits, and one understands why the early Georges failed to make of it a home and were continually hurrying from the fret of politics, when the state of the roads permitted, to the gardens of Richmond with their gothick hermitage and their Merlin's Cave in which you could spy the waxwork wizard seated day or night, in rain or sunshine, amongst wax worshippers; or to the parterres and the mazy Serpentine of Kensington, beloved of Anne.

St. James's was the palace of a formal court with the *bon ton* ever knocking at the door: fashion was too brightly close, crowding on royalty's brief hours of peace. And Whitehall was to be shunned with its shadow of a headless king and memories of a people's wrath and that laughing giant, Cromwell. Out of London must royalty speed if it would free itself from politics and an often too disrespectful mob, out it would race to discard its heavy crown and to hunt, to make merry or to sit in blissful family privacy. And from the days of Henry VIII to those of George II, no palace had such broad parks for hunting, such gardens in which to browse, such a reach of the river, should the day prove hot, on which to be rowed; no other palace near London had both the spaciousness and the intimacy of Hampton Court.

It was in 1837, as largesse on her accession to the throne, that plump young Queen Victoria opened this royal home for the people's delight, giving them the gardens and parklands and all the palace not occupied by those, or the relatives of those, who had shown the country some outstanding service.* Her descendants have followed this generous gesture and it is from the royal purse that the great costs of upkeep are still maintained. We may roam where we will in these grounds, loll on the grass and listen to the drowsy fountain, lose ourselves in the maze or our worries in the peace of the Tudor Pond Garden, watched by the leaden Venus poised guardian, secret and beautiful, over us. This palace is now ours, is yours and mine, save for those apartments given by what is rightly called " grace and favour " to the honoured servants of the nation. To the memory of one of those servants we must pay grateful homage, to the late Mr. Ernest Law, C.B., whose busy antiquarian passions revealed so many of the palace secrets. I cannot speak too highly of him, for when I began this book I was arrogantly certain of making Mr. Law's work out-of-date, and now humbly I confess that almost everywhere I dug I found that Mr. Law had dug before me and few are the facts I managed to find to supplement his three precious volumes. We will be meeting him often in these pages and this mention is merely the first bow, of respect as well as courtesy, before we follow his steps and spy into the palace.

Let us, for the moment, loiter in the grounds, roving around the palace. This is not yet the place to examine its history in detail while a survey of the walls gives us much of that history in panorama. In brick and stone and lead we can detect the different ages, different princes' dreams made solid and beautiful, and, strangely, the dreams do not clash, whatever their periods. From the east front of friendly Tudor brick we are abruptly, without warning, cut into Wren's massive work. Apologists have explained that this front was not built according to Wren's plans, that the top-storey which peeps at us, lurking behind Cibber's tympanum of *The Triumph of Hercules over Envy*, was added as an awful afterthought, the architect being

---

* That the gift was not popular with all classes is shown by the grumbling of the Rev. A. C. Cox in his *Impressions of England*. " Queen Victoria," he wrote, " should give it to the Church, as a college for the poor, and so add dignity to her benevolence, which has already turned it into a show for her darling ' lower classes.' I honour the queen for this condescension to the people; and yet, as I followed troops of John Gilpins through the old apartments, and observed their inanimate stare and booby admiration, it did strike me that a nobler and a larger benefit might be conferred upon them in a less incongruous way. Perhaps the happiest thought would be to make it for the clergy just what Chelsea is to the army and Greenwich to the naval service." Fortunately this " happiest thought " did not occur to the queen who must, indeed, have been surprised—had she happened upon the reverend gentleman's work —to discover that the " lower classes " were her " darlings."

so much more interested in beauty than utility that many court officials were fussing—that being the nature of court officials— because they had been given nowhere to sleep and, if one dare use the word, work. Wren thereupon popped them behind *Triumph over Envy*, surely with no malicious intent, obscuring many windows with that boisterous bas-relief and blotting others from his sight.

The East Front.

There is decidedly something "wrong" about this east front, but whether it be these semi-blotted-out officials' windows, or the Tudor chimneys poking giraffe-like over all, or merely Mr. Cibber's chiselling, it is difficult to say. It depresses me with its suggestion of a tiered birthday-cake, the candles blown out, the icing hardening in its drips, and the child for whom it was made being sobbed to sleep elsewhere. Let us, I pray, turn our backs and soothe our eyes with that long and lovely Little Canal beyond the avenue of limes.

For that is one of the delights of Hampton Court. When one blinks away from too many paintings, mostly bad, from too many musty unlived-in rooms, when one turns from Wren's opulent façade, one enters the ordered pastoral world of Watteau or Fragonard and glimpses the poet, Pope, behind a tree. Or should you prefer a coarse, more human world, there is the exquisite little Tudor knot garden for which we must thank, as we will be continually thanking for many benefits, the memory of Mr. Law. Not that this garden is " coarse," it is most delicately arranged, but it brings us solidly to life, to a world in which virtue might be rewarded with the axe's edge and beauty with men's honour could be cheaply bought. But it is not my intention to conduct a tour of the gardens or the palace; you can buy your guide-book for that and nothing can be more confusing, more exasperating than a catalogue of visual things. The printed word cannot compete with the album, and Hampton Court is open, winter and summer, to your roving. I would be your guide only into the history of this palace so that next time you visit it the ghosts might walk and the stone and timber be nor merely stone and timber but living matter imprinted with the spirit, the ambitions and despairs, of those long dead.

Remember when next you tread these echoing halls that other steps have echoed here, steps of greater men than you, of most probably lovelier women than you, and hold your breath that you might listen, for houses have tongues, if you will only stop to hear. Each house, your own, has its individual echo. You know when you open the door if the silence be friendly or sullen, you know by the crepuscular breathing of boards, by the sigh of the wind in the chimney, by the knock of a distant slate, if you be welcome or hated. No house is ever empty. You may put the key in your pocket and the click of the lock can assure you that all is safe when you leave, but you are no longer there to see and listen. You cannot hear wood creak when ghosts step from the skirting-boards and the witch-lover whistles down the chimney. I have no personal assurance of ghosts' existence, nor do I think them the embodied dead, but I do most definitely believe that the personalities of those who have strongly loved or hated their surroundings remain on those surroundings, as the imprint of an etching remains on paper after the plate is destroyed. At times it might even take bodily form, trapped in a sort of mental prism which glows and shows for a moment something, somebody stirring. For authorities tell us that when seeing a ghost, if you move, the ghost will probably vanish because you have stepped from the viewfinder, as images will slide from a mirror when you step aside. All houses, I believe, are silently bustling with these ghosts, memories of the once living, call them what you will, which we are too egotistically blind to see. Our antennæ are blunted and we stride smugly, blindly on, insensitive to delicate beings we shoulder aside.

There are ghosts, accredited ghosts, it is said, in Hampton Court and although later we will pause to watch them, it is not of these ghosts that I am now thinking. It is of the ghosts that no one has seen, that have never taken on solidity, and yet are soaked into these walls, into that floor, that ceiling.

It is my intention to evoke, if possible, those ghosts for you. Certainly here is the place for ghost-hunting, for there has been tragedy acted within these walls such as we little folk could never experience; there has also been happiness—rare times—and love and marital content—and that indeed was rare—and hatred that was not rare enough. The man who first built this house knew the hell of relinquishing suddenly, at the whim of a king he had thought his slave, all his splendours, this manor included, and of dying in lonely, chattering fear. And the man who had killed him with kingly unconcern was to know anguish at the infidelities of the women he loved and was at last to die in terror lest his dynasty die shortly after him. Nor were his daughters who adored this palace to know much happiness, neither Mary, loving unloved, nor Elizabeth, that weak woman with a man's will. Few have been happy here, and the Tudors in their different ways were all to suffer. Yet Charles II made merry, although his father had lost his head and his grandfather had slobbered in perpetual fears of justified assassination and his brother was to run for his life out of England. Perhaps William and Mary knew some happiness, at least the happiness of tearing down bricks to erect other bricks, while Anne, despite her constant miscarriages and the bullying of Marlborough's Sarah, was a contented soul. But the early Georges, trussed in German arrogance, buttoning their humourless souls even during the ups and downs of tedious love-affairs, were men whom one cannot imagine smiling, save at an enemy's fall or the humiliation of their eldest sons.

All these men and women lived here and, before them, many of whom we do not know, for a preceptory of the Knights Hospitallers of St. John had once had here a manor house with gardens and a dove-cote in a thousand acres of pasturage that fed two thousand sheep. It was their house which Cardinal Wolsey leased in 1514 for ninety-nine years at £50 a year with the right to take from " Seynt Johns Woode in the seid county of Middlesex " four loads of wood and timber yearly suitable for " pyles for the reparacion and sustentacion of the Were called Hampton Were."

It is from the sealing of that lease that our tale begins.

DEDICATION
for
WILLIAM and KITTY GAUNT

My Dear Bill and Kitty,

It is with a certain trepidation that I write your names on this page, for your knowledge, my dear Bill, is so much greater than mine on questions of art and architecture. But friendship brings courage, with the desire to offer some book to you both whom I love so dearly. I ask only that you do not expect too much, for these pages are merely an act of homage to the palace where I have spent so many happy days and I am only too aware of my weak equipment for the task. Before you begin to read, therefore, I would ask your patience while I give warning of the limits of the work. Indeed, it is easier to say what it is not than what it is; for it is not purely antiquarian, archæological, or architectural, while in many ways, it is all three, particularly the first. Mainly it is an historical picture, for while the palace stands to be examined by all those who love the past and beautiful things, I would repeople it with the mighty dead who once walked its halls and slept in its bed-chambers, and would try to show you how they lived and what they ate, how the world looked to them, how they dressed, and with what ceremony they were guarded.

Many other volumes have been written about Hampton Court—you will find some listed in the bibliography—but the greatest, impossible to supersede, remains the late Ernest Law's, while for those interested mainly in architecture and archæology, I strongly recommend Mr. Yates's small, but well-packed, book. Because the ground has been so thoroughly charted by these men and others, I have given as few architectural details as possible, such being for the expert while I write for the ordinary reader who would study the manor and would like to know its history, what was done within its walls. and who were the great men who once lived there.

There are many I must thank in compiling this book and in gathering the illustrations, but it would be invidious to make too small a choice and some are mentioned in the text. I would like, however, to thank Mr. E. T. Croft-Murray, Assistant Keeper of Prints and Drawings at the British Museum, not only for the time he so generously gave me in collecting the illustrations but for permission to print his notes on Kent's peculiar drawing. These will be found in the appendices. There are, however, so many to be mentioned, friends and experts, that I had best stop before this dedication spills into the text. But, like most research-workers, it would be ingratitude if I did not add my thanks to the ever-obliging assistants of the British Museum Reading Room.

It is impossible to give a complete bibliography, for had I listed all the works consulted they would have proved almost sufficient for a history of England from the Tudors to the early Georges. Therefore I resigned myself to recording only those which actually deal with the palace, but I can assure you or any doubtful reader that, unless otherwise stated, nothing has been invented by me. To save paper I have, unfortunately, sometimes had to telescope my quotations, compressing two or three paragraphs into one, but otherwise I have made no alterations.

I shall, of course, quite correctly be denounced for including no index; for this there are two reasons: firstly, the scarcity of paper— the publishers have asked me to delete at least ten concluding pages leading to the victory celebrations—and secondly, I feel that an index would be a cumbersome thing for a work such as this which briskly leaps the centuries.

Next time you visit the palace I only hope this book will help bring the ghosts from the past and you will love it, if possible, the more for the sad, the tragic, and occasionally even happy times men and women have known in its many chambers. That is my one intention. . . . But I had best pause lest I ramble into the history itself which remains to be read at your leisure. Reluctantly I stand aside, hoping you will not be disappointed and that you will accept the book gladly, if only because of the love with which I offer it.

London, S.W.   PHILIP LINDSAY.

CHAPTER I
THE CARDINAL

OF the size and appearance of the preceptory we know nothing, for immediately on leasing it, the cardinal pulled it down; but we may be certain that it was insignificant compared to the manor he raised on its foundations. To our knowledge, nothing of the original building remains, but it is more than probable that the wooden cupola above Anne Boleyn's Gateway was a part of it, as it antedates the palace. This cupola contains the bells of Henry VIII's clock and, when next you hear them ring, listen to history speaking, the tongue of the oldest portion of the building tolling as it has tolled for almost five centuries. In the inventory with Wolsey's lease we find mention, amongst other of the furniture, of two bells in the tower, one broken; and we may believe that it is the unbroken one now ringing. With the founder's initials, it bears this legend: ✠STELLA ✠MARIA✠MARIS✠SUCCVRE✠PIISIMA✠NOBIS✠—*Mary, most holy Star of the Sea, come to our aid.*

From before the conquest a house had stood beside this curve of the Thames, for the Domesday Survey of 1086 shows that it was then the property of a Saxon Earl Algar while being in the possession of one of the Norman enemies, Sir Walter de St. Valeri. By 1180 the Knights Hospitallers had become the owners and it was from their master that Wolsey leased it. Insignificant the preceptory may have been compared to the manor Wolsey was to build, yet Queen Elizabeth, wife of Henry VII, had chosen to lodge therein for a week of prayer that she might have divine assistance in her imminent confinement: assistance which was unhappily withheld, for the delivery was to prove her death. And her husband, miserly, bald-headed, treacherous Henry Tudor, from his nearby palace at Richmond had apparently used the preceptory for what was called a " cell," a kind of private private-house, a bolthole from statecraft and all the Lilliputian twines of courtesy that bound a king, for we find the Bishop of Winchester writing to Wolsey in 1519 when surrendering to him the palace of Esher for which he had begged: " Use it all ways, as often and as long as it shall please you, right as your own, and make it a cell to Hampton Court, as the king that dead is, whose soul God pardon, made Hampton Court and it cells to Richmond."

Henry VII's associations with our palace are slight, although a correspondent in *Notes and Queries* for June 30th, 1927, writes that Sir Hans Sloane is reported to have said that when Bartholomew Columbus was sent to England by his brother in 1486 to try to persuade the king to fit out his expedition around the world to the Indies, the project was set aside and the money that would have been invested in it was spent " in the purchase of a suite of fine tapestry hangings, brought from Antwerp, and afterwards used for the decoration of Hampton Court." This, however, is purely gossip of a later age and Sir Hans gives no authority of which I know. Much as I dislike that grasping usurper, I cannot chalk against Henry this bargain of the Americas for a shipload of tapestries. At any rate, he and our palace have only the slightest acquaintance, and it first appears of importance when Wolsey bought the old house by the river.

The king's cell, the knights' preceptory, now became the cardinal's palace to house himself and his enormous retinue. Quickly, for desire must instantly be consummated in his impatient ruling, he summoned the wandering artists, those freemasons of Christian lands with their chisels and brushes and adzes and gravers, to come at once to Hampton Court. Unfortunately, we have not the name of the ingeniator or magister—architect we would call him—who drew the plans for what was to be the largest post-Roman brick building in all England. Nor do we know the full extent of Wolsey's manor, for the king later added much, and following kings and queens were to tear down and rebuild and alter at their whim, but there would have been no question of expense. Wolsey, with England's coffers wide to his fingers, had no need to trouble about pence, and beauty and size and splendour alone would have been his consideration.

So briskly did he set his artist-army to work that in a little over two years sufficient had been built, painted, decorated and furnished for him not to be ashamed of welcoming his king and queen there for a brief visit. That queen was Katherine of Aragon, because of whom—or rather, because of her husband's passion to rid his bed of her—Wolsey was to tumble from his glory of which Hampton Court was but one symbol, for he was to have other and probably even greater palaces—at York Place in London, at the More between Rickmansworth and Northwood, and at Tyttenhanger—of which the More was his own favourite, the French ambassador considering it of greater splendour even than Hampton Court, while York Place was to become the envy of the king who was eventually to seize it and convert it to the royal palace of Whitehall. But it is by Hampton Court that Wolsey is remembered as a builder and Skelton chose it for symbol of the cardinal's power in that fierce hammering poem, *Why come ye nat to courte?* and as it is of Hampton Court that this book is written, we will not meddle with others of Wolsey's building, for which he had the grandiose passion of his time.

He had never much liking for monasteries—as William Roy miserably laments:

> *What monasteries he hath broken*
> *With out their fownders consentis*

—and was always eager to convert them into cathedrals, and therefore it would have seemed to him nothing blasphemous to raise a palace, if not to the glory of God, to the glory of God's portly representative, on the foundations of the white cross warriors' home. And there is this to be said for Wolsey love of ostentation, of jewels and tapestries and many-chambered palaces, that he could honestly argue that such vanities were not for his honour but for that of England. And this he proved by surrendering Hampton Court to the king with apparently no motive, as it was long before his fall that he made the gift. He was not only cardinal but the royal representative and those were days when men judged frankly by externals. Experience has taught us caution in such surface judgments and, at least in talk, few would confess to assessing a man's intelligence or integrity by the cut of his coat or the polish on his shoes. That they continue to do so is proved almost every week in the columns of newspapers devoted to police court reports, but it is a human weakness of which few boast, for snobbery is now a failing indulged in only with intimates who will not scoff. In Wolsey's days, however, snobbery was no sin and dress and manners did most definitely make the man, while sumptuary laws were continually being issued to restrict the wearing of certain colours and materials to certain classes. If a man then dressed as a duke he was a duke and there could be no mistaking a king or a cardinal.

Therefore, as symbol of his greatness, Wolsey built Hampton Court, a palace sufficiently far from Westminster and London to appear unofficial and in which he could with gaudy bravura dazzle envoys and ambassadors and, perhaps, even the king himself. Besides, he was not by birth a gentleman, which indeed was much in those times, and the parvenu can never resist overplaying his part. Such overplaying was to prove Wolsey's doom, for he made no friends and many enemies. Yet what cared he for friendship when he had a king for gossip ? It seems that with almost spiteful delight he strove to humble others, although he could be merry and loving at times, when it was convenient or wise. He was Power and he permitted no man to forget that for one moment.

Only through the church could one so lowly born have risen to such heights, for without influence an ambitious youth had no choice save to enter priesthood, that seminary from which statesmen rose, as few but clerks could read and write with skill. He was born at Ipswich in the latter half of 1472—or early in 1473—and his father was a butcher, not a killer and seller of meat but a grazier, and was of sufficient wealth to own property in two parishes and to leave bequests to the town. He could therefore afford to send his son to Oxford University where he graduated B.A. from Magdalen College to be ordained priest on March 10th, 1498.

This is not the place to detail his rapid rise to power but there is one youthful episode which should not be passed over if we would understand the many sides of Wolsey's mind, and this is a surprisingly disgraceful episode, but we have only tradition for guide in saying that for riotous behaviour the future cardinal was locked into the stocks. In his later life there is nothing to suggest that he could be so incautious as to offend power without reason; at times he was to act the clown and to spit venom when angered, but it was always when he knew that clowning would delight the king or when venom could be spat harmlessly to himself. Yet in youth he was locked into the stocks by an enraged knight, and it is possible that this degradation before a grinning populace was the turning-point in his career, instructing him in that discipline which must have been necessary for the attainment of a red hat and the king's love.

George Cavendish, who wrote that sweet biography of his master, gives us one hint of the rungs by which Wolsey climbed. The tale cannot be accepted literally, although undoubtedly Cavendish had it from Wolsey's own boastful lips, and indeed its exaggeration tells us much of Wolsey's character. For his story goes that Henry VII posted him to the emperor in the Low Countries one midday, and by jumping into a London barge, he reached Gravesend without a second wasted, and from Gravesend he hired post-horses to rush him to Dover the same night. In the morning, the packet to Calais sped him to France where he raced to the emperor, conducted his business, and was back in Calais the same evening, reaching Dover just over twenty-four hours after quitting it. From Dover he posted to

Richmond so as to reach the palace by night. The tale continues that when on the morning of the third day the king noticed him loitering near he turned to him in fury at such sloth only to be startled to discover that the mission was done and excellently done.

That Wolsey was lying when telling this examplar to young Cavendish cannot be doubted; even had he been lucky enough always to catch the tide and to find post-horses not too blown by previous riders, there are other details which one might kindly label doubtful. Yet the adventure has in it some gold of truth and it is the prerogative of elders to lie a little when admonishing the insolence of the young, and that Wolsey was swift in performing royal orders and ever assiduous to please his master may be accepted as self-evident. Unquestionably he did race to the emperor and back, and if he halved the time in telling the tale, what matters that ? So prodigious a cardinal cannot be fettered with fact when compiling his own hagiology, for as Thomas Becket, son of a merchant, had achieved sainthood, there would seem to him no reason why Thomas Wolsey, son of a butcher, should not also receive his halo, Rome being so obliging to her son on every question, save making him pope and resolving the damned dilemma of the divorce.

For the divorce it was that destroyed Wolsey; but that subject is too involved to be discussed here. We will treat of it briefly in its historical moment when it arrives, for this gallop ahead in time is merely to show what manner of man was this great cardinal who built our Hampton Court. In appearance he was like his master, large and powerful and inclined to fat, little about him it would seem of that scabby sheep which Thomas More so loved to call him in later times when the scabby sheep was in his grave. Nor did the fat weaken him, for he was as agile in body as in mind, " a man of lust and courage and bodily strength to do and suffer great things," although, like many powerful men, he was distrustful of his flesh and was ever physicking himself to such an extent that the king protested. But there was none of the whining hypochondriac in him, rather was he a man of jests, " a gay finder out of new pastimes," and subtle and brilliant in talk with a " filed tongue " and an " angel's wit " that could " beguile all men, and to bind the whole world withal." Nor was that written by some worshipping Cavendish but by Tyndale who distrusted and almost hated him. But that honeyed voice of the " butcher's cur " was such that few could resist it when the honey was spread thickly, and certainly it made the young king a loving worshipper.

5

It is difficult to imagine this man without his scarlet robes; the brown-eyed mask with drooping eyelid was set so firmly on his face that it had become his face, and when we watch him through old print we can decipher only a kind of apotheosis of pride, never a man. Yet that he was sometimes weakly human is proved in his loving a woman, "the daughter of one Lark," who bore him children. Impossible to imagine him alone with her, impossible to see the body unrobed with pendulous belly and fat legs. Nay! on with the scarlet swiftly, pick up the pomander to sniff, clap on the cardinal's hat he so worshipped: it is not right that such men should ever be undressed. Place him at the council board or at the table that literally groans with the weight of food, but do not ever seek to see him alone, for we have that final, that terrible picture painted by Cavendish when he knew that both king and God had abandoned him, and then he is painfully naked, grovelling, weeping, a worm.

But that day of doom was far ahead when he set his seal to the lease of Hampton preceptory. Then was he mighty in his pride and all men, save the king, bowed to him, while even the king himself, as yet a colt uncertain of his strength, must often have flinched before this commoner with an angel's wit and a cunning tempered by fruitful study of Machiavelli's lore. Then he was on the wave of his greatness, being Archbishop of York and expectant of further honours, probably already dreaming of the time when he would find even St. Peter's throne a possibility. Hampton Court was almost a symbol of the future. Here he raised the stones and bricks that were to be the outward and permanent sign of his supremacy.

He was then forty-two, harassed from waking to sleep-time by the duties of the chancellorship, and the physicians had advised him to live outside London where drinking water might be found suited to his ailments. That may have been the alleged reason, but it is more likely that he felt his position demanded a home outside the city where, with hunting and banquets, he could bring ambassadors and other important folk to lay aside officialdom and to blab truth in the accident of laughing relaxation. To me it seems impossible that Wolsey moved from the city so that he might be alone, that a man with such passion for power would ever need peace and silence. Do these monsters, burning with their own ego, ever relax? Even in Berchtesgaden did Hitler relax? or Napoleon at Malmaison? Nay, Hampton Court was needed not for the cardinal's pleasures but as a monument to his pride, where he could smile in comfort after the satisfaction of

seeing men before the common pleas, in the king's bench, in Westminster Hall, in chancery, in the exchequer, in the Star Chamber,
tremble at his nostril's quiver.

Pride raised Hampton Court just as pride eventually struck down the
builder. His ambitions reached beyond England to the papacy while
he gloried in the red hat when it came from Rome. Snarled Skelton:

> *Whiles the red hat doth endure*
> *He maketh himself cock sure;*
> *The red hat with his lure*
> *Bryngeth all things under cure.*

To-day you can see its portrait at Hampton Court under the sill
of the window above the archway on the inner-side of the Clock
Tower. How this terra-cotta relief remained after Wolsey's disgrace
is not known; certainly the king would never have left it as a perpetual
reminder of his dead minister,* but a clue is given by Sir Henry Cole,

---

* On either side of the door to the chapel from the cloister are large finely decorated
panels of the royal arms which, it is most likely, conceal the arms of Wolsey, for the supporters
are angels, unusual ones for royalty but natural for a cardinal. This entrance is particularly
beautiful, not only because of these panels, but because of the arched doorway, similar in
design to the doorways opening on to the Great Hall, except that here the spandrils are plain.

writing in 1839, who mentions " two cherubs of terra-cotta made to support the arms of Henry VIII which ostensibly have supplanted something better." Probably the plaster, hastily moulded to conceal the ghost, either crumbled or was scraped away, which is fortunate for us, the panel being a delightful work, as you will see on your next visit. In describing it we will not be technical with heraldic terms which are mumbo-jumbo to the uninitiated but will explain it merely as a black shield bearing a white wavy-edged cross with a red lion prancing in the centre and with a blue leopard's head on each limb of the cross. At the top of the shield, above the cross, runs a white band with a blackbird either side of a red rose. From behind this shield rises an archiepiscopal cross topped with this cardinal's blessed hat with its twenty tassels. Below is carved his motto, *Dominvs michi adjvtor—the Lord my helper*—while originally there was a segmental pediment above with the date 1525 and the intertwined initials, *TW*, Thomas Wolsey.

There to-day it stands to remind us of this man who built this palace and there reposes in terra-cotta the more than precious Hat. Unfortunately we do not possess the name of the artist who modelled this panel, but the work is definitely Italian, for these are chubby renascence boys of the days when artists seem to have bred them fat to make them look almost deliciously edible. And the man who could carve such pretty boys was certainly the artist for that hat where it stays poised above the cross, for wherever Wolsey went that hat went with him, as Cavendish relates of his setting out for West-minster Hall. " Apparelled all in red " he stepped from his palace, " in the habytt of a Cardynall; which was other [either] of fynne skarlett, or ells of crymmosyn satten, taffeta, dammaske or caffa, the best that he could gett for mony; and uppon hys hed a round pyllion, with a nekke of blake velvett set to the same in the inner side. He has also a tippett of fynne sables abought his nekke; holdyng in his hand a very fayer orrynge whereof the mete or substaunce within was taken owt, and fylled uppe agayn with the part of a sponge, wherein was vyneger, and other confeccions agaynst pestylente ayers; to the whiche he most commenly smelt unto, passyng among the prease [press], or ells when he was pesterd with many sewters. There was also borne byfore hyme; first, the great seale of Englond, and than his Cardinall's hatt, by a noble man or some worthy gentilman, right solemply, barehedyd . . ."

To which we may add the rat-tat of Roy's:

A greate carle he is and fatt,
Wearing on his hed a red hatt.

But let us, however reluctantly, leave this large brown-eyed cardinal and watch his craftsmen busy at his new home, this Hampton Court, which he raised on the ruins of the knights' preceptory.

It was built of red brick with stone for windows, doorways, copings and ornaments, and of a brick apparently unknown to modern builders. We have become so weary to-day of that uniform tomatoish brick which the kilns turn out in merciless numbers that we are liable to despise this beautiful material. The rugged texture of brick is homely; its matt surface is like human skin, so different from the cold repellent feel and look of modern marble or of pocky cement or impersonal stucco. Brick is friendly, it seems to respond to one's touch as though it breathed, to kiss roughly one's fingers. And these bricks which Wolsey's artists used for Hampton Court have the warm tints of nature in autumn, ranging from pink to purple and blending to one jewel of colour. The walls seem to breathe, the whole house to live, for it is not something dumped on to nature, but seems almost a part of trees and grass and sky while the twisted chimneys are like boughs upstretched. Not as the Gothic is a tree of intricate and living loveliness, this is ordered nature, trimmed and mastered by man's hand.*

Those twisted chimneys are, to me, the beauties of Hampton Court. Few of the originals, alas! remain, but the restoration has been carefully done and we can have no quarrel with it.

The presbytery is down, rubble in choking dust, that dust of an old building which has something of the sharp tang of a corpse, and carts come on iron-rimmed wheels bearing bricks hot from the kiln, smaller and more delicately proportioned than those we have to-day. Labourers, masons, bricklayers, carpenters, tilers, paviors, smiths, carvers, painters, glaziers, moulders, joiners, plumbers, all are busy

---

* I cannot resist quoting, if only in a lowly footnote, the opinion of the learned William Howitt in his *The Northern Heights of London.* When discussing Cromwell House on Highgate, he wrote: " The bricks and brickwork of our old mansions, as Hampton Court, the part built by Wolsey [and Henry], this old house, and hundreds of old mansions in town and country, show how far, in this hurrying and money-scraping age, we have gone backward in the quality of brick and bricklaying. And yet this is scarcely a correct expression, for we can go back to no period of our history in which the brick and bricklaying are not far superior to ours. Look at the fineness, the solid smoothness of the brick; at the nice and compact manner in which it is laid; and then turn to the coarse, often very unequally burnt brick of to-day, and the coarse mortar in which it is set, often in rude layers of nearly an inch thick, and the contrast is disgraceful to this age of boasted progress in the arts, but an age in which strength and beauty of building are sacrificed to the sordid calculations of the builder's profits." What Howitt published in 1869 is equally, if not more damnably, applicable to the builder to-day.

at their separate crafts and they sing while they work, for all men could sing in those distant days when lutes were kept in barbers' shops so that customers could play away the waiting time as now we are given aged papers to read. Chalk is carried from Taplow and Windsor, timber from Cobham Park, stone from Reigate. The ground is drained and water brought in leaden pipes from the springs of Coombe Hill. Rapidly out of the skeleton-scaffolding is formed the cardinal's manor and a broad ditch is dug around it, the last moat made in England, to keep enemies or persistent petitioners at bay.

The earliest sketch which we have of the west front is by Antonius Wynegarde and was drawn in 1558 and, as Henry's alterations here were few, Wolsey's manor must have looked very like this when it at last was finished. Then the great gatehouse was two storeys higher than it is to-day, for the rascally "restorers" of the eighteenth century deliberately threw it down, an act of vandalism beyond forgiveness, for the proportions now have gone and the present gateway—if it be possible with so lovely a work—seems almost mean when compared with Wynegarde's drawing. Luckily, the oriel window remains but the panel of arms inserted below is absurdly large, although typical of Henry who would blot out the cardinal with any monstrosity so long as it was large, assertive. The Roman

emperors peering from their plaques on the turrets are Italian-made, the work of Giovanni da Maiano, we discover, for poor Messer Maiano was compelled to write pleading payment as late as 1521, and his letter has survived. Eight plaques were made for the cardinal in or about 1541, but we now possess ten. As there are two others, plainly from the same hand, at Hanworth House, it would seem that these four are from the old Holbein Gate at Whitehall, which had eight such roundels.

The drawbridge and moat which are so distinctive, so appropriate an entrance, were lost for over two centuries. During alterations—Charles's or mayhap William's—the parapets of the bridge had been hacked down and the moat stuffed with gravel, but luckily the bridge itself was not destroyed. It was merely buried until Mr. Law, for whom God be thanked, began probing the gravel, inspired by references in old building accounts, and had it unearthed, adding to it the original heraldic monsters that had been tossed aside, shrouded in dirt, as lumber.

But there is so much for which we must thank Mr. Law that the list of his benefactions is wellnigh endless. There are the huge oak doors to the Great Gateway which George III wrenched down, replacing them with common jail-like cast-iron gates, and flung into a lumber-room where they served as flooring to a carpenter's shop. Now, thanks to Mr. Law, they have been repaired and replaced. They are seventeen feet high and six and a half feet wide, while the main framing is six inches thick and is studded with nails, the panels being carved in the homely yet delicate linenfold design, such as we find in Wolsey's remaining apartments. The holes in the wood, by the by, are alleged to have been the result of shot fired during the Great Rebellion.

It is not difficult to reconstruct Wolsey's manor and Mr. Law reproduces a careful plan in his first volume, but I fear it would only confuse the reader should I continue in detail. Except to the initiates, architectural and archæological terms conjure nothing but a vacuum in the mind and yet it is impossible to describe buildings without their use. Mr. Law's fat volumes will give all information on these matters and there is the excellent slim book by Mr. Yates which is an invaluable signpost. For I am not an architectural but an historical guide and would people for you the great and little chambers of the palace; therefore we had best return to the cardinal who watches these walls rise brick by brick.

When the king and queen rode to the semi-finished manor in May, 1516, it was not their first visit, for on March 20th, 1514, they had visited the preceptory, evidently to inspect the property which Wolsey intended to buy. The Marquis of Mantua had presented Henry with some horses and the king took this opportunity of viewing them, being a great lover of animals until his ulcerated leg kept him cautiously on the ground. At sight of the horses he swore that had the marquis given him a kingdom he could not have been more delighted. So delighted indeed was he that he babbled like a boy, turning from courtier to courtier as he exclaimed on the beauties of the beasts. Giovanni Ratto, who had brought them to England, mounted a bright bay and spurred it to perform its tricks, which it did in the Spanish fashion so expertly, so gracefully that the king could not hold back from caressing it and crying joyfully, " So ho, my minion ! "

The manor's site must have delighted him equally as the horse, for Wolsey thereupon sealed the bargain and set to to pull it down to raise his own great palace.

The king's next visit was to inspect, not horses, but the half-built manor and to make merry at the first of many banquets at the cardinal's table there. Often these banquets were informal and king and cardinal could toss aside crown and red hat and jest and sing together or listen to the musicians scrape and pipe music from their gallery above the screens through which the servitors entered with food and wine. Often would the king sing to his courtiers and ladies, for he was no mean poet. Young and handsome as a god, six feet two inches tall, he was, and the scholars, not only of England but of Europe, prayed that at last they had found a patron who would support them in their little necessities. Responsibilities of kingship had as yet not puckered the tiny mouth nor taught him to mistrust all others. He was a jolly youth, powerful of body and brilliant of mind, who loved to jest or to argue friendlily on philosophical or theological problems with his good friend the cardinal.

" And when it pleased the kyng's majestie," Cavendish tells us, " for his recreacion, to repayer unto the Cardynal's howsse, as he dyd dyvers tymes in the yere, at whiche tyme there wanted no preparacions or goodly furnyture, with vyaunds of the fynnest sort that myght be provided for mony or frendshype. Suche pleasyrs ware than devysed for the kyng's comfort & consolacion as myght be invented, or by man's wytt imagyned. [At] The banketts ware set forthe masks and mumreyes in so gorgeous a sort and costly maner that it was an hevyn to behold. Ther wanted no dames or damsells meate or apte to daunce with the maskers, or to garnysshe the place for the tyme, with other goodly disports. Than was ther all kynd of musyke & armonye, set forthe with excellent voyces bothe of men and childerne. I have seen the kyng sodenyly come in thether in a maske, with a dosyn of other maskers, all in garments lyke shepherds, made of fynne clothe of gold and fyne crymosyn sattin paned, & cappes of the same, with visors of good proporcion of vysonamy [physiognomy], their heares and beards other [either] of fynne gold wyer or ells of silver, & some beyng of blake sylke; havyng XVI torches berers, besids ther dromes, and other persons attendyng them, with visors, & clothed all in satten of the same colours."

The Great Hall we enter to-day at Hampton Court is not Wolsey's; it was built by the king after he took possession; but Wolsey's must have been almost as beautiful. And in such a hall would these merrymakings take place, the king being rowed up the river to greet his friends; then with selected great men and ladies seated on the table on the dais, he would dine and wine, other tables for ladies and courtiers running at right-angles from the dais down either wall towards the screens above which the musicians perched in their gallery. People sat only on one side of the table in those days, their backs to the wall, so that they could be served from the front and feel certain that they would not be literally stabbed in the back. The walls would be hung with heavy tapestries on tenterhooks, for Wolsey was a busy buyer and cajoler of tapestries, mostly of religious subjects.

All the important chambers would be hung with such tapestries— the lesser rooms with painted cloths—to keep out draughts, and the list of those he possessed reads like a summary of Biblical and Saints' tales—Esther, Tobias, Moses, the Forsaken Son, David, Samuel, Jacob, Susannah, Our Lady, Christ, the Passion, David harping, Christ casting the traders out of the temple, St. George, the sacrament of the altar—all these and many others were amongst them; and there were also brightly woven tales from romance and myth and history, of Jupiter, Pluto and Ceres, Paris and Achilles, Priam, Hercules, Jason, Hannibal, the ever popular medieval Wheel of Fortune, the Pilgrimage and Life of Man, the Romaunt of the Rose, and, which sounds delightful, the " Duke of Bry and the gyante Orrible." Wearisomely on and on runs the catalogue, but it would have been far from wearisome to have looked on the pieces themselves in all their shimmering splendour of threaded silks with silver and gold. Some remain: three of the Triumphs—Death, Renown, and Time—can still be seen at the palace, the remaining three of the set—Love, Chastity, and Eternity or Divinity—being now in the South Kensington Museum.

Wolsey had an insatiable love of tapestries; no man he knew went abroad without a commission in his mail to purchase arras. And they were needed in this great manor with ill-fitting windows and draughty halls and its two hundred and eighty guest bed-chambers. As Cavendish relates, pretending it is Wolsey speaking:

> My chambers garnished with arras fine
> Importing personages of the liveliest kind
> And when I was disposed in them to dine
> My cloth of state there ready did I find
> Furnished complete according to my mind;
> The subtle perfumes of musk and sweet amber
> There wanted none to perfume all my chamber.

Not only hangings but carpets, too, were Wolsey's passion and continual need—carpets for tables, for window-ledges, for the floor of important chambers, or as foot-carpets and mats. When Venice thought to bribe him, the doge and senate despatched bales of such carpets at his suggestion.

Wrote the Venetian ambassador, Giustinian: "One has to traverse eight rooms before one reaches his audience chamber, and they are all hung with tapestry, which is changed every week." Colour on the walls, rippling in a wind, colour on the tiled floor, on the roofs and painted glass, it must have been like moving in one huge prism or walking in a rainbow to visit Hampton Court those opulent days. Ceilings were mostly painted in Wolsey's colours, gold and byse—byse being a fierce light blue—and were moulded or carved with scrollwork and cinquecento designs. The arras would tremble besides you, as though moving with you, when wind came through open windows with their rich painted glass set in lead lozenges, and always, on every side of you, you would see Wolsey's arms, his colours, and his motto. In your chamber, were you a guest, wine would be ready for your drinking when you arrived and your bed would be cupboarded behind hangings of satin or velvet or silk, with the counterpane, when you opened the hangings, of blue damask, perhaps, with flowers of gold, or of red satin with a mighty rose in the midst, wrought with needlework. Your pillowslips would be of silk and would be stuffed with carded wool, and the silk would be embroidered with, mayhap, flowers or foliage. The four posts of the bed would be carved and gilded, it is most likely, with cardinals' hats. The ceil, your cloth ceiling when you lay abed, would be of satin embroidered with flowers or heraldic monsters, while the testers, when you drew them shut for sleep, would gleam with thread showing in the dark, perhaps, a hunt or babies bathing and splashing water. There were ceils and testers for every mood, from the pious to the amorous, but if you preferred to sit and read you would most likely be given a stool—chairs being rare in those days—and there would be numerous cushions of velvet, green or red or blue or cloth of gold, tasselled and embroidered with Wolsey's arms for you to sit on. Your round table would be of cypress, your cupboard of panelled oak, and your clothes would be folded into a great flat chest of wainscotte or in one bound with white plate or with iron.

Come, now we are furnishing the palace afresh, let us be guests for one night. Let it be in October, 1527, after a raw day with frost webbing the fields and glistening crystalline on the leaves outside our window. We have come, almost frozen after our ride, from London, our horse, like a dragon, snorting smoke; the long leather gloves cannot keep our fingers steady on the bridle and the riding-hood, lined with fur, drawn far forward has not shielded our eyes from the icy wind. Our beard is stiff and hard, it crackles when we smooth it, while the leather riding-boots reaching to above our knees have not protected our legs, so that we fall rather than climb out of our saddles. But the grooms are waiting, the guards salute with dipping halberds, and the chamberlain greets us and he has a small iron box in his sleeve, a box stuffed with hot coals, to keep his fingers warm.

A marriage has been sealed between Princess Mary, then but ten years old, " the pearl of the world, and the jewel that his Highness, Henry VIII, esteemed more than anything on earth," and the young Duke of Orleans, and we have travelled to England with great nobles, humbly in their meinie, to confirm the compact and invest the king with the order of St. Michael. These were dark days for the cardinal, days of doom's gestation, for Anne Boleyn, that black-haired witch with the almond-shaped eyes and wide tight mouth, the sallow skin and the swan-neck that was in time to feel an axe's edge, sorceress

Anne with the extra little finger and the sharp tongue, was slyly, adroitly teasing in and out of the king's embrace, never letting him hold her longer than a kissing-time. But neither the queen nor the cardinal bothered as yet about her, thinking her merely an amorous whim of the king's, for he had already possessed her sister, Mary, and each believed the other to be the enemy. They did not understand, plotting with the bones of diplomacy, that this shrewd shrewish wench, no longer very young, was their implacable enemy, their doom in the flesh.

But to our embassy. . . . Before our coming, my lord cardinal has called together his principal officers, his steward, his comptroller, his clerk of the kitchens, and told them to spare neither expense nor travail in preparing a banquet that would startle England with its magnificence and humble us proud Frenchmen that we might return dazed and babbling like sailors from lotus land to our own country. From the steward, the comptroller and the clerk of the kitchen the order is given to the caterers, the purveyors, the cooks and others to prepare the rarest foods, to gather them by friendship, threats or money from intimates of my lord. And my lord's own cooks are shamed and furious, sharpening knives, when stranger-cooks are called to assist them with curious recipes, cooks from other great households and from London shops, who have boasted they possessed secret methods of preparing food deliciously. The purveyors have bought or bullied from tenants, cattle and sheep and birds, and the cooks have wrought both day and night divers subtleties, and these subtleties needed artist's skill to prepare, being ornamental or emblematic groups made of sugar, tinsel and wax, symbols of saints or royalty, many having labels issuing from their mouths with words painted on them, speaking wisdom or welcome.

These kitchens are still to be seen at Hampton Court, although what is now open to us is but one-third the entire length of the original Great Kitchen. Yet what we have contains three gigantic stone-arched fireplaces, two with a span of eighteen feet, rising to a height of seven feet in the centre. In the south wall, one fireplace still retains its roasting fittings with the iron brackets for the spits that were turned by greasy kitchen-boys, wretched lads about whom an enactment of Henry's commands that they " shall not goe naked or in garments of such vilenesse as they now doe, and have been accustomed to doe, nor lie in the nights and dayes in the kitchens or ground by the fire-side."

If, standing on the hearth of this kitchen, you crane upwards, you will see the sky through four flues up which rolled the spiced smoke of those days. Between two chimney-breasts on the north there opens a little chamber which I like to believe was, in Wolsey's time and later, the office of the Master Cook, and there is certainly no reason why it should not have been his. This master cook was a great man, he did not blister his fingers at cooking, but was similar to the chef in a modern hotel who merely sniffs to find whether the exact pinch of spices or salt and no more be administered to the sacrifice. Dressed in velvet and satin, with the gold chain of office clinking around his neck, this Master Cook would perch in his tiny office, aloof in his regality, and only when his advice was needed would he stalk out to taste the latest sauce, while the cooks around him watched and waited in challenging silence. On ordinary occasions, when there were no important visitors to feed, he would have twelve of these cooks to superintend, and they in their turn had eighty under them, down to the filthy scullions. But now, with the French lords coming, it must indeed have been a miniature hell in the kitchens with all the stranger-cooks in their brief authority shouting for further stores from the butler in the buttery.

Apart from this Great Kitchen, to the east, stands the Privy Kitchen, now unfortunately half shut to the public, and there would be cooked simple meals when the cardinal was alone in residence. Its beautiful brick chimney-stack and high roof with carved louvres through which the smoke could curl can still at least be glimpsed from Tennis Court Lane.

Not only is food to be prepared for our arrival with the French mienie, but the beds must be aired and made and the chambers sprinkled with fresh herbs. Cavendish tells how the yeomen and grooms of the wardrobes were busied in hanging the chambers with costly handings, and furnishing them with beds of silk and other furniture. Being the cardinal's gentleman usher, Cavendish himself would here be in command, and with two underlings he worked from morn till dark, rushing from chamber to chamber, to chamber from chamber, hooking up tapestries and making certain that the floors had been swept and sprinkled with vinegar to ward off plague and were strewn with fresh rushes from the river to hold dirt and dust and gobbets of waste food. Then the carpenters, the joiners, the masons, the painters, and all other artificers needed to glorify the house and feast were set to work. There was carriage and re-carriage of plate, stuff, and other rich implements. There were also fourteen score beds provided.

All is now prepared for our arrival; we lick our lips at thought of spiced wines, warm for our chilled bellies, while we jog in the long train of the Marshal of France. But we have been too eager. Cold and thirst have whipped our horses ahead of time and as we trot over the drawbridge, under the tower, into the grass court, respectful yet worried officials await us. Would we hunt for a time? there are forests in the royal park of Hanworth, only two or three miles distant: would we pray hunt there until night?

Shrugging up our clammy cloaks against the chill on our spines, woefully we turn our horses and canter off.

At last it is sunset. At last we can race our horses back to Hampton Court; we are warmed by hunting but the wind is chill and our blood needs wine. And wine awaits us. We have each his chamber, fresh-smelling with new herbs, and those with fireplaces have sea-coal bustling, snapping in the grate, while others must be content with charcoal in metal pans shaped like that blessed cardinal's hat turned upside-down on the floor, the charcoal being protected under a wire mesh. And there, ah, there is wine on the little table, a cup of hyppocras—that spiced sweet red wine strained through a woollen bag. Our curtained bed awaits us; it is a feather-bed we find when we press our hands into it, and the counterpane is of blue damask with flowers of gold, while the pillowcases are seamed with black silk and have embroidered golden fleur-de-lys in our honour. The curtains are also of blue, fringed with Venetian gold, and are embroidered with scenes of hunting and hawking. We should sleep soundly here and have sweet dreams, for there are two mattresses on which to lie, both stuffed with carded wool and covered with stout Holland cloth. The blankets are soft and white and furred with fine lamb's wool, the sheets are silk of Rennes.

A carved oak chest gapes to swallow our clothes and green velvet cushions embroidered with golden birds are on the window-seat. This window, its diamond-shaped leaded lights painted with the cardinal's arms and his hat, opens—should we think to open it in such weather—on to the cardinal's garden. We shiver and keep it shut as we unlock our male, or travelling-bag, and select and warm our chosen garments—round breeches padded with tow to make them swell about our hips, fat jewelled embroidered codpiece exaggerating masculinity, gaily coloured hose, round-toed shoon, silk shirt, and tight-laced doublet with padded chest. We comb the damp from our beard in the tiny mirror we carry tucked in our sleeve and are ready to meet the cardinal.

But we do not meet the cardinal, not for many hours do we even see the cardinal, so we roam into other chambers and chatter with friends also roaming with impatience, and we spit when we talk of the English, these tailed men of legend who are animals on two legs trying to imitate our graceful French manners and appearance. We are determined not to be impressed, yet, secretly, while we curl our nostrils and spit on the carpets, we are a little shaken by all this luxury.

The first waiting chambers are draped with magnificent arras, rich in colour and texture, showing scenes from the Holy Book, and tall yeomen in the cardinal's livery stand ready to attend us. Tables are placed against the walls and have fine cloths of diaper, neatly pressed and clean, and there stands a cupboard with its tiers of steps displaying gold plate, parcel gilt, with candles placed to glitter on the gold and silver. Even the presence chamber we will not allow to impress us when we stroll to it and hood our eyes at the gorgeous cloth of estate above the empty chairs, with sewers waiting to serve the viands, the mere smell of which, from the far kitchens, starts our bellies biting us. And all is sweetly smelling with herbs on the floor and with perfumes on the cloths and arras, and here are cupboards with their steps of plate, and here the high table has been taken from under the cloth of estate and placed in the middle of the chamber, covered with linen cloths of damask-work, all warmly perfumed. One cupboard, six steps high, seems afire with rolling eyes of gilt plate watching us; and there are two huge silver and gilt candlesticks on one cupboard with lights of wax as fat as torches, and these candlesticks, we are carefully told, have cost three hundred marks, a little fortune. The English dogs appear to deem their cupboards precious for they will not let us approach too near, each cupboard being railed about. Here, too, flares a merry fire while many candles burn against the wall with huge reflectors of silver and gilt behind them.

But the time for dinner is near and it would not do for us to be seen snuffling at the table like dogs, for gentlemen should not show hunger; we must scurry back to our chamber and pretend we have been picking our teeth or combing our beards or merely reading some leather-covered book of hours.

Then sounds the trumpet and, leashing our impatience, we stroll to the banquet. Officers of the household with their white wands of office greet us courteously and escort us to the chamber of presence which we have recently examined. In their little gallery the musicians strike up with trumpet, drum, viola and hautbois and other sweet-sounding instruments as we are conducted to our seats against the arras. The tables are placed at right-angles from the dais on which stands the table for the ambassadors.

At last, to music, the food is brought, sewer after sewer running from the kitchens, over the cold court, up the stone stairs, under the screens into the presence chamber, trotting around the great wood fire on its stone slab in the centre, offering us food and wine, serving us from across the table, while carvers are busy with knives with four-inch blades, carving, carving, as the sewers wait with silver dishes.

Course swiftly follows course, food and wine and wine and food, until as we sniff the new dishes, suddenly the cardinals steps into the centre of the room. He has come without warning and is booted and spurred, having just left his horse or mule in the court, and he smiles as he welcomes us gaily, standing red-faced, his whip curled in his hands until he tosses it to an attendant. We all rise to bow, kicking against our stools; but he will have no ceremony, he says. Fat and smiling, brown eyes gleaming with the pleasure of seeing us, his guests, he bids us remain seated and calls for a chair.

The chair is immediately brought and placed on the dais, wedged between the great men seated there, under the canopy. Cardinals' hats are carved on it and its high back is of black velvet fringed with black silk and embroidered with a cardinal's hat on a cross of crimson and Venetian gold. There now the cardinal sits, still wearing his tall leather boots that reach to over the knees and with the prick-spurs on his heels; nor will he talk of serious matters. Such are for the council table, not for this festive board, he says, and laughs.

Seemingly endlessly food is carried to us, together with subtleties between each course, over a hundred in all, so that we can merely blink and know not which to choose, like a man in a nunnery. There are castles and churches made of sugar and pastry and icing, St. Paul's with its steeple, as well counterfeited as any painter could paint on a wall; there are birds, beasts, insects, and all edible, with shapes of men and women, and of saints and angels, too; some tiny sculptures fight with swords of sugar, some with sugar guns, some with crossbows, some are vaulting, some leaping, some dancing with sugar or pastry ladies, some in full armour joust with other armoured knights: so many figures and conceits, indeed, that we cannot examine them all. But one none can help but notice and admire: a chess-board cunningly wrought of spiced plate, having all the correct men, knights, castles, king, queen, rooks and all. The cardinal rubs his hands and swears that Frenchmen are notoriously expert at the eastern game and therefore they must eat it, too, and he insists on one nobleman—he with the greediest gloat —taking it and commands that a case be yarely made so that it might be carried to France.

Then while all smile and envy his sweet-toothed comrade with the chess-board, the cardinal swallows his grin and stands to his feet. In both hands he lifts a golden bowl worth fully five hundred marks and calls to have it brimmed with hyppocras. When that is done and the sewers have backed, bowing, away, he lifts in both hands that brimming bowl, after taking off his cap, and says loudly: " I drink to the king my sovereign lord and master, and to the king your master," and thereupon drinks deep a drunkard's draught. To the grand master he passes then the bowl and asks for him, too, to drink that pledge, then calls on each of us to drink to our royal princes. Then is there running of sewers and butlers, cups are filled, and all men drink deep to the Kings of France and England, God defend them in their right.

Eventually the cardinal leaves, the fat rogue steals off to eat alone in his privy chamber, but soon he is back in scarlet robes and scarlet cap to see which of us have iron bellies and can yet drink. He drinks with us until the arras seems to quiver alive to our drunken eyes, saints and figures of fantasy seem to step from the embroidery to dance a measure for us amongst the broken bread and pastries and the slops of wine and the crumbled subtleties. We have struck a Moses' rock that has no bung and here be wines aplenty, even for a Frenchman.

And while we sit, swining and wining in that arrased chamber, servants are making ready for when we should need to sleep. Then as morning burns close, we stagger or are carried to our chambers, fires have been stoked for us and on the table stands a silver basin with a silver ewer for washing, and a huge silver pot with wine and another pot with beer, and a silver goblet with a small silver pot, and two candlesticks with lighted candles pale in the dawn, their flames shrinking like shy girls from our drunken breath: one white candle and one yellow candle, with a stiff torch spluttering resin; and may the Lord protect our bellies from English generosity! a loaf of manchet-bread made of the finest white flour and a chetloaf of bought bread of the purest are ready should we need to eat after such a banquet. . . .

Draw swiftly the curtains, yarely, yarely . . . we must be up in the morning, this being a cardinal's house, to hear mass, if our stomachs permit.

That was one of the huge feasts prepared by Wolsey to impress foreigners, and we from our peak in futurity can sigh to realise that all the gold was waste, for the king at Greenwich Palace was, in jealousy of the cardinal, preparing yet another feast even more appalling to our modern stomachs.

Always there was food in the hall of Hampton Court, ready for any chance visitor, while officers were continually in attendance: a steward who was also a priest, a treasurer who was a knight, and a comptroller who was a squire. Altogether, the cardinal must have maintained at least five-hundred servants, many of them of noble lineage, for in those days the young were sent to other nobles' homes to be reared in courtesy, learning, and martial arts without the danger of parental love weakening them. These squires would do the carving and serving and would be proud to wait on the proud cardinal. Others had tasks beyond the walls; with the clerk of the stable and the master and the yeoman of horses, there was the saddler, the farrier, the yeoman of the chariot, the sumpter man, the yeoman of the stirrup, the muleteer, with sixteen grooms and many others to tend the horses and mules of which there were fully a hundred; but the youths here would not always be of the nobility, although most would be well-bred. The stables begun by Wolsey and, like so much else in the palace finished by Henry, are on the road to Hampton near the river, about two-hundred yards beyond the entrance-gate.

And all this was the cardinal's. . . .

Yet he gave all to the king, without reason we know of, in 1524-5. Pollard suggests in his biography of Wolsey—and it seems likely— that he was so stung by Skelton's gibes in *Why come ye nat to Court?* that " he ' gave ' the lease to Henry, but continued to occupy it till his attainder. . . . He then ' gave ' it once more to Henry, this time ' in exchange ' for Richmond . . . and on 5 June, 1531, the prior of St. John's ' granted ' it to certain trustees for Henry's ' use.' " No matter who was the nominal owner, Wolsey continued to live in Hampton Court until his fall and Henry's appearances were as a guest, but as a guest who might command and take whatever he desired.

Before closing this chapter on the first and, to my thinking, most splendid era of the palace it is impossible to ignore another event like that already described of the early times when king and cardinal were as brothers.

We have eaten, the crumbs and wine-stains and meat-slops are on the damask tablecloth as we lean back to belch and drink under the bright eye of my lord cardinal in festive mood. And as we sat talking in the subdued fashion of those whose stomachs are at peace, we are startled by a sound as of enemies at the gate.

Cannon are thundering, cannon roaring on a hushed evening in the English countryside when there are no possible foes save beyond the Channel or nearer than the heather of Scotland. The cardinal sits with his guests, head to one side as he listens, and he makes pretence to be troubled, yet there is laughter in his eyes and the drooping lid seems to wink at us, for he knows that there is only one man in the realm who would dare fire guns at Hampton Court, yet with the pretence of fear he sends attendants with torches and drums and fifes to welcome these strangers, whoever they be, coming as if to Camelot.

In rush the maskers, gentlemen and ladies, disguised in hoods and masks and with false beards of golden wire or wearing vizards cut with slots through which eyes sparkle against the dark. In rush and dance the merrymakers, disturbing this portly churchman's meal; they dance and leap amongst the rushes, ringing bells and beating tabors—little drums—slung from their shoulders; some pipe like Greek shepherds and others howl like devils. It is the young king on a frolic. The dragging skirts of the ladies sweep over rushes and bones, their little feet peep with flat toes beyond the hems, their hoods are awry, their coifs pushed back to show the white parting in the centre of their hair, their corsage is dragged down becomingly, if wickedly: for old Queen Katherine is not present.

Some play dice, shouting as they kneel on the floor, and the cardinal leaps the table to play with them, his red gown almost tripping him as he joins the sport. But which is the king amongst these many maskers? Wolsey plays his part; he peers here, there, snaps his fingers as though annoyed when he chooses the wrong tall man: which is the king amongst these men disguised? And the king is twisted with suppressed laughter to see his friend the cardinal choose always the wrong man. At last his laughter cannot be contained. He roars like a boy and tears off his mask, and all of us laugh at the cardinal who laughs back at us.

It was right merry at Hampton Court in those days before the Lady Anne came back from France. The cardinal was master of all England. " He is," wrote Guistinian, " in very great repute— seven times more so than if he were pope," and that he desired " not so much to be honoured as a prince as to be adored like God." When he first arrived in England, Guistinian records, Wolsey would say to him, " His Majesty will do so-and-so," then he said, " We will do so-and-so," but later he would say, " I will do it." Although as the Venetian ambassador, Guistinian was enraged by the Cardinal's policy and infuriated by his pride, he adds that his reputation was good in that he was just, favouring the poor above the rich, hearing their suits in person and despatching them swiftly while ordering counsel to plead without fee. He broke the legal tyranny of the barons and made the king's court a court of justice and he was surprisingly tolerant on religious matters. Not a single man or woman was burnt to death for heresy while he commanded ecclesiastical jurisdiction; when Thomas More succeeded him there were three burnings; and after More's retirement within three years there were fifteen or sixteen. Yet More's comment may be recorded here as the best summary of Wolsey's character: " Glorious was hee very farre above all measure, and that was great pitie; for it dyd harme and made him abuse many great gyftes that God hadde geven him."

Now must come the tragic fall, now must Wolsey leave Hampton Court for ever, for he had failed the Lady Anne Boleyn. She had always hated him. Years before she had been loved by Henry Percy and Wolsey, probably under royal orders, had forbidden the marriage. Anne did not forget, nor did the queen forget that he had assisted in the divorce; both women were eager to tear him down, and Anne succeeded. Disgraced, Wolsey had been practically banished from court; and there is here a strange coincidence to be recorded. He had always had a horror of the name of Kingston and would never pass through that town if he could avoid it, although it was on the direct road from Hampton Court to London. Always he would make a detour or travel by water. Then when he lay sick unto death, an envoy

24

came from the king and he learned that the envoy's name was Kingston, the constable of the Tower.

" ' Mr. Kingstone,' quoth he, rehearsing the name once or twice; and with that clapped his hand to his thighe, and gave a great sighe." His superstition had come true and, likely enough, the coincidence hastened his fatalistic death,* although we cannot dismiss the possibility of suicide. For so proud a man to face his enemies, ruined, at their merciless mercy, suicide would have been the one escape. But of that we do not know. He died, this mighty builder of our palace, when the clock struck eight on the morning of Tuesday, November 29th, 1530, as on the day before he had prophesied to the hour.

---

* Strangely, we find the same coincidence in the death of Ferdinand the Catholic, Queen Katherine's father. He always avoided the town of Madrigal, where one of his bastard daughters was a nun, beeause a wizard had once warned him he would die at a place of that name. He remained certain that he would live indefinitely if he could avoid this town, but when at last he fell mortally ill, he discovered to his horror that he was in a village named Madrigalejo. If is of course more than possible that in both cases the coincidence hastened death with superstitious fear.

CHAPTER II
HENRY THE EIGHTH

THERE was plague in England when for the last time Wolsey looked on Hampton Court. He had been living there as in a fortress, permitting few to see him, for men were dying in hundreds, until the royal dismissal came. It would seem that this periodic plague, this "sweating sickness" which Henry VII is said to have brought with him, along with foreign troops, from Flanders when he invaded England, was either malaria or some virulent form of influenza. Henry's brother, Arthur, had apparently died from it, although "consumption" was diagnosed; but a consumption in those times meant wellnigh any wasting disease. Almost every year this sweating sickness sweated hundreds to death. Anne Boleyn shivered with it but her vitality won the battle although, while she lay ill, her royal lover had kept his unromantic distance, sending instead of himself his second-best physician; for Henry had a strong man's terror of illness, particularly of this "English sweat" which had small reverence for kings and shook to his grave the lord with the commoner.

Wolsey would not run before the plague; unlike his master, he would remain in Hampton Court or some other palace while the epidemic raged and continue working, although, as the French ambassador tells us, he was at such times difficult of access, allowing the ambassador to approach no nearer than the village "when he will consider whether I shall speak by trumpet or by myself."

But more certain death than the sweating sickness struck down Wolsey, and this is perhaps the place to record a quaint superstition of which Mr. Law tells us in his monumental work. There is, he states, a spider "found in extraordinary abundance in the old nooks and corners of Hampton Court" called the Cardinal Spider. "This enormous insect, with its fat reddish-brown body and its long jointed hairy legs, often attains the size of five inches in width; and, when seen crawling about a bedroom at night, will startle even persons of tolerably composed nerves. It is alleged to be a kind of spider peculiar to Wolsey's palace, and being in some mysterious way connected with his disastrous fate, to be destined for ever to haunt the scene of his former greatness. Such is the story. The fact, however, is, that this supposed unique specimen of the arachnida is well known

Kent's Design for Drayton's *Polyolbion*

to zoologists under the name 'Tegenaria Guyonii or Domestica.'"
And, he adds, although abundant at Hampton Court, it "is not
unknown elsewhere in the valley of the Thames."

Yet, one may ask, should not the cardinal go visiting?

With almost indecent haste, the moment the cardinal was banished
to Esher, the king seized Hampton Court. It is true that Wolsey had
already given him the manor, but the gift had been purely a token one,
a magnificent gesture that meant nothing. Now Henry started
hurriedly rebuilding, adding to his palace. It is difficult to be certain
where his work begins and where Wolsey's leaves off, both being of
the same style of architecture, but he definitely added a new gallery,
a new great hall, a new library and study, and various chambers. Nor
must we forget the bowling alley and the "close tennys play" built to
the north-east of the palace in 1529, for the court is still in use. My
friend, Ralph Straus, has been busy the many years I have known him
in compiling what will be the definitive history of the game and he
has often played on this court, of which he speaks highly. The
original game was very different from lawn-tennis—although Henry
had at Hampton Court also an "open tennis play" which may have
been more like the modern kind—for you used a hard ball and had a
curved racket with diagonal gut-strings, while you played over, not
a net, but a cord with hanging fringe. The dedans—the spectators'
gallery—at Hampton Court, beneath the penthouse, must have held
many courtiers and ladies to applaud when the king in his tennis coat
of blue velvet and with tennis shoes on his great feet, proved himself,
as he did continually, one of the finest athletes in the country. "He
is most fond of tennis," writes Guistinian, "at which game it is the
prettiest thing in the world to see him play, his fair skin glowing
through a shirt of the finest texture."

You can walk that court and men still play where Henry played;
it is the oldest now in England still in use and has been taken as
model for all other courts. It had twelve windows covered with wire
to stop them breaking should wild play drive a ball high, and each
window was divided into three lights. One above the other, two
passages ran from the "lodgings"—apparently rooms for the marker
and attendants—to the palace, so that the king could visit when he
liked, even when it rained, and could walk thither without ceremony.

Tennis was by no means the only sport beloved of Henry which he
could enjoy at Hampton Court. There was hunting to be had
in the parks, and he reared rabbits, partridges and pheasants for the

joy of later murdering them, shooting and hawking being his great delights; and he built a Tilt Yard—which William III turned into six kitchen-gardens, four of which are now open to the public, two as hard tennis courts and putting greens and two as tea gardens; a fifth is now a car park and the sixth an informal garden—and five towers from which the jousting could be watched, but of these towers only one remains in a tragic state of " restoration." Here were thrilling scenes with mounted steel-clad men trundling each side of the wooden tilt raised to keep the horses apart, their lances aimed athwart the horse's ears; although not pointed but tipped with a coronal—a trefoiled button—these lances could do harm enough when they caught you and lifted you out of your saddle to crash in full armour to the sanded ground.

To-day, Henry's armour can be seen in the Tower of London, and it is sad, looking on the two suits there, to brood on the wicked ways of the flesh, for one was hammered for a lad and has beautifully fluted taces—or skirt, in non-technical language—while the other is almost huge enough to contain, as one antiquary has remarked, a hansom cab. On examining armour it must, however, be remembered that when empty the plates naturally huddle together and often give an entirely false idea of size when worn by an active man. After the plates were buckled on, they would naturally expand at the joints and there were therefore always unprotected spots, or protected purely by mail—linked rings—through which an enemy might stab. It is this illusion, the difference between an empty and a worn suit, which has caused many people, including even occasional antiquaries, to argue that men of the middle ages were smaller than men to-day. That argument becomes nonsense when we note the recorded heights of kings, many of whom were almost giants, like Henry VIII himself and his grandfather, merry Edward IV. Most of our medieval kings, after the early Angevins—yet Richard I was no small fellow—were tall.

Henry was an expert jouster—the difference between joust and tournament being that a joust was a duel between two men and the tournament was a battle of sides, like a football match—and Guistinian tells us that his skill seemed almost supernatural, the agility with which he could jump on and off his chargers—and phenomenal strength was needed for that when in full armour—" making them fly rather than leap, to the delight and ecstasy of all."

While speaking of Henry as sportsman we must not forget archery, at which he was renowned, for archery needs both skill and strength when the longbow of yew or witch-hazel is used, the string being drawn to the ear, the six feet bow held at arm's length, with a bracer of bone or metal on the forearm to catch the sting of the string when it is released. Henry was at the butts in Hampton Court park when Cavendish arrived with news of Wolsey's death. " And perceyvyng hyme occupied in shotyng," writes Cavendish, " I thought it not my dewtie to troble him; but leaned to a tree entndyng to stand there, & to attend hys gracious pleasyr. Beyng in a great study, at the last the kyng came sodynly behynd me where I stode, and clappt his hand uppon my sholder; and whan I percyved hyme, I fyll uppon my knee; to whome he sayd, callyng me by name, I woll, quod he, make an end of my game, and then woll I talke with you, and so departed to his marke, whereat the game was endyd. Than the kyng delyvered hys bowe to the yoman of hys bows, and went his way inward to the place, whome I folowed. . . ."

Of other games which Henry liked to play at Hampton Court we should mention that he built two close bowling alleys, one of about two hundred and seventy feet in length; both of these have vanished under the hands of some rascally, if royal, " improver "; and that he was fond of fishing, either in the Thames or in the garden ponds which were always stocked for his and his courtiers' sport.

Wherever you turn in the gardens of our palace, or even in the apartments and grounds laid out by later monarchs, Henry is somehow there. His ghost and Wolsey's are stronger than the wigged ghosts of later kings. Even Wren with his precise building could not exorcise the past, the true builders of our Hampton Court. Henry is there; in the knot-garden with his ladies, in the park hunting with his gentlemen, in the tennis-play leaping for the ball, in the tilt yard thundering in his steel, Henry is always there, his golden shadow warming us with dreams of a dangerous yet vivid past in which one walked stealthily, sword at one's side, ambushed by scheming ladies or sullen courtiers. Not William and Mary, not even the Georges, could exorcise that ghost with hammering, with plaster, with tearing down precious bricks and mortar. This remains his and Wolsey's palace above all; and that is why I love it.

When Wolsey went despairingly to Esher, Henry raced to Hampton Court. For the next three years enthusiastically he altered and built and added to the manor, until his expenditure mounted so vastly that Cromwell—the new, less gorgeous Wolsey—was forced to protest, sighing to consider that should the king cease building for only one year " how profitable it would be to him." Hampton Court was not, of course, the only channel for this outrush of gold—Mistress Anne's garments and trinkets must have made a pretty sum—but it slashed its by no means small gap in the royal money-bags.

Henry was raising here new kitchens and offices for the kitchen, a new buttery, pantry, pastry, spicery, larder, dry-fish house, and so on; he was raising also that dignified Great Hall which stands to this day as warning of our artistic degeneration, although in parts it has been altered and here and there miserably " restored." We have lost the louvre, for example, through which the stinging smoke from the tarred log-fire ascended: all painted and gilded and carved it was. The glass in the windows, of course, is modern, although not so frighteningly bad as most modern stained-glass which seems copied from some nineteenth century schoolbook. It is the louvre, however, we miss most, for it rose in three tiers, pinnacled and cunningly carved in wood, was lead roofed and had glassed sides. Thanks to some lucky accident, the huge bay window still rises from behind the dais with its forty-eight lights and its vault of miniature fan-groin with delicately carved pendants. The halpace, the raised step before this window, was originally paved with green and white tiles, for in Tudor times, almost everything was coloured.

They had not then our bloodless love for flat boxes like biscuit tins gashed monotonously with mean one-sized windows; they had not our watery love for bleak walls within showing not a dab of colour, rarely even a painting on their blind desert. So far have we reacted from the overcrowded interiors of Edwardian days that we have leaped into a vacuum in which " taste " means lack of any colour or ornament and is equally as " vulgar " as the junk-shop appearance of our grandparents' sitting-rooms.

Wolsey and Henry set chimneys of all sizes, of all shapes, side by side; they pierced a window where they wanted a window of the most convenient size, with the result that the whole becomes as fascinating and lovely as nature itself where trees do not dwarf themselves and uniformly shorten branches. Men of those times loved colour, and rightly so. Little was left unpainted or ungilded in their homes; woodwork, sometimes even stonework, was painted, and this glorious Great Hall of Hampton Court would have blinded the watery-eyed æsthetes of modern architectural "taste," for lovers of painting at least, thank God, have not grown dark glasses through which to reveal nature. We possess the building accounts for Hampton Court and in them we find the painter recorded with due honour, as for example: "Payde to John Hethe, paynter, of London, for gyldyng and payntyng of 272 badges of the Kyngs and Quenys, standyng abowghte the vowghte, and the caters within the Kynges new haull, at 12d. the pece"; and again: "For lyke gyldyng and payntyng of 28 hedd, standyng uppon the hammer-beamys in the rouff of the said haull, price the pece, 2s.—56s." Bright colour on roof, on walls, in windows; and on the floor, colour again. And the men and women, too, then were prismatic, moving in richly dyed clothes and purring velvet. All this we have lost, we modern convicts in our jail of uniformity, drably existing in drab surroundings.

It is ironic, and fortunate for us, that in time Wolsey triumphed over his destroyer. His arms have reappeared on the Clock Tower and, while the royal apartments have become dust under the assault of William's workmen, his private chambers have come back. They overlook the garden on the south and the Inner Court on the north and are reached to-day through William's State Rooms. Under the early Georges, court officials roosted here and, when royalty deserted the palace, the rooms were adapted to "grace and favour" apartments. Where the massive cardinal plotted and sometimes slept, ladies lived for many years, as if the jealous ghost would keep all male rivals from his rooms; and he was a benevolent ghost, it seems, for one of the residents, Lady Frances Beresford, found such peace there that she managed to cling to life for 106 years.

Tudor decorations were out of favour and the lovely panelling, the decorated ceilings, and even the fireplace, were hidden behind papered canvas and partitions, while a mullioned bay window was demolished and an ordinary sash-window inserted, yet much has been recovered. When, in 1913, these rooms became vacant, antiquarians had their opportunity to tear away the concealing boards and canvas, and the four hundred years-old walls were found, having been hidden for over two hundred years. Much has been saved but, alas, much, too, has been lost. The painted glass was powdered centuries ago; many decorations and ornamental cornices and friezes are now dust; while the colour has vanished; although in one room, probably Wolsey's privy chamber, one can detect a faint glitter of gilt and paint on the ceiling. This is a very lovely ceiling with panels geometrically arranged, with flat moulded ribs and gesso-work decorations, and with little turned bosses of lead-leafed wood at the intersection of the ribs. In this chamber, under that ceiling which generations of whitewash have not entirely ruined, one can meet most vividly the ghost of the cardinal, can see him before the stone fireplace with its back of herring-bone brick, warming hands and feet while he sips his wine and dreams of the tiara.

The other rooms are not quite so valuable to us, although the first one you enter, Wolsey's ante-chamber, has a somewhat rare linen-fold pattern and a mullioned window that must originally have overlooked the Inner Court. It now looks out on to the wall of a staircase behind Wren's colonnade. The third room has suffered most. Its mullioned bay window through which Wolsey must often have gazed upon his garden was destroyed so that some " modern " fool might have a common sash-window. Only a part of the ceiling remains and still has a little of the paint-pot left, while a few of the plaques bear Wolsey's badges, such as the pillars and cross-keys. But the room called the Cardinal's Closet has escaped almost wholly, although now made smaller, for freize and ceiling are wellnigh perfect. Here we find the Tudor rose and the Prince of Wales's feathers and therefore it must have been designed during Edward's childhood, and we can conceive some idea of the richness of the original with the gold on a blue field on the moulding. Similar in design to this ceiling is the decorated cornice with the arabesques of human and animal creatures, a pageant on which Wolsey must often have gazed and which his great hand has touched. Therefore look on it with reverence, on those queer creatures in relief, and on the moulded fillet under them—although it is undoubtedly not in its rightful place—with Wolsey's motto: " Dominus michi adjutor." Look also with reverence on the frieze on the cornice, the narrow panels of wood painted with the Passion of our Lord, for it was almost certainly there in Wolsey's day, with the mullioned window opening on to the Fountain Court and with the fireplace and the cast-iron fireback, the oldest in Hampton Court.

Almost miraculously, it seems, after those centuries, the cardinal has returned to us. Not the hand of Henry, not the impious destruction of William and the early Georges, have exorcised him. By right of building, by right of dreaming this palace into existence, he has come from the past and here, in these chambers, can you meet him. No history book can bring him to us so vividly as can these walls, that panelling, that frieze, that ceiling, that fireplace. In this room it is well to pause when you visit the palace, for if your country's past means anything to you, here you will find it living yet.

In the kitchens, too, you will enter the Tudor world for, thanks again to the energy and persistence of Mr. Law, much has been recovered. Wolsey's kitchens were not large enough for the king and under the Great Hall and Great Watching Chamber he constructed his own " Newe Boterie, Newe Bere Seller and Newe Wyne Seller," and they were in use until after the Stuart times. Perhaps men drank less in the late seventeenth and eighteenth centuries, but that is indeed doubtful. If anything, it would seem they drank more, for English drunkenness—at court, at any rate—became outrageous under James I when his wife's Danish relations imported habits that shocked Elizabethans like Sir John Harington. Of the state visit of the King of Denmark he complained that " the Dane hath strangely wrought on our good English nobles; for those whom I could never get to taste good liquor, now follow the fashion, and wallow in beastly delights. The ladies abandon their sobriety and are seen to roll about in intoxication." That could not have been written of the court of Henry VIII, but we must remember that ale was then a necessity, water not being drunk save in emergencies, and most likely it was not very strong.

From the Clock Court you enter the buttery, but there is little of interest to be found, no trace of its original use being seen, for here were kept the stores to be passed through the hatch to the officers of the cook. It is to us merely a large rectangular cellar with little windows slightly above ground-level giving a dim light, and the exhibits are of small value—pieces of ancient crockery and floor-tiles, beams from the hall-roof to show the wicked work of the death-watch beetle, with iron work, including some exquisite pieces from Tijou's gates and screens, and a very incongruous Carolian altar-rail from the Chapel with a chain-dredger dredged from the moat.

Under the archway and into the beer-cellar you go to find equally disappointing barrenness, for only the stairs remain to remind you that it was in Tudor days entered also from the cloister, and a big fireplace is there that you may remember how cold it must have been in this dank dim underworld. From here you enter the wine-cellar running off at right-angles under the Great Watching Chamber. And now you are not disappointed. When the tons of rubble and rubbish were carried away from here and the floor discovered, brick benches built around the walls and running down the centre, eight inches higher than the passages between them, were revealed. On the brick stands hollows had been cut to hold the barrels steady. This cellar, sixty feet by thirty feet, is divided into two equal aisles by a row of stone piers with vaulting ribs of brick rising from them and the stone corbels in the walls. This was built, we find from the accounts, by a certain Williams, priest and surveyor, who had also worked for Wolsey. Two brick arches open into the serving-place and here the yeomen-waiters and others came to be served through the hatches with their moulded oak frames and shutters hinged at the top.

The Great Kitchen.

The Great Kitchen, however, is our goal, for it is thirty-seven feet long and twenty-seven feet wide and has in the north wall a huge fireplace under a stone arch with a brick relieving arch above, although a later fireplace has been built inside it with a row of brick ovens. Opposite are two further fireplaces of noble proportions, one being sixteen feet wide, with a roasting-spit ready to turn for roasting. In the west wall, two doors open into Wolsey's kitchen, of

34

which we can see but little, for parts have been partitioned off and two mighty fireplaces are therefore hidden. Yet enough remains for us to be able to repeople these kitchens, shutting our eyes on the collection of ornamental bosses gathered from the ceiling of the Great Watching Chamber, with pieces of carved stone. Interesting as these exhibits are, particularly some of the cooking utensils, I would have them swept out had I my way, for they bring to these spacious chambers the musty depression of a museum, and nothing can exorcise ghosts like a museum where all is glazed from us. These odds and ends of the past merely help to kill the past for, by their disconsolate air of being put by, broken and discarded, they wrench us sharply into the present and sadden us to think of all that we have lost.

Swiftly rose the king's manor about the cardinal's manor, even freemasons being employed, although Henry VI had issued a statute against them. We have the roll of artists' names and it is interesting to find Mr. Law remarking that all were "Englishmen, nearly without exception, and almost invariably the inhabitants of the neigh-bouring towns and villages—such as Kingston, Moulsey, Hampton, Epsom, Teddington, and Chertsey. Even the most delicate carvings and paintings of the roof, which are sometimes stated to have been the work of Italian and other foreigners, are proved to have been entirely executed by Englishmen." To English genius and English craftsmanship this splendid house owes its conception and its birth, and these men worked briskly under the king's impatience as is shown in the following item of expenditure: " Empcion of tallow candells, spent by the workmen in the nyghte tymes uppon the pavyng of the hall, for the hasty expedecion of the same at 18d. the dosyn "; and this for building the bridge: workmen " workyng in theyre owre tyms and dryngkyng tymys . . . for the haystye expedycyon of the same." Fierce indeed must have been that royal impatience to have English workmen squander drinking-time.

And, to stamp that impatient ownership on the walls, wherever Wolsey's arms showed, Henry tore them down or had them plastered over with his own arms. His arms, indeed, were set everywhere and heraldic beasts were carved on pinnacles and copings, on the gables and battlements, all of which now are gone. Not only his own name but the name of his new wife, his sweetheart, must be carved wherever possible, often her initials interlacing with his own; for even before the fall of Wolsey, men were building " Anne Bouillayne's lodgynges at Hampton Courte."

Under Anne Boleyn's Gateway you can see the fan-tracery vault—a modern but exact reproduction as the original was becoming dangerously cracked—with the king's badge of the portcullis and fleur-de-lis with Anne's of the falcon, and the initials H.A. entwined in a true-lovers' knot that was shortly to be severed with an axe.

Anne Boleyn's Gateway.

For Anne, the falcon was safe in the royal mews, domestically sewing and embroidering at which, like most ladies of the time, she was well skilled. Hentzner in his *Travels in England* during her daughter, Elizabeth's reign, tells us that visitors to Hampton Court were shown a bed-tester worked entirely by Anne for her huge husband and her to sleep within; and George Wyatt, grandson of the poet who had loved her, records that " those who have seen at Hampton Court the rich and exquisite works by herself, for the greater part wrought by her own hand and needle, and also of her ladies, esteem them the most precious furniture that are to be accounted amongst the most sumptuous that any prince may be possessed of. And yet far more precious were those works, in the sight of God, which she caused her maids and those about her daily to work in shirts and smocks for the poor."

. Anne was not always blinding herself at needlework, by any means; there were also days for hunting and hawking and for bowls and shovel-board—the original shove-halfpenny and still played on ship-deck in a more expansive fashion, for in Henry's time, circular pieces of wood were pushed down a low-walled table by long shovels—and nights for cards and music and backgammon— then called tables. It seems that she was not always lucky, no luckier indeed than she was in love, for the royal privy-purse expenses detail such horrific matters as gifts to her of from £40 to nearly £200 for her losses. But that was not a pinch of gold compared to the cost of her wardrobe in which one nightgown alone, made of black satin and edged with black velvet and lined with black fur, cost £101. 15s. 8d.—a sum so huge that it is impossible to inflate it to our present fantastic currency: we might multiply it by five and yet fail to be correct, for while then necessities seem to us comparatively very cheap, luxuries appear appallingly expensive. This nightgown, by the by, would not be worn in bed, it would be used like a modern dressing-gown: most people then slept naked or, at most, wore only a thin shift.

Yet for all the lovely apparel, for all the jewels about her long white beautiful throat and on her slim fingers, Anne's can be no happy ghost in our palace. Queen Katherine yet lived, noble and proud, and she was worshipped by the people, while Anne's efforts to humiliate her by demanding from her her jewels were petty and but revealed how deeply herself was hurt and ashamed.

This book, however, is a history of the palace and not of England and, I confess reluctantly, we must leave the complexities of Anne's character and her torments when she found, after bearing no prince but a girl, that she was in the same dangerous corner to which she had forced Katherine, that the king was lolling about young Jane Seymour, neglecting and even insulting her.

We must leave her while, as briefly as possible, we examine Henry's royal household. Many historical novels reveal how ignorant are most people about the rigid etiquette which surrounded, and still surrounds if in a lesser degree, a king and queen. I have read novels in which courtiers walk casually into a queen's chamber to see her alone, in which a queen like a commoner steals abroad to meet a lover; but the details of Katherine Howard's adventures with Culpeper reveal how trapped in envious mirrors was a queen, how few, how precious were those moments when she could creep to her lover, and how dangerous. One of their meetings was actually in the privy, and a privy in those times—before Sir John Harington wrote so delightfully of his invention, the water-closet, in Queen Elizabeth's reign and was considered a nasty crank for having such ideas*—must have been a revolting and very far from romantic trysting-place. Yet even to such vile assignations must a queen stoop if she would elude her ladies-in-waiting, all spies, and the hundreds of servants watching her every move from every side.

In the royal ordinances for the Tudor household—published by the Society of Antiquaries in 1790—we are given in detail the formalities of Henry's court and can visualise the world in which trapped Anne Boleyn moved, no longer the free falcon, no longer able to tease her lover-husband who now turned his broad back on her to toy with Jane.

We cannot examine all these regulations—that would require a volume—but will take a few examples, such as the order to stop men from gambling, playing dice, tables or cards in the presence chamber when the king was absent, and for the attendants to " have a vigilant and reverent respect and eye to his Grace, soe that by his looke or countenance they may know what lacketh, or is his pleasure to be got or done." From such enactments we can deduce the opposite, that it was the custom for men to gamble when Henry

---

* Yet, if we may judge by Harington's *Epigrams*, Elizabeth was not unimpressed by his invention, for one verse is headed: " To the Ladies of the Queen's Privy-chamber, at the making of their perfumed privy at Richmond "—alas ! not at Hampton Court.

was absent and to be a trifle myopic when his impatient highness wanted something he was too lazy to mention. Again, the following reveals the everyday bickerings and mutterings of courtiers in a palace like Hampton Court, weary of performing the endless ritual of courtesy:

" Item, it is ordeyned that such persons as be appointed of the privy chamber, shall be loving together, and of good unity and accord; keeping secret all such things as shall be done or said in the same, without discloseing any parte thereof to any person not being for the time present in the same chamber; and that the King being absent, without they be commanded to goe with his Grace, they shall not onely give their continuall and diligent attendance in the said chamber, but also leave harkening and enquiring where the King is, or goeth, be it early or late; without grudgeing, mumbling, or talking of the King's pastime; late or early going to bed; or anything done by his grace, as they will avoyde his displeasure; and it is also ordered, that in case any of the said privy chamber shall heare any of his fellowes, or other person, of what estate or degree soever hee bee, speake or use any evil or unfitting language of the King, he shall with diligence disclose and shew the same, with the specialltyes thereof, unto his Highnesse, or to some of his privy councell, such as he thinketh meete, to shew and declare the same unto his Grace."

Each man here is commanded to turn informer on his fellows so that the court, the merry Tudor court, must have been a court of spies, each man eager to lie or cheat for preference, to earn the king's love with tattling treachery, repeating any grumble, any of those exasperated expletives of which we are all capable when we vent our anxieties on a popinjay as substitution for ourselves. And the king, we note, is ever watchful of his dignity and is not the romping over-grown boy he is usually depicted in books or on the stage. When he turns his huge royal back he wonders, suddenly human away from others watching, whether those who fall on one knee to speak to him do not curl their lips and wink when he has gone. What do they chatter about? he wonders; then, in fear of loss of dignity, he commands them not to chatter, not to speculate about whose bed he seeks, which minister he would confer with, not to blab together of his affairs; for pride can be blasted by scandal and even a royal godhead become tarnished with whispers and chuckles that he was late abed last night.

39

In such enactments as these do we see the court far more clearly than in travellers' tales or ambassadors' reports which record mainly the surface and, save for occasional anecdotes, do not show the ordinariness of these men and women who lived and loved and hated in Hampton Court and other palaces four hundred years ago. Here we see them spiteful and lazy and truculent and gossiping and dirty. To our thinking, they were often very dirty, as this enactment shows: "All such as have their lodgeings within the court shall give straight charge to the mynisters and keepers of their chambers, that they do not cast, leave, or lay any manner of dishes, platters, saucers, or broken meate, either in the said galleryes, or at their chamber doores, or in the court, or other place . . . soe that broken meate and drinke be in no wise lost, cast away, or eaten with dogges, nor lye abroad in the galleryes and courtes, but may daily be saved for the reliefe of the poore folks." Not for need for cleanliness must you desist from throwing your bones or spitting the gristle amongst the rushes or putting your dirty plates in gallery or court, but to feed the poor. And that mention of dogs recalls another of these enactments which does make some attempt at sanitation, for dogs' fouling with rotten rushes and other refuse must have made the palace often stink in summer. " The King's Highnesse," it is announced, " alsoe straightly forbiddeth and inhibiteth, that no person, whatsoever he be, presume to keepe any grey-hounds, mastives, hounds, or other dogges, in the court, other than such few small spaniells for ladyes or others."

All the various officers at the palace are dealt with in these regulations but their tasks are too many and often too unimportant for us to loiter with, for they include, apart from lesser attendants under these attendants: the sergeants of the bakehouse, the pantry, the cellar, the chaundry (candle storehouse), the ewry (for ewers and towels and table linen), the larder, the acatry (containing provisions brought by purveyors scouring the countryside), the poultry, the squillery (a scullery for the cleansing and keeping of silver plate), the pastery (where pastry was made), the porter in his lodge, the butler, the clerks of the spicery and of the kitchen, the master cooks, the officers of confectionery and wafery, the purveyor of sea-fish, the marshals and ushers and sergeants of the hall; not to mention the sergeants-at-arms, the heralds, the pursuivants or messengers, the minstrels, the huntsmen, the footmen. . . .

All these are far too packed a gallery to fit between the covers of this book, and indeed, deserve a volume to themselves with their many duties, but the list explains the need for large palaces. To be served, the king must have hundreds of followers, all eating into the revenues and, large though it was, Hampton Court must often have seemed cramped, with six men sleeping in one small chamber and others having to lie under tents in the grounds, when visitors were many, for the visitors would bring with them huge retinues, hundreds of strangers also to be housed and fed. Surrounded by men, each with his duty that might be done in a few minutes, the king was rarely, if ever, alone, for he was escorted even to that one chamber of the house where every man demands solitude.

From dawn to bedtime, he was watched, and his bed-chamber was so guarded that none could slip in unseen, while his love affairs must inevitably have been trumpeted through the palace. To close these enactments let us quote the following that you might have some conception of a Tudor king at home:

" It is ordeyned, that there be daily one yeoman usher at the said [outer-] chamber doore, by eight of the clocke in the morning at the furthest, to attend to take the charge thereof, and not to depart from the same, except he deliver the same charge to some other yeoman usher of his company; and that he permitt nor suffer any man to come in the same chamber, but lords, knights, gentlemen, officers of the King's house, and other honest personages, as by his wisdome and discretion shall be thought good; resorting in all cases doubtfull to the lord chamberlyn, and in his absence to the vice chamberlyn, for knowledge of their pleasure and minde in that behalfe. And over this, that no man presume or be suffered to come within the said chamber after the King be served for All-night, but onely the esquires for the body and pages, except such as be of the King's privy chamber, who in their passing and repassing through the said chamber shall soe use themselves, as they doe not disturbe the said esquires of their rest and sleepe; nor alsoe that there be no manner of playing at disse or cards, used within the same chamber, after the King be served for All-night, except it be by the King's commandment or lycence. And over this, it is ordered, that dayly the yeoman ushers and yeoman wayters for the day, be within the King's great chamber by eight of the clock in the morning at the furthest, giveing their continuall attendance without departing, except they shall be otherwayes lycensed by the lord chamberlyn or vice-chamberlyn in his absence; and semblably that the groomes of the chamber be there by the same houre, and give their like attendance accordingly; and that one of the yeoman wayters shall dayly take the charge of the door of the same chamber, not permitting or suffering any person to enter, but such as by his discression shall be seene good and meete for that place; nor any gentleman's page to come within the same chamber, except it be to speake with his master; and his message done, incontinently to depart."

And such was not the divinity but the human ramparts that did hedge a king like Henry VIII . . . I have said that we would now have done with these enactments, but let us pause to repeat one tribute to the yeomen of the crown, for these were those who did the real and dirty work, and here we find them rightly honoured as the " most semely personages, clenely and strongest archers, honest of conditions and of behavoure, bold men, chosen and tryed out of everey lordes house in Englond, for theyre cunnyng and vertus. . . ."

That is a tribute worth our repeating and one that most definitely could not be given most of their betters, the lords and ladies of Hampton Court.

Anne had failed. In his lust for a son had the king married her, and she gave him one daughter, Elizabeth; then when she was again with child she was to learn the martyrdom of Catherine, for she miscarried. One story goes that " the king seeming to affect Jane Seymour, and having her on his knee, as Queen Anne espied, who was then thought to be with child, she for anger and disdain, miscarried." The Spanish ambassador, Chapuys, suggests a similar episode by blaming the disaster on Anne's fear lest Henry " treat her like the late queen, especially considering the treatment shown to a lady of the court, named Mistress Seme [Seymour], to whom, many say, he has lately made great presents." I prefer Wriotheseley's explanation—and he was of the court and should have known— that " it was said she tooke a fright, for the King ran that tyme at the ring and had a fall from his horse, but he had no hurt; and she took such a fright withall that it caused her to fall in travaile, and so was delivered afore her tyme, which was a great discomfort to all this realme."

We may question Wriotheseley—pronounced Riseley—about Henry's " no hurt " for Chapuys tells us that his fall in full armour was so heavy that everyone thought it a miracle he was not killed;

while in a later letter he attributes the miscarriage directly to this tumble. Therefore we can dismiss the scandal of Anne catching Jane on Henry's knee; although there is no reason why it should not have happened, it was plainly not the immediate cause of the miscarriage. It was this fall, incidentally, which broke the vein in Henry's leg and caused the running sore his enemies gleefully denounce as a syphilitic ulcer; but there is absolutely no evidence that Henry was ever diseased and the lie should now have stopped since the publication in 1932 of Frederick Chamberlin's *The Private Character of Henry the Eighth*, where the evidence is exhaustively examined.

Because of this tumble and the breaking of the vein, Henry was unable afterwards to continue his violent sports, for he was forced to hobble with the aid of a staff—you can see it in his portrait in the possession of the Earl of Warwick—and therefore grew so huge that silly legends have been invented about cranes being needed to lift him on his horse.

This is no place to argue Anne's alleged adulteries in which I certainly do not believe. The tragic tale of the trial is well known, and her proud death less than four months after Katherine's funeral when she stepped from the Tower in her nightgown—dressing-gown —of damask with red damask skirt and with a netted coif about her raven hair, " as gay as if she was not going to die." While she knelt, praying on the scaffold, the executioner slyly drew the sword from where it lay hidden under straw, and lifted it, and swung. She was the first English queen to be beheaded and for so notable an occasion an expert headsman had been despatched all the way from Calais at the cost of £23. 6s. 8d.

That same night Henry supped with Jane Seymour and the next morning they were betrothed.

CHAPTER III

HENRY AND FOUR WIVES

O N May 30th, 1536, Henry married Jane, defiant of superstition, for May was considered the black month for marriages. This was ten days after the betrothal; but a betrothal then, if sworn before witnesses, was considered as binding as the marriage ceremony itself. He was still busy building Hampton Court, for one never stops altering and adding to a house one loves. Always there is something more to do; one feels like an artist fiddling with a painting who is reluctant to drop his brushes. The Queen's New Lodgings, planned for Anne, were completed for Jane, and painters and moulders were scurrying about the palace, tearing down Anne's badges or painting them out to replace them with Jane's quarterings. We have seen that, fortunately, they neglected to destroy the carving in the groined ceiling under the Clock Tower, but they even plucked the figure of St. Anne in painted glass from the chapel window, for now the poor saint must be martyred for her namesake's wickedness. Outside the chapel door, the carved tables from which already Wolsey's arms had been painted out, were now painted again with a *J* over the *A* in a true lovers' knot with *H* for *Henry*. Jane's castle bubbling fire and Tudor roses under a crowned phœnix was painted or carved wherever possible, so that all should be made ready to proclaim at last a permanent queen, for who could dare doubt that this placid little alleged virgin would breed the needful sons and would keep breeding wellnigh yearly for years and years ?

Few of these emblems remain, but in Henry's Great Watching Chamber to the north-west of the Round Kitchen Court and at right-angles to the so-called Haunted Gallery you can still see them in the ceiling. This chamber remains by some extraordinary good luck as a perfect example of Tudor architecture and is, to my thinking, the most precious at Hampton Court, with its tall stone clerestory windows of a simplified Gothic and its mighty semi-circular oriel of thirty-six lights, a winking twinkling sun rising from the stone. But it is towards the low ceiling of cunningly arranged ribs and pendants that I would ask you to look. At first glance all may seem haphazard until the design takes form with its angles and squares enclosing fleur-de-lis and Tudor roses and other emblems, including Jane's. You cannot mistake hers for, as I have remarked, they include a phœnix, Tudor roses of eight petals, and a castle enclosed in some form of papier-mâché. To-day, alas, they lack the original colour and you must try to imagine them as they were, gaudy with gilt and reds and pinks.

Originally this chamber was intended as the Guard Chamber at the entrance to the royal Presence Chamber and State Rooms, all of which have been destroyed. The painted glass in the bay window was made in 1846 and is not so bad as one might fear from that date. It shows the four arms of the four sees held by Wolsey—Durham, Bath and Wells, Winchester and York—with his motto and badges. The king's head is also, inevitably, there to glower on the cardinal's honours.

It was now that further beauty was added to our palace. In 1535-6, Henry built the stone bridge in place of Wolsey's which had probably been of wood. Long was this bridge lost to us until Mr. Law and other antiquaries cleared it and brought it again to stand over the moat. It is of four spans, each eight feet wide, and is twenty-five feet wide, made with a core of red brick faced with stone from Headington in Oxfordshire. Originally, twelve heraldic beasts bearing shields stood on it, six a side, and Mr. Peers surmises that " it is not unreasonable to suppose that six of them bore the king's arms and six the queen's. The greyhound, the lion, the dragon, and the bull are clearly the king's beasts, all having been used as his supporters at various times, the dragon standing for Cadwallader, the greyhound for Beaufort, and the bull for Clarence. Now the queen's supporters were a lion with a prince's crown and an unicorn. As to the jall or yale, he is a rare and strange animal partaking of the nature of the heraldic antelope, that is to say, wearing horns and a large pair of projecting tusks." There was also a panther which was probably Jane's. " If this chain of reasoning holds good," continues Mr. Peers, " it seems that the dragons, bull, and greyhounds, and probably the ' jall ' on the bridge bore shields of the king's arms, and the panthers and unicorns the queen's arms, while the lions were divided between them. The panels on either side of the west door of the chapel afford a useful contemporary model for these shields."

This was the bridge Henry raised and which was lost for so long, and bright in the sunlight it must have shone with its paint and gilding when Tudor gentlemen trotted over it, little round caps aslant their cropped heads, gay short cloaks curling over the saddle at the back and open on the padded and gold-embroidered doublets, as they came to lout low to the new young queen.

Jane has few associations with Hampton Court save her sad death, despite her badge being so often discovered on the walls, for as she did her duty by the King he honoured her memory by, on marrying again, not tearing down or painting over her emblems, and therefore they remain. Most probably she would have resided in the apartments that had been building for Anne, with the Queen's Long Gallery—destroyed by William III—which was 180 feet in length and twenty-five feet broad, lighted by many windows on either side, all gay with painted glass reflecting multi-coloured on the carpeted or rush-covered floor as though scattering diaphanous flower-petals. The brightest of Wolsey's tapestries were hooked against the walls and there was a ceiling of over a thousand balls of burnished gold with golden leaves. All this have we lost because of William's damned passion to out-build French Louis.

In this glorious gallery Jane awaited her accouchement, sewing and embroidering with her ladies, or chatting with Princess Mary, whom she had begged the king to love and let return to court, while all prayed that at last the King would have a prince.

And at last was that prayer granted. At two o'clock in the morning of Friday, October 12th, 1537, Prince Edward was born in Hampton Court.

Now was the Tudor dynasty, it seemed, assured. The blood shed on Bosworth Field would at last be soaked without stain into the earth and the memory of a noble yet murdered king thrown naked into a nameless grave would be forgotten in England. At last, after fretful years lest all be for naught while the Tudors had killed every man they could snatch who had a drop of Plantagenet blood, the second Tudor king had a Tudor son. High had flourished the seed of that Welsh lover of the widow of Henry V; these descendants of a base squire and a royal French widow with madness in her veins were rulers now of England and were safe with a prince to follow them.

In almost every town in England, bells pealed and fires were lit, for civil war was now a memory, cold ash of a dangerously recent fire. There is a lie that Henry, on being told that either mother or child must die, cried: " Another wife is easily got, but not so another child "; yet such was Henry's mood. We cannot doubt if he had been asked the question he would, and quite rightly with his shaky throne, have chosen the prince's life. But Jane did not die in childbirth, she died shortly afterwards, apparently of puerperal septicæmia.

The boy, Edward, was baptised in the Chapel of Hampton Court which had recently been enlarged and improved by the king, new painted glass being fitted into the windows and new stalls carved, with a new organ in a new organ-house, and with the beautiful arched roof freshly gilt and painted. Of the original chapel only the roof with its pendants of angels and escutcheons of the king's and queen's arms is what remains to us. The painted glass, the pictures, the images, all were destroyed by ordinance of parliament in 1645, and Wren tore down to rebuild what little remained, save for this ceiling. Even the tiles have been altered: instead of Henry's green and white floor, a checkered pavement has been laid. Yet at least we may be grateful for the ceiling, as it is lovely work: a fan vault of the kind usually made only in stone, rarely in wood like this, while the winged cherubim with their musical instruments are genuine renascence babies, chubby and gay and seeming ready to laugh.

In this chapel—or should we say, under this roof?—little Prince Edward was baptised, three days after birth. At the north of the Chapel Court, the procession entered the Prince's Lodgings and turned left into the Council Chamber which opens into the Haunted Gallery. All carried torches of virgin wax, to remain unlit until after the ceremony, and behind the eighty knights and gentlemen and squires, walking two by two, came the children—the singers— and the ministers of the chapel, with the dean and chaplains, all in surplices and copes. Next walked the king's council, the great men of the realm, both spiritual and temporal, and they were followed by two lords carrying " a pair of covered basins, and a towel upon that, with a cup of assay " in which wine would be first poured that it might be tasted for poison. " Next after, a taper of virgin wax, borne by the Earl of Wiltshire, with a towel about his neck," and then, " a salt of gold, richly garnished, borne by the Lady Elizabeth, the King's daughter, the same for her tender age [she was not quite four] was borne " by two lords. Lastly, came the royal baby himself, carried by a marchioness with the assistance of a duke and her husband, a marquis, the train of the baby's robe being upheld by an earl and a lord, and with them walked the proud midwife, her vulgar milk to feed a prince, and a nurse. Four gentlemen of the king's privy chamber lifted a rich canopy over the child, and beside them walked four other gentlemen with torches. Lady Mary, the godmother—so dearly loved was the poor princess by the queen—concluded the procession with a rout of "ladies of honour and gentlewomen, in order after their degrees."

Solemnly, in reverent pomp, the god-baby was carried on his cushions: England's future Prince of Wales and already honoured, his chuckling majesty, as though he were a little Christ, and these lumbering lords and heavy-skirted ladies were the kine worshipping: solemnly they paced the Council Chamber, along part of the Haunted Gallery—through which we shall shortly venture—to the king's great Watching Chamber at the upper end of the Great Hall, then down through the Hall, under the Screens, down the Great Stairs, under Anne Boleyn's Gateway with above them her initials still twined in a true lover's knot with Henry's to scowl on the babe; into the Second or Clock Court, then through the Cloister to the Chapel door, they went. Almost on tiptoe, heads erect, they paced, while hushed servitors watched from behind barriers that were hung with cloths and tapestries to keep them from the sacrilege of touching or even of breathing on this most precious prince. All the way, men-at-arms stood with their halberds on either side while servitors held blazing torches.

The courtyard had been strewn with fresh rushes from the river that these great men and women should pad noiselessly in their velvet shoes, as soundless as stalking animals: all silent, those who walked and those who watched, save for the baby which, perhaps— we do not know—wailed at the pinch of cold air. In this fashion, with all due ceremony, they went through the palace, into the court and into the chapel. The people of England were not there to watch their prince's christening; almost was it a family ceremony with only the palace household present, for the plague was abroad and all were forbidden to approach Hampton Court lest they kill this child of a middle-aged man who had dreamed so long, so seemingly hope- lessly of its coming.

As the procession neared the chapel door, gentlemen ushers guarded the way where a large porch, " covered with rich cloth of gold, and double-hanged with rich arras," had been built, "its floor boarded and covered with carpets." Still soundlessly, they went, heads erect as though they acted some sacred fertility-rite, as if themselves had bred this prince, as if they were, men and women, the symbolic body of England which had, at last, with prayer and labour given birth to this little raw infant mewling on his cushion of cloth of gold.

Both chapel and quire were draped with tapestries, and the high altar seemed aflame with gold plates and cups and a gold crucifix. A font of solid silver gilt stood in the centre of the quire, " set upon a mount or stage, made of four degrees in height and eight square in compass, inclosed with double barriers of timber, with two or three entries, one to come in, another to pass to the travers [the screen], the third to the altar," to build which the carpenters had worked " in theyr owre tymes and drynkyng tymes." These barriers were hung with cloth of gold while over the font was stretched a brilliant canopy. To the south of the font a space was screened or curtained off, to which the babe was carried to be made ready for its performance. A pan of coals kept this screened chamber warm, and it was headily perfumed to delight a week's old child, and there stood basins and chaffers of silver and gilt holding water with which to wash the child, should that be necessary. Concealed behind these screens, the nurse prepared the prince while the quire sang the *Te Deum;* then was it carried forth to the ceremonial christening.

These christenings were elaborate ceremonies and the full ritual would, I fear, take more space than we can give, but when at last it was over and the baby had become God's, torches were lit and flared in the chapel. Then Garter King-at-Arms stood forth in his tabard of bright colours and proclaimed: " God of his Almighty and infinite grace, give and grant good life and long to the right high, right excellent and noble prince, Prince Edward, Duke of Cornwall, and Earl of Chester, most dear and entirely beloved son to our most dread and gracious lord, King Henry the Eighth."

The King waited with his Queen in her bed-chamber while the ceremony proceeded. We do not know which room this could have been, but Mr. Law conclusively demolishes the tradition that it was the one in the south-east corner of the Clock Court which is sometimes pointed out to visitors. It would, however, have been somewhere in the new apartments planned for Anne that now were Jane's; and to the royal couple here the slow procession returned and the sacred child, now a Christian, was given to his father and mother who would be eager to learn whether he had cried, for such matters were omens in those days. And thus, we are told, he " had the blessing of Almighty God, our Lady, and St. George, and his father and mother."

Ten days later there was another solemn scene enacted at Hampton Court: after the ceremony of dedicating a life to God came the ceremony of sending a soul to Him.

Queen Jane died at eight o'clock on Wednesday morning, October 24th.

She who had recently suffered the pains of labour knew now the pains of death. So young, she who had been so healthy, to die so swiftly. Only a little over a week before, *Te Deums* had been intoned to heaven to glorify her in her labour and the King in his joy had sent her fat quails to eat, while cannon had thundered from the Tower, fires had been lit in the streets, and the people had danced and rejoiced. Now all was mourning with the young queen dead. She who was " bound to serve and obey " had served most nobly, and, in grief, the King fled Hampton Court for Windsor so that the melancholy task of embalming the corpse might be done without him to watch through tears.

On a hearse covered with a rich pall of cloth of gold and with a cross placed on it, the body was carried to the Presence Chamber and there in the middle of the room lowered to the floor. The walls were black; not a blink of light showed save from death's candles, while the mourners knelt, Princess Mary chief amongst them, all in black save for white kerchiefs on heads and shoulders, praying for the late Queen's soul. Even the altar was black, draped with a pall and shining only with its crucifix, its images of saints, its censers and candlesticks, metal polished against man-made night. For a week, masses were said and dirges sung; night and day, without pause, they craved the easy passage of this soul to God.

Then blessed with holy water, censed with incense from sweet-smelling censers, on the last day of October the body was carried to the chapel, priests and the quire holding tapers and singing about it. On November 12th, the offices of the dead being finished for the time, the coffin was borne to the Clock Court, to the waiting funeral car that was yoked to four horses trapped with black velvet and bearing escutcheons of the King's and Queen's arms in fine gold on double sarcanet with a chamfron of the same arms on each horse's head. On the bier, in wax, a figure of the Queen lay in her robes of estate, such being the fashion of a royal funeral, with a golden crown on her waxen head, the fair hair rustling loose from under it; in the right waxen hand, fingers glittering with rings set with precious stones, was caught a golden sceptre. Gold and precious stones collared the neck, for the effigy had been dressed with the care that would be given a living woman, naught being forgotten, not even the hidden smock and stockings, while garters were probably buckled under the knees, and cloth of gold shoes were on the feet and a pillow of cloth of gold tissue lay under the waxen head. Had Pygmalion been present this Galatea need have suffered no embarrassment, so modestly garbed was she.

On horses trapped with sombre velvet sat the mourners, Princess Mary chief amongst them; then slowly they paced beside the coffin on its cart, the Queen's effigy glaring upwards with glass eyes, on the road to Windsor and burial in St. George's Chapel.

They say that poor Queen Jane can yet be seen, late at night or early in the morning. They say that she steals out, dressed all in white, as a ghost should dress, in her shroud, from a door on the eastern side of the Inner or Clock Court. This door is set back under its arch, while carved in each spandrel over the arch are winged cherubim holding blank shields that once had been painted with Wolsey's arms. Out of here steps Jane, they say, and peers forlornly about her, wandering, as if lost, up and down the stairs, seeking something somewhere, flittering near the Silverstick Gallery, never still, poor soul who was so brief a time a queen.

There you may see her if you care to watch, or so it is said. Miss Agnes Strickland vouches for her and she was a careful historian with whom we must not argue, save on slight questions of fact. And who ever said that a ghost was a fact, like a beetle, to be pinned beneath your thumb?

Now is the palace a nursery. For fully a year, the King did not return to Hampton Court; perhaps the memory of Jane, the one wife who had done her duty, was too poignant. He stayed elsewhere while the workmen remained, as ever busy altering and building, and gardeners dug those delightful Tudor gardens laid out in medieval fashion. They were cut into small beds of different designs and were called knot-gardens, and there were pebbled walks around them and they had beds raised from a few inches to two feet, faced with boards or brick, which could be used as seats as well as flower-beds.* These gardens were small. As late as 1665 we find Rea

---

* To describe such a garden it is best to quote from the late Sir Frank Crisp's *Mediæval Gardens*. He wrote: "Knots were of two kinds, open and closed. Open knots had the design set out in lines of box, rosemary, hyssop, thyme, or other plants that were low growing or could be clipped. The designs would be merely geometrical in complicated as well as simple forms, the intervening spaces were filled in with different coloured earths, and the paths when not of grass were covered with loose sand."

E   51

writing in his *Flora* that twenty square yards were sufficient to make one. Small though they were they were very beautiful as you will see in medieval miniatures. Mr. Law has reproduced at Hampton Court as well as he was able an excellent example of one such garden, but the originals would have been even more beautiful. They would have had arbours trellised with roses and other climbing

The Tudor Garden

Henry VIII and Family

plants, and sundials would have stood to slice away the minutes darkly, while numerous sculptures would have been there, heraldic beasts with painted shields gripped in stone claws. But of Hampton Court's pleasaunces only remains the Pond Garden, separated by a narrow path from what is called the Cardinal's Garden which is actually Mr. Law's garden for, by happy inspiration, he had it laid out in imitation of a contemporary knot-garden, with ribbons of box, thyme and lavender. This is reproduction as it should be, and to walk in that delicately arranged garden is to return, in spirit, to the days of Henry and Elizabeth.

The Pond Garden was probably the first to be dug at Hampton Court. Here stand guardian the King's heraldic beasts, once brightly coloured and gilt, about the beds. The accounts give details of its making and we find amongst them a note of " laberers lading of water out of the Temmes to ffyl the pondes in the nyght tymes." Here must Henry often have strolled with his courtiers and ladies, between the flower-beds railed with white and green, such as can be glimpsed in the " conversation piece " of the jester Will Somers and Jane the Fool standing in the arches between the royal family in the painting which still hangs in Hampton Court in the Cartoon Gallery. Not that the garden shown here was this garden, being more probably that of Whitehall or Westminster. In a most royal pavilion, under a canopy of state, Henry sits with Katherine Parr and Prince Edward on either side of him and with Princess Mary to his right and Elizabeth to his left.

Will was a very famous person, for jesters were privileged and, at the risk of a whipping, could tell even a king the truth under the guise of wit. There were jest-books of Will Somers', as there were jest-books of Archie Armstrong's, James I's fool, but such books did not mean that they recorded pranks actually perpetrated by the men whose names were on the title-pages. Just as popular stories of the day not so long ago were fathered on a stage-comedian, Joe Miller, and published regularly under his name, so in the past was a jester's name tagged on to any collection of popular jokes. Not only professional jesters, but even poets, have been honoured this way. We have, for example, jest-books of that fine Elizabethan dramatist, George Piel.

Will Somers was famous as Henry's jester and, as you can see in this Hampton Court painting, he did not wear the convential cap and bells. Such a costume was rarely, if ever, worn, save perhaps on state occasions, and here Will seems no different from other men of the period, save for the monkey on his shoulder. In an illuminated psalter in the British Museum we have another portrait of Somers, showing him singing to Henry's accompaniment on the harp, and here again he is dressed in contemporary fashion of hose and shirt and jacket with his hair cropped short and receding either side, and with a scruff of a beard, very unlike the popular conception of a jester such as is acted nowadays in *Twelfth Night* where he prances in parti-coloured hose, wears a cap with bells, and has a bladder on a stick. Had you been fortunate—or mayhap, unfortunate—enough to visit Hampton Court when Henry lived there you might have passed Will without a second glance as merely one of the servants. He was the professional comedian who, when the court was weary, had the appalling task of rousing it with quips and songs, with juggling or dancing with his monkey.

Jane the Fool, who shares with Will a panel in this painting, was the woman jester attached to Princess Mary's retinue. As with Will, she is dressed in ordinary garments, although her head was regularly shaved like a nun's.

While Henry, on the death of his queen, fled Hampton Court, the prince remained in the care of his wet-nurse, and a year later, of his dry-nurse, Sibill Penn—or Pen or Penne—whose ghost allegedly walks these ancient corridors; but of that ghost we will speak at the historical moment. She is, at the date of which we write, very much alive and she proved herself so efficient a nurse that Henry granted her a manor and a rectory, and she was so affectionate, which is more important, that her grateful foster-son was to keep her at court until his early death.* Both Mary and Elizabeth also loved her, giving her a permanent home in Hampton Court, while her tomb can be seen in the church with a life-size effigy under a marble canopy supported by Corinthian columns and pilasters and with a long rimed inscription to her virtues, in which, inevitably, the writer could not resist the pun of his pen with Mistress Penn. His boast of her being " a Hampden by discent " was no poetical license as can be seen by consulting Mr. Gordon Roe's scholarly article in the *Connoisseur*. " On both sides," writes Mr. Roe, " Sibill came of branches of the parent stock that

---

* Among the Holbein drawings at Windsor Castle is one inscribed " Mother Jak," which Mr. Law suggested is possibly of Sibill Penn. The portrait, however, is wrongly labelled and actually represents Margaret Griggs as can be recognised in the Nostell Priory picture of the More family, Margaret having been a relative of Sir Thomas's who married Dr. John Clement, later court physician.

was to bear the patriot who received his mortal wound at Chalgrove Field," her father being " William Hampden of Dunton (Duddington) and Wingrave in County Bucks, eldest son and heir of Sir Edmund Hampden, knight, of Woodstock. Her mother, Audrey, was one of the two daughters and co-heiresses of Richard Hampden of Kimble." Although her tomb remains under the tower staircase leading to the organ loft, it was desecrated when the original church was pulled down in 1829, having been struck by lightning in the mighty storm of August 17th, 1827, and—this, it is suggested, explains the ghost— we are told that no body was found, " only a little yellow hair and a few hair-pins."

With Mistress Penn as nurse under Sir William Sydney as chamberlain, the baby's household reads like a man's, for we find in it all the needful officers: chief steward, vice-chamberlain, comptroller, cofferer, dean, down to—or should we say up to ?— Mistress Penn herself. He was strongly guarded, none daring to approach him without special permission, or even to touch the royal cradle. The food he ate, the water he drank, were elaborately tested for poison; and we cannot wonder that he became sickly, being thus fenced from the natural, inescapable dirt of the time, for too much pampering must have broken the resistance of his body and left it open, when it was exposed to ordinary conditions, to a multitude of germs.

Since his fall in the lists at Greenwich, Henry had being growing fat, very fat, as was inevitable with an athlete no longer able to wrestle or run, to play tennis or joust, the only active sport remaining to him being the hunt. And as a hunter in need of fresh pastures, he began to steal ground for Hampton Court—if a king can be named thief for taking from others what he considered by divine right to be his own. The people, seeing their meadows and pastures seized for habitation for deer which they dared not kill, were unable to protest until Edward VI's reign when the council explained—as they would not have dared to explain while Henry was alive any more than the commons had dared protest at the loss of their livelihood by these encroachments—that " his highness waxed heavy with sickness, age, and corpulency of body, and might not travel so readily abroad, but was constrained to seek to have his game and pleasure ready to hand." The Royal Chase grew rapidly, stretching out from Hampton Court on the Surrey side, and was enclosed with wooden palings wherein birds and deer might live in safety, save when the king and his retinue came hallooing for their death; and those unfortunates who found their homes hemmed in, their fields trampled in the hunt, were not permitted even to maim the beasts that were ruining them by destroying the crops.

While expanding the parks into forests, Henry had also made certain of his ownership of the manor by acquiring the fee simple from the prior of the knights hospitallers on May 30th, 1531, shortly after Wolsey's death. Now none could argue that the palace was not his, the gift of the cardinal sealed by the prior. And he was still building, still adding further apartments, although himself did not live there during the first year of his son's life, until the fame of Hampton Court grew so great that King Francis in France was plucking his lip in envy and sharply questioning ambassadors about the amount of gilding Henry used, complacently remarking that himself used little or none, preferring the natural tints of wood which, he said, were richer than any gilding, and more durable.

Not that such jealous criticism could keep Henry from the royal gilding-pot. Gold was splashed on Hampton Court, as metal, as paint, and as leaf, while the fat little prince was learning to stand on his two fat legs.

It was doubtful whether Henry and his next queen, gross Anne of Cleves, ever slept at Hampton Court—it is more than doubtful if they slept together anywhere—therefore does she remain but a dim ghost in our palace, staying there a few days while she awaited the divorce which was pronounced in July, 1540.

But with the rapid coming and going of this German Anne, love once again brightens the palace, for little Katherine Howard arrives to play her tragic part.

On August 8th, 1540, she was openly revealed as the new queen and sat beside Henry in the royal closet in Hampton Court chapel and then dined publicly with him, the Princess Elizabeth at her side.

Katherine was a charming young girl under five feet in height and had reddish hair and hazel eyes. The portraits of her obviously fail to do her justice and the hook-nosed elderly one in the National Portrait Gallery I cannot accept as genuine, for it is dissimilar to those by Holbein while conflicting with my impression of her as seen in the records, for this painting is of no light-hearted foolish girl, but a complacent woman; and that Katherine most certainly was not.* Holbein's portraits of her in the Buccleugh and J. H. Dunn collections and the miniatures at Windsor are nothing whatever like this portrait. There is also the Holbein sketch at Windsor which, unfortunately, is more than doubtful, although I find it difficult to relinquish; had it been by any less careful artist I would accept it wholeheartedly, but it does not fully agree with those we know to be authentic and sadly we must let it go with the alleged sketch of Anne Boleyn in the same—in every sense—royal collection.

Apparently Kate was not beautiful. The French ambassador rated her no higher than of mediocre attractions and said that she was graceful rather than beautiful; but to Henry she was his " rose without a thorn," his " jewel for womanhood." Unquestionably she was graceful and dainty, childlike, quick to merriment, and like many wenches with that air of bland innocence, she had known love from early years. Such girls are incapable of passion and therefore place little value on the flesh. It is to them merely an instrument of pleasure and they cannot understand the idiotic price which romantic men put on it. If man demands that value they are prepared to play the part and wear a virgin's mask. Such was Kate who should never have been a queen.

Brought up under the feeble supervision of a grandmother who seems to have let her romp as she willed with the servants, at an early age she had loved her music-master, one Mannock, and then adored a distant kinsman, Francis Dereham, of her uncle Norfolk's household. We have many details of those young days in her confession, printed, for some odd reason, in the appendix to Bishop Burnet's *History of the Reformation*. It is a pathetic document, for in it the poor queen strips herself naked, then hurriedly, in panic, gathers up her rags of shame and tries to hide with lies behind them. One moment remorsefully she confesses and the next, in terror, denies her own confession. Reading it, one has the impression of listening to a half-mad babbling baby and one pities Cranmer who

* My suspicions have been proved correct. Since writing the above I have begun work on a biography of Katherine Howard and, wishing to make certain of the painting's authenticity, I wrote to the National Portrait Gallery and asked for its history. Mr. G. K. Adams, assistant to the director there, kindly gives me permission to quote from his reply. It was, he tells me, " purchased from a dealer, and according to the minutes of the meeting at which the picture was purchased, the portrait came from Condover Hall. I presume that it was purchased by the dealer at Christies on the 6th March, 1897, when there was a sale of Condover pictures, catalogued as the property of ' the late Reginald Cholmondeley, Esq. . . . sold by Order of the Rev. R. H. Cholmondeley.' No portrait named Queen Katherine Howard was included in the sale but there was a portrait which from its description was almost certainly the one that is now here. It was lot eight and was described thus: ' a Lady in black dress embroidered with gold lace, and white embroidered sleeves, with jewelled necklace and pendant, on panel 29in. × 19½in. from Overleigh.' Overleigh was the family seat of the Cholmondeleys who had inherited Condover from the Owen family." It is with genuine pleasure that I can now turn my back on this dark predatory-looking female with the calculating eyes, hooked nose, and mannish hands.

had to sit in this palace and watch a terrible sight, a child broken and weeping who for the first time feels death close and knows it to be terrible and final. " In a state " she was, said Cranmer, " it would have pitied any man's heart to see," and he strove to quieten her with promises of royal mercy in which himself did not believe. " He had proposed first," he writes, " to exaggerate her demerits, then declare the justice of the laws, and lastly, signify the king's mercy; but for fear she would enter into a frenzy, he was fain to begin with the last. When she broke out into any ' extreme braydes ' he told her there was some new fantasy come into her head and asked what it was. She said that this ' sudden mercy ' made her offence seem more heinous. About six o'clock she fell into another ' pange,' which, she said, was for the remembrance of the time, for about that time, as she said, Master Hennage was wont to bring her knowledge of Your Grace."

Small wonder that her ghost is said to walk in Hampton Court.

I had not intended to quote so largely but, turning up the confession again, I sat musing on that passage and felt I must continue, although we are running ahead in time, for it troubled me to think of this poor creature tangled in that political web. She babbled such terrible truths. " And," she cried, speaking of Dereham, " he used many times to kiss me; " then remembering her peril, she added: " and so he did to many other commonly in the house. And, I suppose, that this be true, that at one time when he kissed me very often, some said that were present, they trowed he would never have kissed me enough. Whereto he answered, ' Who should lett [hinder] him to kiss his own wife ? ' Then said one of them, ' I trowe this matter will come to passe, as the common saying is.' ' What is that ? ' quoth he. ' Marry,' said the other, ' that Mr. Deram shall have Mrs. Katherine Howard.' ' By St. John ! ' said Deram, ' you may guesse twice and guesse worse,' But that I should wink upon him, and say secretly, ' What and this should come to my lady's ear ? ' I suppose verily there was no such thing."

The wild contradictions of a girl on the edge of hysteria, the tug of sentimental memories against the terror of the axe, the sudden bursts of pride, the boasts of how she had been loved abruptly denied, reveal a picture like few in history. Clearly, while we read, we see Kate in the darkening gallery, weeping, imploring, lying, confessing, unable to hold her tongue, while sadly Cranmer listens and remembers that he must write down later this report which we possess.

"As for carnall knowledge," she cried, " I confess as I did before, that divers times he hath lyen with me, sometime in his doublet and hose, and two or three times naked: but not so naked that he had nothing upon him; for he had alwayes at the least his doublet, and as I do think, his hose also: but I mean naked, when his hose was put down. And diverse times he would bring wine, strawberryes, apples, and other things, to make good chear, after my lady was gone to bed. But that he made any special banquet, that by appointment between him and me, he should tarry after the keyes were delivered to my lady, that is utterly untrue. . . . And sometimes Deram hathe come in early in the morning, and ordered him very lewdly, but never at my request nor consent. . . ."

Thus she rambled, telling of the past of before marriage, only once casually letting slip the truly dangerous name of the lover of after-marriage, Thomas Culpeper, one of the gentlemen of the chamber, clerk of the armoury, steward and keeper of several royal manors, and rascal enough once to have been indicted and later forgiven for rape of a poor countrywoman whom he had had his servants hold down for his lust.

Let us, however, turn back from that dark day in Hampton Court when Katherine babbled these terrible truths to Cranmer; let us return to when she was first queen, worshipped by her King.

Revitalized by her youth, King Henry seemed to become young again. For her device she had taken *Non aultre volonte que la sienne*— No other will but his—and in his longing for peace and love and children, he accepted the motto without questioning and there was merriment again in Hampton Court. Such was his maudlin love that, even in public, he could not keep his hands from her, as though he must be ever touching, squeezing her skin to make certain she was real. Each morning he was up between five and six, for life was too precious to squander in sleep, and despite his ulcerated leg he would ride for four or five hours in the park. Not since his youth had the king been so happy and all men noticed it with wonder. Nor did Katherine twist his passion to unworthy ends; all lovers of poetry should remember her for she begged Sir Thomas Wyatt's freedom from the Tower in which he had been locked on suspicion of treason and papal tendencies. She was kind, too, to Mary and Elizabeth, and when Anne of Cleves arrived with New Year's gifts of two horses with violet velvet trappings, and insisted on addressing her on her knees, Katherine protested and " after the king had retired the queen and Lady Anne danced together and next day all three dined together. At this time the king gave his queen a present of a ring and two small dogs, which she passed over to Lady Anne." To the unfortunate Countess of Salisbury, imprisoned in the Tower because she was of Plantagenet—and therefore dangerous—blood, Kate sent a furred nightgown, a worsted kirtle, a furred petticoat, another nightgown—this time of saye, a kind of silk, lined and faced with satin—a bonnet, four pairs of stockings, four pairs of shoes and a pair of slippers.

Like a child on the throne, heedless of the sorry ghost of Anne Boleyn, Katherine probably believed she had nothing to fear, so plainly her slave was the king. Now were there merry times in Hampton Court, with this little laughing girl a queen and her big lame king singing to her in the garden; and, of course, building was still going on.

We must not forget the astronomical clock which this happy summer was inserted in the tower of the Clock Court, where its brass face can be seen to this day, a thing of beauty cunningly constructed. The date of its being placed in the topmost storey of the tower is stamped, with the initials N.O.—apparently of the maker, Nicholas Oursian—on an iron bar inside the dial, 1540.

Set in a fifteen feet square frame of stone carved with Henry's badges and initials, the dial has roman numerals for twenty-four hours —I to XII, then again I to XII, so that a XII is at both top and bottom of the face. There are three dials, or rather, three copper discs, one above the other, of different sizes and revolving at different speeds. In the centre of the inner disc is a faintly projecting globe for the earth, surrounded by four divisions representing the moon's quarters. Behind this disc is another, showing through a circular hole the varying sizes of the moon. On the third or outer disc are painted the names of the months and the days and the signs of the zodiac, while along the rim runs a circle subdivided into 365 parts for the days of the year. Out from the second disc projects a long arm bearing a gilt sun, and by the direction in which this points, you can tell, with two smaller arms on the inner discs, the hour, the month, the day of the month, the position of the sun in the ecliptic, the number of days since the beginning of the year, the phase of the moon, its age in days, and the hour of the day at which it souths and thereby the time of high-water at London Bridge.*

---

* Mr. Yates tells us that this clock " has been called the Clock of Death, the tradition being current that the stopping of the clock portends the imminent death of a palace resident."

At least, that is what one should discover from a study of this beautiful face—the works are comparatively modern—but I confess that, after almost cricking my neck, I have failed to understand it wholly; but I am glad to note that it behaves like an honest Tudor conservative and refuses to heed that nonsense promulgated by heretics like Copernicus and Galileo, for the sun, as it should, revolves obediently around the earth. When first set in the tower it was, in the fashion of the day, richly painted, " all wrought in oil colours as vermilion, &c., and guilded with fine goulde."

Royal revenues being low at the time of this, his fifth marriage, Henry took his tiny bride on a royal progress to show her to his people, but they had returned to Hampton Court before Christmas and remained there for the following four or five months while the privy council, the king presiding, met daily there to discuss the business of the realm. Then off Henry carried his Kate for a brief summer progress, returning to Hampton Court on October 24th, 1541, when his happiness was such that on hearing mass in the chapel he must give " Him most hearty thanks for the good life he led and trusted to lead with his wife."

But his good life's ruin was already plotted. Great pity it is that love and politics must often shift together in a palace and that this royal marriage of one of the Roman catholic Norfolks must bestir the protestants to drag Kate down. Cranmer, during mass, slipped into Henry's hand a little terrible note, the very day after Henry had prayed so noisily about his marital satisfaction and had desired " the bishop of Lincoln, his ghostly father, to make all prayer and give all thanks with him on All Souls' day " because of his new-found peace. Now came this damning little note about Katherine's early merry-making with Dereham. Henry could not believe it when he read it. So suddenly it struck into his joy that it stunned him, although, as yet, nothing was known of Culpeper. Kate's grandmother, trying to convince herself, had sighed that " the girl cannot die for what was done before," and at first it seemed that she had been correct. For all his horror at this thorn on his darling rose, Henry might have forgiven Katherine had not the truth of later loving been revealed.

She was ordered to keep her chamber and her musicians were taken from her, for, she was told, this was no longer time to dance. Henry as yet was dazed: he " so tenderly loved the woman, and had conceived such a constant opinion of her honesty, that he supposed it to be rather a forged matter than the truth." But the truth could not be hidden; Cranmer heard it all that fearful day of which we have already spoken when, unable to lie in her panic, Katherine sobbed her confession. Others were questioned, others who blabbed all, ladies-in-waiting, maidservants, and the king could no longer shy from the truth. At the council table Wriotheseley showed him proofs, and "his heart was so pierced with pensiveness, that long it was before his majesty could speak and utter the sorrow of his heart unto us, and finally with plenty of tears (which was strange in his courage) opened the same." Under the stilted official phrasing, one feels the startled horror of these great men when, which was strange in his courage, the king suddenly burst into tears.

After so many years of unhappiness with women to find that she whom he had thought perfection was a traitor almost killed the king. From that moment he aged, became prematurely old, bald, and wrinkled, the royal spirit fled. This was the ultimate betrayal, last hope of love gone, leaving him lonely for death in his great palace that had become the tomb of happiness.

Small wonder then that the French ambassador records: " The king has changed his love for the queen into hatred, and taken such grief at being deceived that of late it was thought he had gone mad, for he called for a sword to slay her he had loved so much. Sitting in council he suddenly called for horses without saying where he would go. Sometimes he said, irrelevantly, that that wicked woman had never such delight in her inconstancy as she should have torture in her death. And finally he took to tears, regretting his ill-luck in meeting with such ill-conditioned wives, and blaming his council for the mischief. The ministers have done their best to make him forget his grief, and he is gone 25 miles from here with no company but musicians."

Out from Hampton Court, away from the ghosts of happiness, the king fled, but flight cannot cheat those ghosts who ride with one; and out of the palace to nearby Syon went Katherine in disgrace, but Chapuys tells that, when the first shock at discovery left her, she childlike was " making good cheer," was " plumper and more beautiful than ever, taking great care to be well apparelled, and more imperious and troublesome to serve than even when she was with the king, although she believes she will be put to death and confesses she has deserved it." And put to death she was, her head chopped off in the Tower, this wayward over-loving girl who, the true bill against her tells us, had " led an abominable, base, carnal, voluptuous, and vicious life, like a common harlot, with divers persons " while " maintaining outwardly the appearance of chastity and honesty. That she led the king by word and gesture to love her and (he believing her to be pure and chaste and free from other matrimonial yoke) arrogantly coupled herself with him in matrimony."

Bravely she died, where Anne had died, and to the people she spoke a few sad words; then turning to the headsman she bade him be swift, saying: " I die a queen, but I would rather die the wife of Culpeper. Good people, I beg you, pray for me."

Her ghost, it is said, yet walks in Hampton Court, although her headless trunk lies in the Tower church. The alleged Haunted Gallery is on your right hand as you walk down the Queen's Great Staircase. The story goes that when confined to her chamber, Katherine pushed by the guards and ran to speak to Henry who was hearing mass in the royal closet in the chapel, but the guards caught her and dragged her, shrieking, back. To this day, her ghost runs, screaming for pardon, for pity, along this gallery, it is said. Some say they have seen her dressed all in white hurry to the royal pew, then as she reaches it, she turns and runs back, her clothes disordered, with terror in her eyes and on her mouth, while she shrieks until she vanishes through the door at the gallery end.

Details of alleged hauntings are given at the close of this book, and I wish the evidence was conclusive; but that is for you to judge. If ghosts are bred by terror, Katherine's ghost should walk in Hampton Court. Certainly, I would bargain much to see this visual memory of poor Kate trapped in the gallery, repeating those few moments of agonized eternity, her anguish being so powerful that even dumb bricks remain impressed with it, as a sensitive plate is impressed by the image in front of the lens. Of such I believe are ghosts made—not poltergeists which seem some impish projection of oneself, the unconscious incarnate, but the visible memories of those now rotten under earth—of spiritual torments so appalling that they are photographed on the atmosphere. And this visible figure of Kate, it is said, yet runs along the gallery to intercept a king who is not there, to be barred by guards who are not there, from entering the royal pew, and to be dragged back by those same non-existent guards to her chamber, while her voice re-echoes, waves of sound like wireless boxed within walls, to shriek and shriek, as once the living woman shrieked to know that she was doomed.*

The Haunted Gallery

Henry now was old. The false rejuvenation given by Katherine's vitality drained from him at the horror of her betrayal. " He had wonderfully felt the case of the queen," we are told; although not old in years, he was old in misery. Life to him had lost all meaning, although he was soon back in Hampton Court, entertaining Charles V's ambassadors and trying to dodge from being involved in Charles's war with France. He could not entirely avoid it, but his full energies he expended in efforts to conquer Scotland. Politics absorbed him, for he must, at last, have realised that happiness was never for him and he had now no hope of breeding future sons. His dislike of Mary, the girl who should have been a boy, was passing, and he presented her with various jewels and, later, willed her the crown, following sickly Prince Edward. And he married again.

* According to Philip W. Sergeant in his *Historic British Ghosts*, Katherine's ghost has also appeared in the Tower where her body, buried in quicklime, was laid in the Chapel of St. Peter-ad-Vinicula. If this be authentic, it is further proof that spirits are purely atmospheric phenomena. Queen Elizabeth, for example, who died at Richmond, is alleged to appear at Windsor Castle.

But this final marriage was not for love. He chose Katherine Parr, an intelligent woman schooled in the art of consoling old men; twice widowed, she was thirty-one or -two, about five years older than Princess Mary, when Henry chose her, and was already in love with Thomas Seymour whom later she married. But the King called to her in his loneliness and although she is alleged, on most dubious evidence, to have cried: " It were better to be your mistress than your wife!" she at last agreed to marry him, probably because she realised that Henry could not live much longer and, being a strong protestant, felt that she must not shirk this opportunity of helping the reformed church. In a letter she was to write to Seymour, after her marriage to him, she explained that she became queen on God's instructions, for, wrote she, " I can say nothing but as my lady of Suffolk saith, ' God is a marvellous man'."

In Hampton Court, in the Queen's Closet, on July 12th, 1543, was the marriage performed and the same day she was proclaimed queen; and as though to warn her that he was not to be converted to Luther, Henry promptly pounced on some heretics at Windsor and had them burnt; but one was John Marbeck, a singing-man, and the king, who loved poetry and music, reprieved him. " Poor Marbeck," he said, " it would be well for thine accusers if they had employed their time no worse."

On Christmas Eve, the Knights of the Garter held a chapter of their order in the palace and it was probably now that the Earl of Surrey—who was to lose his head under Queen Mary—first began to love that Geraldine of whom he sang:

> Hunsdon did first present her to mine eyen:
> Bright is her hue, and Geraldine she hight.
> Hampton me taught to wish her first for mine;
> And Windsor, alas! doth chase me from her sight.

Who was this Geraldine whom Surrey spied, in Nashe's words, in " thrice imperial Hampton Court, Cupid's inchanted castle," we do not know for certain, but she is, with strong evidence, believed to have been Lady Elizabeth Fitzgerald of Princess Mary's household, then fourteen years of age, the age for marrying. Egg-faced Surrey can be seen to-day at Hampton Court in a painting attributed to Holbein in which he stands in red with legs apart; in red from head to toe he stands, save for the white shirt with dark embroidery. His flat cap is red, and red the gold-studded shoon, while in his left-hand he holds the grip of a long golden sword, and his right-hand rests on his hip above a heavy-tasselled dagger that is richly chased.

Thus, with Katherine Parr, in domestic peace, the great King ended his unhappy life, his children about him; and there is only one more event to be recorded before we turn the page on his reign: the coming of the French ambassador to ratify the treaty of peace. With a long retinue, he rode from London to where, some distance from Hampton Court, he was welcomed by Prince Edward with a train " of five hundred and forty in velvet coats; and the Prince's livery were with sleeves of cloth of gold; and there were the number of eight hundred royally apparelled." Edward, then almost ten years of age, embraced the ambassador " in such courteous and honourable wise that all the beholders greatly rejoiced, and much marvelled at the said Prince's high wit and audacity."

For six days in the palace Henry entertained the Frenchmen with " banquetings, huntings, and triumphings, with noble masks and mummeries, with divers and sundry changes; insomuch that the torchbearers were clothed in cloth of gold," while tents, pavilions, and small wooden houses were built in the Tilt Yard to lodge so many visitors.

That is the last historic reference to Hampton Court of any importance in Henry's reign. He died, not within these walls he had helped build and which he loved, but in Westminster Palace on January 8th, 1547, having left Hampton Court towards the end of 1546. It was treason to prophesy a king's death, therefore none dared tell him he was doomed until, towards the last flicker of life, one took courage and warned him, so that he might have the opportunity to make a last wish. But no: Henry mumbled that he was certain that God would forgive his sins, through the mercy of Christ, even should they have been greater than they were; and he asked for Cranmer. Cranmer hurried and came just in time to press the royal hand before the great king died.

Both Wolsey and Henry who had plotted and built this house now lay dead. And the palace, this creature of wood and brick and stone, this solid memorial of their dreams, waited for its new master, the boy king, Edward VI.

CHAPTER IV

EDWARD THE SIXTH

THIS is but a tragic interlude, the brief yet promising reign of a boy. Edward had been born in this palace, reared and educated here, and it was therefore more his even than it had been his father's, but he did not live long enough to add or alter anything. His is a frail coughing ghost, for he was sickly from early age, being fat and puffy—dangerous signs in babies. All the Tudors were sick folk. Despite his vitality and physical strength, Henry was not truly strong: he aged quickly and died only a little over fifty, old both in spirit and appearance. His elder brother, Arthur, had died young and his other brother and two sisters all died in infancy; his illegitimate son, the Earl of Richmond, went at seventeen of some unstated illness; and although Mary and Elizabeth were to cling to life for comparatively long periods, they were both neurotic and rarely well. The argument, of course, is that Henry was syphilitic but—apart from the sore on his leg already mentioned—there is absolutely no evidence of Henry ever contracting the disease.

Families were naturally large in those days yet few children reached man- or womanhood. Brought up to be grown up, tied immediately after birth in tight swaddling-bands under the delusion that they would make the limbs grow straight, and fed on salted meat with few vegetables, the only wonder is that so many reached middle, let alone old age.

Poor Edward was allowed few pleasures and was jealously guarded, so that it was almost inevitable that he should become physically weak, while at the age of ten he had the intellect of a man. They are pathetic creatures, these children of a king, with the learning of philosophers at an age when they should have been playing with dolls and living in that world of self-created fantasy so essential to childhood. They were not permitted to behave like children, for parents then had not our sentimental fondness for the young; they considered children as luxuries who must be swiftly reared so that they could be used in bargaining to be sold in marriage for property and wealth.

Those who detest King Henry, and they are many, insist on reading syphilis into every illness that touched him or his children, but the medical evidence, diagnosed by the highest authorities, as printed in Mr. Chamberlin's already mentioned book, does not endorse the theory that the weaknesses of his children were the result of the father's sin. Edward was never strong and he died at sixteen of what was apparently consumption, having undergone the usual childhood ailments of measles and smallpox. In his diary, now in the British Museum, we see his hand becoming weaker when, in April of his last year, the disease took firm grip of him. Some call this a priggish diary because in it Edward talks like an over-wise man, but such a judgment could be made only by those ignorant of the period and of a royal education. Yet even in the stilted prose we catch a few charming glimpses of the boy, and the records give us such delightful anecdotes as when, playing cards with little Jane Dormer, he said: "Now, Jane, your king is gone: I shall be good enough for you"; and when he tried to calm Princess Mary who was weeping because of the protector's attack on her religion by telling her "to have patience until he had more years and he would remedy all."

These are not the utterances of the prig which religious historians persist on seeing in him. And there is a boy's humour in his reply when asked whom the protector should marry. "My Lady Anne of Cleves," he said, then added after a pause: "Nay, nay, wot you what? I would he married my sister Mary to turn her opinions."

In appearance he was startlingly like his father. Indeed, when looking at Holbein's portrait of Edward one could believe it to have been a painting of Henry when young, for there is the same prim little mouth, the same bone structure of the head. His teachers were chosen for their antipathy to Rome and from earliest years he was instructed in the New Learning so that he grew to love scholarship for its own sake and would often be found studying some theological work and, while still a child, he wrote that book of alarming maturity, *Discourse of the Reformation of Abuses*. Not that he was discouraged from physical exercise, for a king must be able to hold his own with any man at anything. In Hampton Court we can conjure his ghost, thin and grave and courteous, and in the palace and grounds there he would have been taught dancing, archery, riding at the quintain, while in his diary we find notes of challenges he had received for shooting and riding at the ring; and with young comrades it was natural he should learn to swear, too, like a man, and the boy who taught him the wicked words was well flogged for it while the little king suffered what was probably worse, a lecture.

Six months after his accession, in June, 1547, he rode to Hampton Court for the first time as king, and he remained there while the protector, the Duke of Somerset—his uncle, Jane Seymour's brother —rode north to chastise the Scots at Pinkie Cleugh. Far from being given any power, Edward was almost a prisoner in his uncle's strong grip while the protector's scheming brother, Lord Seymour, who had married Katherine Parr, plotted to be his friend, secretly sending him money and inciting rebellion. Seymour was a man almost insane with ambition: he even attempted to seduce young Elizabeth, while she was obviously half in love with him in a girlish fashion, until she realised she was playing with treason, and the shock was sufficient to send her into such terror of love that could betray her to the axe that, I feel certain, many of the complexities of her emotional character, her desire for lovers and her physical inability to love—if Ben Jonson spoke truth to Drummond—can be placed to this girlhood episode.

Somerset was a great man, a man of vision beyond his time, and once he smelt his brother's game, he sent him to the axe. But he had overreached himself, all the firm forces of reaction feared his reforms, while powerful enemies plotted to rise against him and take the king away. Hearing that they had gathered in London, Somerset started furiously to fortify Hampton Court.

Edward, who must have been rather bewildered by all this flurry which did not concern him in the least, records in his diary that five hundred suits of armour were carried from the armoury to arm the servants. The moat was filled in, the gates were manned, and cannon were placed in readiness. For the first and last time, Hampton Court became a citadel noisy with steel and tramping warriors, but to think to defend it was absurd. With its soft walls it could never have withstood cannon fire, as it had not been built for any such emergency. Yet, for its brief hour, Hampton Court became a fortress with armed men clanking in steel as they sped through the galleries or mounted the roofs to watch for the enemy, leaning against the carved beasts and painted vanes. Probably, of all those present, the prince enjoyed himself the most, but with a typically dirty trick, fate robbed the excitement of half its joy by giving him a cold, and it is difficult to play Lancelot with a running nose.

To the people, Somerset issued pleas for them to repair to Hampton Court armed in defence of their king while he scattered abroad leaflets denouncing his reactionary enemies. " Good people," were the words he wrote into the people's mouths, " in the name of God and King Edward, let us ryse with all oure power to defend hym and the Lorde Protector agenst certen lordes and gentilmen and chief masters, which wolde depose the Lorde Protector, and so endanger the Kings royall person, because we, the poore comens, being injuried by the extorcionse gentylmen, had our pardon this yere by the mercye of the king, and the goodness of the Lorde Protector, for whom let us fyght, for he lovithe all just and true gentilmen which do not extorcyon, and also us the poor commynaltie of Englonde."

And the people rose with him, for him, seeing clearly that he was the one hand that kept them from the greedy clutch of landlords enclosing, evicting. Ten thousand brave men answered his call and trooped to Hampton Court. But they were, alas ! indeed the poor commons and many had not even a knife or a bow with which to battle. Bare-handed they came to fight and they filled the palace. Somerset realised then that he, with only the people and the king's authority, could not withstand the great men and that if he remained in Hampton Court he would be trapped. So off he rode to the strong castle of Windsor that could hold armies at bay, taking Edward with him.

For that one noisy night, Hampton Court, which until then had heard only the tread of soft-soled men and women, echoed with the thunder of steel, the click of swords pushed into sheaths, the twang of bowstrings tested, the rattle of pikes and voulges on its floor and against its walls. Walking its many chambers to-day I find it difficult to visualise that night, for here steel seems out of place. One must go to the Tower to find the ghosts of armoured men; there the walls seem damp with blood and the lofty chambers whisper still with the shouting and praying of the doomed. But in this pastoral world such men are alien, sharp-edged figures, frighteningly faced with bars of metal, shouldering aside Kate Howard and Anne Boleyn, tramping even before the ghost of Henry. Of all the past I find that night most difficult to recall. Our palace is no arsenal and we should be glad that the scare passed, that armies did not meet, that no cannon smashed its bricks. Later there was to be a murder committed here, a very foolish crime, but murder is not battle, and only at the hands of builders and restorers has the palace suffered, save for a few unimportant fires and the threat of bombs in the recent war.

Somerset had over-estimated the forces against him, they were not yet organised to strike, and within a few days he submitted to them, was locked into the Tower for three months, then reinstated in his old position, for there was no more able man in England. Soon he was back in Hampton Court, unarmoured now, in July, 1551, when the sweating sickness drove him and the king from London. Edward was probably glad to return, for he could have found few amusements in the city, while he had always hated Windsor, complaining that it was like a prison with no galleries or gardens; and not long after his return he was visited by the Marshal St. Andre, envoy of the King of France, who had come to England to initiate him into the Order of St. Michael. Proudly Edward notes in his diary how the hall and his lodgings were hung with tapestries for the occasion. Very gravely, the young king, conscious of his dignity and of the curious eyes of these Frenchmen eager, if possible, to carry home a scornful report of his behaviour, greeted the ambassador, then dined with him in the Great Hall; afterwards, " being brought into an inner chaumber," he writes, " he told me he was come not only for delivery of th' ordre, but also for to declare the great frendshipe the king his master bore me, which he desired I wold thinke to be such to me as a father beareth to his sonne or brother."

Next day came the ceremonial investiture of the Order in the Chapel, for—as with the Order of the Garter and even with the accolade—such honours were semi-religious, binding the recipient to keep faith with God and to be ever prepared to fight His battles. After communion, the envoys kissed Edward on the cheek, then all trooped to a tremendous dinner in the Great Hall where, in the pauses between eating, polite suggestions were made about Edward marrying the Princess Elizabeth of France.

Edward was doomed to marry no one. Already there was death in his body, although he led the envoys in the hunt and showed them his skill with a gun, on horseback, and at strumming the lute. On the last day of their visit, he plucked from his finger a diamond ring valued at £150 and presented it to the marshal. So successful had been the visit that a permanent resident ambassador was thereupon appointed to the English court; on September 28th, he was presented to Edward and the next day being the Feast of St. Michael it was celebrated with particular splendour in honour of the King of France and to prove, despite all rumours, that England had not forgotten God in the reformation.

Now came the destruction of proud Somerset. At Hampton Court, he flushed to see the armed tide rise against him, for his mortal foe, the Earl of Warwick, was there created Duke of Northumberland, and Somerset had to sit and smile and pretend not to hear the whispering of his enemies. Within a few weeks, reaction back in power, he was executed and the little king scribbled in his diary: " The duke of Somerset had his head cut of[f] apon Towre hill, betwene eight and nine a cloke in the morning."

Warwick now became the king's guardian and he loosened many of Somerset's restrictions, giving him more time for sport and play; but Edward had not long to live and Hampton Court ceases to be of importance in his diary. The last record is of the visit of the Queen Dowager of Scotland, Mary of Guise. There was feasting and merriment and the following day, as noted in the royal diary, " The dowagier perused the house of Ampton court, and saw some coursing of dere."

That is the last mention of our palace, although Edward visited it on July 27th and September 29th, 1552, and he was to die at Greenwich, writing with his own hand his " Devise for the succession." He willed the crown to the male heirs of Frances Brandon, Duchess of Suffolk, his cousin, then to her daughter, Lady Jane Grey's heirs male, thus remitting his two half-sisters, Mary and Elizabeth, to the old accusation of bastardy. It was said, of course, that he was poisoned; everybody said so, according to Henry Machyn in his diary; but to-day we cannot doubt that he died naturally, if disease be natural.

CHAPTER V
QUEEN MARY

L IKE all the Tudors, Mary was not healthy. After such a childhood, seeing her mother put aside and her religion assailed,
one can only wonder that she did not become even more
neurotic than she did; yet, strangely, she loved her father and
when Katherine Parr married again, she was aghast at this betrayal
of the royal ghost. It must be remembered that, despite her sufferings, Mary's mother loved Henry and he remained to both women
a good man misled by evil counsellors; nay, more than a man, he
was almost a god to Mary and, in contrast to Henry's feminine
squeak, her voice was gruff and wellnigh masculine. Nor was she
beautiful. Of middle-height, she was remarkably like her father
in appearance, particularly about the mouth—that tight little Tudor
mouth buttoning on pride—while, Marillac writes, she " has a
voice more man-like for a woman than he [Henry] has for a man."
Long-necked she was, he adds: " with a fresh complexion she looks
not past eighteen or twenty, although she is twenty-four. Her
beauty is mediocre, and it may be said that she is one of the belles
of the court," which is scarcely complimentary to the court. Although
physically of small attraction, she was brilliantly educated, as another
ambassador tells us, being " more than moderately read in Latin
literature, especially with regard to Holy Writ; and besides her
native tongue she speaks Latin, French and Spanish, and understands Italian perfectly, but does not speak it. . . . Her majesty
takes pleasure in playing on the lute and spinet, and is a very good
performer on both instruments; and indeed, before her accession
she taught many of her maids of honour. But she seems to delight
above all in arraying herself elegantly and magnificently, and her
garments are of two sorts: the one, a gown such as men wear, but
fitting very close, with an under-petticoat which has a very long
train, and this is her ordinary costume, being also that of the gentlewomen of England. The other garment is a gown and bodice,
with wide hanging sleeves in the French fashion, which she wears
on state occasions, and she also wears much embroidery, and gowns
and mantles of cloth of gold and cloth of silver, of great value, and
changes every day. She also makes great use of jewels, wearing

them both on her chaperon [hood or cap], and round her neck, and as trimming for her gowns; in which jewels she delights greatly, and although she has a great plenty of them left her by her predecessors, yet were she better supplied with money than she is, she would doubtless buy many more."

Below middle-height yet well proportioned and slim, she was unlike both her parents who grew fat. Bright and piercing were her pale eyes, although she was so short-sighted that she was forced to hold a book or letter against her face while she read. But always thought of her ghost evokes that voice, " rough and loud, almost like a man's so that when she speaks she is always heard a long way off."

Poor romantic Mary, she was to suffer both spiritually and bodily, for she adored the husband who did not care for her and she was rarely free from pain, suffering continual headaches and palpitations. Anæmic, tormented during menstruation which was very irregular and often ceased for long periods, she was pale and melancholic and, according to modern medical opinion, had ovarian dropsy.

This is the unhappy queen who steps, for a brief reign, the halls and chambers of Hampton Court, strolling with her ladies in the gardens in springtime to see fields sprinkled with the white of daisies on the green with yellow buttercups, to stay hours in the Chapel, praying for the Pope's power to return to England while she offered burnt heretics to pacify God, or sitting melancholy, brooding in the galleries, sunlight glittering through the painted glass to dapple richly the floor, while her husband was off hunting or whispered with young Elizabeth.

At Hampton Court in 1554, the Imperial ambassador, after passing through London where the citizens, far from cheering, had hung down their heads when he passed, was joyfully welcomed, for his master, the royal bridegroom, was expected before Lent. There " they had great cheer as could be had, and hunted and killed, tag and rag," while the ambassador made the formal proposal of marriage. Already Mary loved the long-jawed Hapsburg, but etiquette demanded that she appear shy. Looking down at the coronation ring on her finger, she said that it was not right for a maiden to discuss publicly so delicate a matter as her marriage, which could be argued by ministers, but she would, she said, have him understand that her first husband was her realm and that none other should induce her to violate her coronation oath.

Thus went the public discussion, as formal as a mask in which each player knows his part and acts with due solemnity, but at the banquets that followed, Mary's myopic eyes were bright with acceptance of her bridegroom. "Towards the end of the dinner," we are told, "the Lord Admiral, who had dined in an adjoining chamber, came in and stood before her, who seemed pensive. He said something to her in English, and then turning to us [Spaniards], asked us

The Great Hall.

whether we would like to know what he had said. Although her majesty did her best to prevent him from translating it to us, he went on to say that he had wished that his highness [Philip] had been seated there at her side, pointing to her right, in order to banish her melancholy. She blushed at this and asked why he said it, to which he replied that he was sure she was not cross, and liked to hear it; whereupon the queen and everyone else laughed, and it all went off in good part."

Very happy was Mary in Hampton Court these days, and brief must have been her bouts of fearsome melancholia which at times drenched her moods with inarticulate despair. She did not heed the threatening murmur in the land, the mutter of rebellion against Spanish and Roman domination. Wyatt rose, the son of the poet, but he had misjudged the time and suffered with his head; and in that dangerous moment, with her throne uneasy under her, Mary showed her mother's courage and dauntlessly refused to run, while Bishop Gardiner, on his knees, implored her to take barge to Windsor. " Shall I go or stay ? " she asked the Imperial ambassador, her beloved's representative, and he gave wise advice. " Stay," he said, " or lose your crown "; so Mary stayed and triumphed.

We will not pause to contemplate the martyrs burning. History has too long been written with religious bias and the truth is forgotten under the brilliant roaring of men like Froude and Belloc, each blind to the other's side, each hating and loving too much. If we remember the Spanish blood in Mary and that her grandmother was that Isabella who lit the inquisition's fires in Spain, destroying Moorish culture and throwing the people to Torquemada's hot mercy, we can understand these burnings. Mary cannot be blamed for them. According to her faith, heretics were already damned and it was right to kill them lest they damn others with their poison, and we to-day have seen slaughters enough in the name of different faiths that we can throw no stones. Nor is it our task to argue religious history; our interest in Mary is, not as a ruler, but as a woman in Hampton Court; and she was a most pathetic woman.

Yet she was to know brief happiness when Philip came to England. Golden-bearded, with bulbous forehead and worried blue eyes and a heavy thick mouth dragged open by the hanging jaw, he was, like Mary, tormented with melancholy, that *accide* of the monks, which seems to colour the lives of many earnest Christians contemplating their own and others' sin in Satan's world. Not that he was monkish in habits: he had bouts of furious debauchery in the Low Countries, but these were only occasional outbreaks of Baudelairean energy in which he seemed to seek the devil in revolt from God.

His erect bearing and stiff dignity were armour for shyness, and he must have sweated torments in England with his determination to win his wife's subjects by a gaiety ill-suited to him. He could not look you in the eyes but would stand with lowered lids while you talked; and when he opened his eyes it was only for a moment before the frightened glance shifted away.

That Mary adored him there cannot be any doubt. All her years of loneliness, of dreams of love, after her mother's death, were now exploded on to Philip who cared naught for her and whose one and natural desire was to get out of England as soon as courtesy permitted.

The honeymoon was spent in our palace and these were probably the few truly happy days that Mary was ever to know. " Their majesties are the happiest married couple in the world," wrote one who was with them, " and are more in love with each other than I can write here." That Mary loved Philip is beyond argument but that Philip loved Mary is more than doubtful; yet ably he acted his part, concealed his shyness, and rode with her and knelt with her at mass in the Chapel. It is well to recall those merry months because of the tragedy to follow and to listen to laughter that was soon to fade.

A royal Johanna Southcott, Mary was certain that she was with child, but as with Johanna, the swelling was merely dropsy. During Easter, 1555, she awaited in Hampton Court the confinement that was not to be, and she called for her half-sister—the first gesture of possible forgiveness shown Elizabeth since the suspicions that she might have been involved in Wyatt's rebellion—yet held her so closely guarded that she might as well have remained in jail. Mary herself kept to her own chambers, in daily expectation of being brought to bed, and already letters were drawn up—" Given under our signet at our house of Hampton Court "—and signed by king and queen, ready to be sent to the continent announcing the great event. Somebody started the wicked rumour that she had borne a son—they were so assured of the baby's sex that in the letter which was to be sent to Cardinal Pole the word *prince* was actually written, although all other documents more cautiously left sex and date blank, writing only *fil*, to which could be added either *s* or *le*—and bonfires were lighted, church-bells pealed and feasts were made ready while the rumour even echoed as far as the emperor. At Hampton Court the nursery was prepared with midwives and nurses and rockers and "a cradle veri sumptuouslie and gorgeouslie trimmed."

Pathetically, as the time passed, Mary still clung to her belief that she would bear a prince, while on April 23rd, St. George's Day, Philip, as Sovereign of the Order of the Garter, heard mass in the royal Chapel, then went in procession, with the knights and the lords of the council in their robes, around the cloisters and the courts. It was indeed a royal procession with the knights in their gay coats, the bishop in his mitre with priests and acolytes upholding three golden crosses, lighted tapers and censers smoking incense, while they paced slowly, solemnly round the cloister of the Inner Court—now the Fountain Court—the priests in copes of cloth of gold and tissue singing *salve festa dies.*

Although it was a breach of etiquette, Mary could not resist peeping from her window to watch the ceremony so " that hundreds did see her grace "; but perhaps she thus revealed herself to dispel rumours of her death, perhaps to show her reverence for all things popish, or perhaps—for few historians bother to see the simple human impulses behind acts of royalty—she merely wanted to watch her handsome husband in his robes.

And all the time, anxiously she waited with growing despair for this child for which she longed, while chirurgeons, with blank pretence of wisdom, cruelly fed her hopes, and "to comfort the queen and give her heart and courage three most beautiful infants were brought last week to her majesty to see, they having been born a few days previously at one birth, of a woman of low stature and great age like the queen [she was thirty-eight] and who, after the delivery, found herself strong and out of all danger; and the sight of this woman and the infants greatly rejoiced her majesty."

But it was almost too late now for such sights to strengthen hope while the prophecies of physicians and priests began to lose meaning and the queen despaired, although she told Philip, who told the Venetian ambassador, that she felt " certain pains which indicate the announcement of childbirth." What was even more galling than disappointment, the long waiting had become a jest. " Two gentlemen," we learn, " of no ordinary repute, were imprisoned in the Tower on a charge, according to the report, of having spoken about this delivery licentiously in a tone unbecoming their rank "; and the Polish ambassador, sent to sympathise with Philip about his grandmother's death, went on to congratulate him on the birth

Old East Front—Danckerts

of an heir—so definite had rumours grown that the poor fellow with his little English had apparantly misinterpreted a jest as truth —" to the laughter and amusement of many personages who were there." To this had Mary's tragic illusion come, that even before her husband's face, men could laugh at her and not be rebuked. Yet she had the appearance, the symptoms of child-bearing; it was too bitter a jest of nature to cheat her thus. One can imagine her lonely, weeping, in this palace, shrinking from the eyes of her women while midwives attempted to be cheerful with chatter of Gargantuan gestations, and she, feeling her stomach, mystified, tortured with doubt, shyed from the mockery in their smiles. Even the husband she worshipped must often have revealed his irritation as he longed to be out of this England which he detested.

Continually prayers were said in the Chapel for her safe delivery, continually public processions paced to implore God's help: but God did not heed. He did not turn even at the stink of heretics, burnt sacrifices that went unrewarded, while the king fidgeted and whispered to Princess Elizabeth or rode out hunting to return expectantly only to find there was no news, or rather, the same news: the queen expects. . . . And there was quarrelling between Spaniard and Englishman, hatred that was ill-concealed under lowered lids, the Spaniards being contemptuous of English manners and the English enraged by the Spaniards' scorn. Philip had to issue a warning that the first Spaniard to use a weapon would have his right-hand lopped, while he forbade the carrying of guns and threatened to hang any man who raised the cry of " Spain ! "

Even physicians began to give up calculating the date of the unborn's arrival. At first they had been professionally optimistic, protecting their ignorance behind the mumbo-jumbo of their art. We hear: " Her majesty's having greatly declined, a sign, they say, of the nearest approach to the term;" then talk of it happening at the next change of the moon; then after " the full moon and its occultation." . . . Mary sat, listlessly, half-dead, it seemed, with despair, on cushions on the floor, for hour after hour, not moving, her knees drawn up to her chin, while the wise women nodded their heads, saying that she could not be with child, for the position in which she sat would have been most painful and she would have smothered the babe. In the summer heat, the palace stank and the rooms were drenched with perfumes, while rumour tattled that the queen had been delivered of " a mole or mass of flesh," that she was seeking a baby somewhere to smuggle into court to pretend was hers, that she was dead and the tidings not given for fear of justice on these damned Spaniards who had murdered her.

From November, 1554, to August, 1555, hopes rose, only to die. To the last, Mary clung with tragic desperation to the belief that at any moment she might be delivered; and we know to-day sufficient of the subtle workings of the mind not to be surprised that she exhibited all the symptoms of pregnancy, morning sickness, and even the " swelling of the paps and emission of milk," for her desire was so huge that it forced the body to obey it. And with apparent submission the body cheated her until at length even she had to face the appalling truth and to know that, by confessing she had not quickened, she would lose for a time, at least, the man she loved.

The cradle, never to be tenanted, remained at Hampton Court with its mocking inscription in Latin and English:

> The child which thou to Mary, O Lord of Might, has sen[t],
> To England's joy, in health preserve, keep and defend;

while Mary departed for nearby Oatlands, so that Hampton Court could be cleaned, and " as her grace went through the park for to take her barge there met her grace by the way a poor man with two crutches, and when that he saw her grace, for joy he threw his staves away, and ran after her grace, and she commanded that one should give him a reward."

But the people's joy at learning that she had not been murdered was no compensation to her when Philip was going, disappointed of the heir that might have brought England into his Roman Empire. In 1557, he returned, hoping to drag the country into his wars. For a brief scene we see him and Mary again at Hampton Court on June 10th when they went " to hunt and to kill a great hart, with certain of the council."

No longer in Mary's reign is our palace of importance and small wonder if she detested it after those terrible months within its walls; but there is a mention in August, 1558, of her being there and of her not permitting her faithful friend, Jane Dormer, to travel by barge to London, because she was ill, but making her go by land in her own royal litter with her own physician to attend her.

That is a pleasant scene on which to close this unhappy chapter, drawing the curtain over the sad months of pregnancy that was not pregnancy, for when we open them again it is almost with a flourish of trumpets to announce the coming of Queen Elizabeth.

Chapter VI
QUEEN ELIZABETH

HAMPTON Court had few happy memories for Elizabeth when she succeeded to the throne, yet she loved the palace. During those months of waiting for Mary's alleged accouchement she had been brought here to be kept almost a prisoner, although Philip was astute enough to pay court to her, in fear least Mary die and he and his followers be murdered. At her sister's call she hurried to the palace, probably hoping to be forgiven all suspicion of having been involved in Wyatt's revolt, but instead, she found herself conducted like a prisoner through " the Backside, the doores being shut upon her, the souldiers in their ancient posture of watch and ward," while she was locked into what was most likely the Water Gallery—now demolished—which stood away from the palace proper, near the river; and there she remained isolated, with only her chamberwomen to attend her, for a fortnight, save for a visit from Philip. Men from her sister's court told her that she must throw herself on Mary's mercy, but Elizabeth was no fool, for as she remarked: " If I have offended and am guilty, I then crave no mercy, but the law; which I am certain I should have had ere this, if it could be proved by me." Next day, back came the councillors, wilily arguing that if she would not confess her guilt she insulted the queen by suggesting that her justice had been at fault. But they could not move her: she was guiltless, she insisted, and therefore had no guilt to confess; they went on their knees to her in submission, " and so departed, she being fast locked up again."

In that now vanished gallery, the girl waited in proud suspense; misfortune had stiffened her will to make it strong for any disaster, and the body had suffered for it, being ever ailing, tortured by neurasthenia. Then at ten o'clock one night came the dreaded summons to go to the queen, and it must have sounded to her like the summons of death. She begged her servants to pray for her, as she feared, she said, that she might not return. Through the gardens that early spring night they led her to the stair leading to the Queen's Lodgings. With their torches, the gentlemen ushers and grooms remained in the garden, lighting the sleepy flowers to sudden colour, while Elizabeth hurried to this first meeting in two years with her half-sister. Small, indeed, must have been the love between the daughters of Katherine of Aragon and Anne Boleyn, and it would have been inhuman of Mary to have forgotten her mother's humiliations. On a chair of state in her royal bedchamber, she sat like a judge, revealing no hint of affection.

Elizabeth gave the three prescribed bows and kneelings of etiquette and said, the story tells us, that she desired God to preserve her majesty while she would remain her true subject, and as such she wished to be judged. " You will not confess your offence," answered Mary, " but stand stoutly to your truth: I pray God it may so fall out." " If it doth not," said Elizabeth, " I request neither favour nor pardon at your majesty's hands." " Well," said Mary, " you stiffly still persevere in your truth. Belike you will now confess but that you have been wrongfully punished." " I must not say so, if it please your majesty, to you." " Why then," said the queen, " belike you will to others." " No, if it please your majesty," answered Elizabeth, " I have borne the burden, and must bear it. I humbly beseech your majesty to have a good opinion of me, and to think me to be your true subject, not only from the beginning hitherto, but for ever, as long as life lasteth."

Behind the words each strove to read the other's meaning, Mary uncertain whether she could trust the harlot's bastard and Elizabeth dreading to find an axe's edge at the end of the meeting. " And so," we are told, " they departed, with very comfortable words of the queen in English: but what she said in Spanish, God knoweth. It is thought that King Philip was there behind a cloth, and that he showed himself a very friend in that matter." But whether it were Philip's counsel or no, Elizabeth's imprisonment grew laxer, and even some courtiers were permitted to visit her.

Yet when she became queen, Elizabeth bore no ill will to the bricks and stones that had enclosed her in her hours of peril and, although we have no dramatic scenes to watch here during her reign, that is mainly because of her love for Hampton Court. For her it became what Wolsey had intended it to be—a refuge from court, a country home—and here she would retire or make merry when exhausted by state affairs. That she needed such a bolt-hole cannot be doubted, for she lived tensely on her nerves, a neurotic who would at times scream abuse even at her most faithful followers and who strove desperately to flatter her ego in the mirrors of others' admiration. From all men she demanded this admiration and the hyperbole with which she was addressed seems to us often fantastic, but when we read the popular books of the time we realise that this exaggerated metaphorical way of speaking was the fashion of the period. Kings and queens have ever demanded flattery, as Disraeli well realised, yet the adulation offered Elizabeth was different from that offered most monarchs because it had a frankly sexual basis. Poets wrote of her with the imagery of a lover. She was not only every Englishman's queen but also his mistress; even when she grew bald and toothless she remained Gloriana, for the memories of a tortured youth, ever trembling on the brink of terror in her mind, needed this soothing adulation.

So many are the portraits of Elizabeth that there is small need to describe her in detail, but as we evoke her ghost let us dress her in her fanning fardingale and tight bodice, the torso seeming tiny, a vase on a table, as she sways through the galleries of Hampton Court. Her skin was olive, her body slender, her hair reddish and her eyes light blue, her nose aquiline and her lips tight, Tudorish. Her main charm seems to have been her grace, her agility in the dance of which she was passionately fond, so that when in later life an ulcer above her ankle caused her to limp, and her hair fell out to be replaced by a red wig, she seems to us a tragic ghost hobbling in the knot-garden with her anxious ladies about her. Yet we dare not pity her. One cannot pity an eagle even when it is in captivity, for the glare of its hooded eyes rejects all weakness.

After her crowning, nine months later, on August 10th, 1559, we find Elizabeth at our palace; and soon we see her there teasing with the first of many offers of marriage. It was a Scottish offer from the protestants to keep the Roman catholic Mary from the throne and the suitor was the regent, the Earl of Arran. He was certainly not the fellow to inspire love, being neither handsome nor intelligent—later he was to become insane—but Elizabeth played with the idea, while at the same time tormenting the French ambassador in Hampton Court by showing him Mary of Guise's portrait hanging in one of the galleries. Mary was regent in France and Elizabeth gushed about her kindness, honesty, and uprightness, and sending most affectionate greetings to her. For the time, the ambassador was deceived, but at a later meeting his opinion changed. " There is more dissimulation in her than honesty and good will," he reported to the regent; " she is the best hand at the game living."

Such was the opinion of most ambassadors afterwards. In that game at Hampton Court Elizabeth showed her skill at diplomacy—in other words, in lying—and all through her reign we see her maddening the wretched ambassador unable to untangle truth from lie. She maddened her own ministers, too, sitting in council in Hampton Court and other palaces, for brilliant though she was, there was a flaw in her genius—her desire for, and her terror of, love lest her possession by a man mean loss of power.

Yet she loved Robert Dudley, Earl of Leicester, a clever almost too handsome man, and rumour soon was whispering that he had moved into a chamber close to hers on the plea that the ground-floor rooms were damp and unhealthy, while he was soon openly visiting her with a casualness that shocked the ceremonious court and sent worried ambassadors ferreting to find whether she were virtuous or a liar. Tall and nobly proportioned, Dudley was a brilliant talker and an expert jouster; although Ascham lamented that he had skimped his study of Cicero and Euclid, what mattered that when he had charm and beauty? Inevitably, his favour made rivals sharpen wits and swords while the Imperial ambassador prophesied that should the queen marry him, she might lie down Queen of England but she would wake up plain Mistress Elizabeth, and others bewailed that the country was so poor in spirit that none could be found to assassinate the upstart. There were rumours of the queen having been brought to childbed and, even more sinister, of plots to poison Amy Robsart, Dudley's wife.

And Amy Robsart was found dead at the foot of the stairs in Cumnor Place near Oxford, on September 8th, 1560. Unfortunately, here is not the place to argue the mystery of that convenient demise but, because of the scandal it aroused, any hope of Dudley marrying Elizabeth was finished. But that did not stop her from loving him and, while many watched their chance to tear him down, she tapped his cheek in open court and smiled on him. Once while he was playing tennis with the Duke of Norfolk in the tennis court which still stands in our palace grounds, she watched and, when he grew sweaty, he took the kerchief from her hand and wiped his face as casually as if he were her husband. Whereupon Norfolk, in rage at this insult to his queen, swore that Dudley was saucy and threatened to hit him with his racket. " Here vpon rose a great troble," we are told, " and the queen offendid sore with the Duke "—but not, you will note, with Dudley.

The Tennis Court

Yes, there still stands that tennis court in which two fierce and dangerous men stood ready to brawl while the queen rose in anger and made them stand back. Those walls, indeed, are history and poorly spirited is the man or woman who cannot feel the past when he or she looks on their warm brick. Houses are history. That brick there mayhap was tapped by Dudley as he strove to calm his heart, and in that gallery the great queen walked before her ladies and had men kneel to her. And within these palace-walls Elizabeth fell dangerously ill with smallpox towards the end of October, 1562, the epidemic having been fierce for the last few years, taking even some of the great ladies. On September 19th, she reached Hampton Court and, feeling unwell, foolishly took a bath, thinking it might revive her; then she strolled in the gardens that would have appeared very little different from those laid out by Mr. Law. Amongst the small beds of autumn flowers she walked with her ladies and naturally she caught a bad chill and was hurried to bed, shivering in high fever, and there she lay, semi-conscious, while her hushed ladies listened fearfully to her deep breathing and the physicians sucked in their lips with pretence of wisdom until at last, reluctantly, they hinted that mayhap she might not live. Death, Elizabeth herself said, possessed every joint of her, and the court prepared mournfully for mourning.

Cecil, the queen's great adviser, gathered the few of the council who remained in London and hurried them to Hampton Court, for, should the queen die, the succession was a dangerous matter. Who should succeed her? Some were for Lady Katherine Grey, some for the Earl of Huntingdon, but none dared mention the rightful heir, Mary of Scotland, for her coming might have meant the disastrous return of the late queen's Roman catholicism. But towards midnight of the 16th, the fever began to cool and Elizabeth called for her council and, not yet fully conscious, she babbled of dear Robert. Her first words were of Robert: she begged that he be made protector, gave him a title and twenty thousand pounds; she said that she loved him dearly, that she had always loved him, but as God was her witness, nothing improper had ever passed between them. Her weak voice muttered on while her councillors paled and the maids looked slyly at one another as the queen's heart was spoken to the arras-draped walls of a bedchamber in this palace. If echoes remain, closed within a room, the voice of that queen should still be heard had we the method of catching the sounds of the past; but it is unfortunately unlikely if that chamber remains, for it was probably one of those pulled down by William and Mary.

By October 29th, we hear that " she is now out of bed and is only attending to the marks on her face to avoid disfigurement," and England rejoiced to see vanish that bogy of a Pope. But we might mourn a little, for after this illness Elizabeth never had the same love for our palace and visited it less often.

We have previously mentioned Mrs. Penn whose tomb, containing a hairpin and some hair, is in Hampton Court Church and whose ghost, it is alleged, still walks the palace. She died on November 6th of that same smallpox which brought the queen near death and her ghost, stated Mr. Law, is vouched for with details " more definite and circumstantial than are usually forthcoming in such cases." If you accept the evidence, she apparently slept in peace until the irreverant shifting of her tomb in 1829, although it is difficult to understand why this desecration should have troubled her when her bones lay in some other, more secret place of which we do not know. Nevertheless, after this shifting of her monument, the disturbed spirit made its indignation known, for, writes Mr. Law, a " strange noise as of a woman working at a spinning-wheel, and muttering the while, were heard through the wall of one of the rooms in the large apartments in the south-west wing of the palace. When search was made by the Board of Works, in the direction whence these mysterious sounds proceeded, an ancient, and till then, unknown chamber was discovered, in which an antique spinning-wheel and a few other articles were found, and the old oak planks were seen to be worn away where the treadle struck the floor. The idea broached at that time was, that on account of the desecration of her tomb, her spirit had returned to haunt the rooms which she had occupied in life."

That would seem to be an intelligent enough explanation, for ghosts do not haunt graves so much as houses. Indeed, I know of no authentic haunted churchyard, for the bones are merely the gibbet of the spirit. Yet the moving of bones—or, as in the alleged case of Mrs. Penn, the monument of her tomb—does seem to disturb these strange creatures for which we have only the frightening puff of a word, " ghost," or the exhilarating, " spirit," with its suggestion of alcohol. Yet why should Mrs. Penn keep on spinning to eternity, if spin she does? Spinning, I wonder what? Shrouds? Or new garments for Kate Howard and Jane Seymour to replace those rotting with grave-time?

But the discovery of the spinning-wheel did not exorcise Mrs. Penn, still furious at the pulling down of her church, as well she might be, for the old building was probably far more lovely than any later architect could build. About five or six years after the discovery of the spindle, Mr. Law records that " the phenomena were renewed, and have since become frequent and startling. One of the recorded occurrences is the apparition of Mrs. Penn about four years ago, in the dead of night, to a sentry on guard not far from the haunted chamber, who, on seeing her, ran in abject terror to the guardroom, declaring he had seen a spectral form pass through the wall. Other accounts describe the constant prevalence of mysterious sounds—such as the low whirring of an unseen spinning-wheel, the weird mutters of a sepulchral voice, and the stealthy tread of invisible feet. It is even affirmed that Mrs. Penn's tall, gaunt form, dressed in a long, grey robe, with a hood over her head, and her lanky hands outstretched before her, has been seen in the haunted chamber—a supernatural visitation, which was rendered the more impressive from the narrator being a recent arrival at the palace, and consequently ignorant of the legend. And when, afterwards, attention was drawn to Mrs. Penn's monument (the existence if which was, at that time, unknown to anyone in the palace), and it was found that the description of the ghost exactly corresponded with the appearance of the effigy, the coincidence was so startling as to shake the judgment even of the most sceptical."

Altogether an inexplicable ghost when we consider that empty tomb, the long silence since burial, and the appearance after the shifting of the tomb. If ghosts, as I believe, are projections from the past, I can see no reason why Mrs. Penn should change residence. My theory may possibly be wrong, and I confess it to be shaken after the exposure of the famous apparitions at Versailles to be probably not apparitions at all, yet I can find no other that is plausible. Even should there be an after-life, I still cannot understand why Mrs. Penn should desert it to come spinning at Hampton Court, particularly, so far as we know, there was no tragedy in her early existence. Not believing in an after-life, I can merely conclude that—if the ghost be authentic—the poor creature when she lived was kept so busy at the wheel that her very soul entered the wood; now that the wheel has gone, the bewildered spinner can but wander seeking it, to the terror of the residents. To " lay her," one should, perhaps, go with the lure of a wheel. It is, at any rate, a pursuit worthy of that great ghost-hunter, Mr. Harry Price, and, if not so interesting, the prize at least is more authentic than the ghost of Kate Howard.

But from ghosts to the shadows of the past, let us return . . . let us attempt to revisit the palace one day when Elizabeth was in residence and try to see her and her anxious ladies at work and sport. We will take no famous occasion, no ambassadorial visit, but an ordinary day.

Breakfast was at six o'clock and, the queen being always abstemious, it was probably a small one, a cup or so of ale, perhaps, with a small loaf of bread. Immediately afterwards, she with her maids of honour walked in the gardens. So ably has Mr. Law reconstructed the gardens at Hampton Court that it needs little imagination to see her there, erect, chin up above the laced collar, the huge skirts sweeping dust and leaves and pebbles after her, while she chatters with the maids: for this is her brief hour of relaxation before affairs of state imprison the woman in the queen. This was the hour for scandal while the girls in white and silver giggled secrets to the queen, for they often knew more than ministers. Well born, well educated and most of them beautiful, these maids are essential for any picture of Elizabeth; to see her in her splendour we must have the girls grouped about her, a setting for the royal jewel, but a setting that must never separate, never become individual jewels sparkling for a man's eyes. Instantly then fell the queen's displeasure and the girl was fortunate, should she marry without permission, not to find herself locked into the Tower. Some of these wenches were, indeed, beautiful, and I regret we have not the space to examine them individually; but let us linger on one charming vision, the picture of Mary Fitton—the alleged Dark Lady of Shakespeare's sonnets—stamping into the garden in the moonlight, wearing a long white cloak to conceal her gown while she swaggers like a cavalier to meet her lover. Such were the tricks these ladies had to use should they love, for Elizabeth's spinster jealousy was huge and dangerous. It was, however, not wholly jealousy that made her keep her maids literally maids for as long as possible. They were her wards and she had the right of wardship, a very lucrative one, and " possessed " the right of marrying them for money down.

The brisk walk in the garden over, should there be no state affairs to attend to, most likely the queen would dance in the galleries, for at dancing she was skilled. Even when death knuckled her joints, she tottered out to spring and leap and kick like a girl. Or she and the maids would sew or embroider, while courtiers would come to make extravagant love to the queen and secret assignations with her ladies. We can see them in the Haunted Gallery, as this was probably a favourite for the morning, for the door on the right leads to the Holy Day Closet and the Royal Pew—in which Henry knelt when Katherine is said to have run to him for mercy—a gallery at the west end of the chapel. The Gallery's arched windows would then be bright with painted glass and, should the morning be warm and they open, one could look out into the Round Kitchen Court as it is called to-day. Opposite these windows the walls were spiky with antlers and because these antlers were later tossed into the room separating the Great Watching Chamber and the Great Hall, that has been called the Horn Room.

All the queen's days, however, were not so quiet. On Sundays the visit to the Chapel was one of almost ponderous ceremony and more vividly than I can describe it is the description given by a traveller, Hentzner:

" First went the gentlemen," he wrote, " barons, earls, knights of the garter, all richly dressed and bare-headed; next came the chancellor, bearing the seals in a red silk purse, between two, one of which carried a royal sceptre, the other the sword of state, in a red scabbard, studded with golden fleur-de-lis, the point upwards. Next came the queen, in the sixty-fifth year of her age, as we were told, very majestic; her face oblong, fair but wrinkled; her eyes small, yet black and pleasant, her nose a little hooked; her lips narrow and her teeth black: (a defect the English seem subject to, from their too great use of sugar). She had in her ears two pearls, with very rich drops; she wore false hair, and that red; upon her head she had a small crown, reported to be made of some of the gold of the celebrated Lunebourg table; her bosom was uncovered, as all the English ladies have it, till they marry; she had on a neck-lace of exceeding fine jewels. Her hands were small, her fingers long, and her stature neither tall nor low; her air was stately, her manner of speaking mild and obliging. That day she was dressed in white silk bordered with pearls of the size of beans and over it a mantle of black silk, shot with silver thread. Her train was very long, the end of it borne by marchionesses. Instead of a chain, she had an oblong collar, of gold and jewels. As she went along in all this state and magnificence, she spoke very gracious, first to one, then to another, whether foreign ministers or those who attended for different reasons, in English, French, and Italian: for besides being well skilled in Greek, Latin, and the languages I have mentioned, she is mistress of Spanish, Scotch and Dutch. Whoever speaks to her, it is kneeling; now and then she raises some by her hand. While we were there, W. Slawata, a Bohemian baron, had letters to present to her; and she, after pulling off her glove, gave him her right hand to kiss, sparkling with rings and jewels,—a mark of particular favour. Wherever she turned her face as she was going along, everybody fell down on their knees. The ladies of the court followed next to her, very handsome and well shaped, and for the most part dressed in white. She was guarded on each side by the gentlemen pensioners, fifty in number, with gilt battle-axes. In the antichapel next the hall where we were, petitions were presented to her, and she received them most graciously, which occasioned the acclamation of, Long live Queen Elizabeth! She answered it with, I thank you, my good People."

Thus must you picture her when next you visit the Haunted Gallery, but you must remember she was not always old. She was twenty-five when made queen and it is as well to strip aside ceremony and see her as another visitor saw her, Sir James Melville, a young courtier sent by Mary, Queen of Scots. On his first visit she was just over thirty.

Melville was young and handsome and Elizabeth liked such gallants. In Sir James's memoirs she stands out vividly, coquettish and gay, proud yet almost kittenish at times while she strove to make him admit that she was lovelier than his queen. Melville, however, was too cunning a courtier to be trapped and adroitly he evaded all direct answers while, with his eyes, showing his admiration.

He first appears at Hampton Court in 1564, carrying the portrait of one of Elizabeth's suitors, Hans Casimir, the eldest son of the elector palatine; but for all his cleverness he could not snare Elizabeth into accepting her political lover. Casually he told her of his dislike at having to leave so charming a fellow, and to keep some remembrance of him, he said, he had carried with him portraits of the elector, his wife and all his sons and daughters—he did not tell Elizabeth that he had refused to take a painting of Casimir alone as being too blunt an attack on her heart. Naturally, Elizabeth wanted to see the paintings and he, to disarm suspicion of ulterior intent, said that he had left them in London and that he was immediately leaving from there for Scotland. That was sufficient for feminine Elizabeth. At all costs she must see these paintings and she forbade Melville to leave until he had shown them to her.

When next day he delivered them at Hampton Court, Elizabeth said she would like to keep them for the night; apparently, however, her maiden dreams were not of Casimir for, after showing the paintings to Leicester—it is not difficult to guess Leicester's dry comments—she returned them to Melville, giving him thanks for the sight of them. If only she would return him those of the elector and his lady, said the perfect courtier, she might keep the others; but Elizabeth would have none of them. Leicester had spoken well and Casimir had no hope of entering the virgin's heart. " I had also sure information," wrote Melville, " that first and last, she despised the said Duke Casimir. Therefore I did write back from London to his father and him in cypher, dissuading them to meddle any more in that marriage." There were always spies in palaces, not merely servants, but ladies and gentlemen agog to sell their mistress or their master for the touch of gold, and Elizabeth's court was no exception.

Soon, however, Melville returned as Mary's accredited agent and, for nine days, was continually in and out of Hampton Court, riding over that drawbridge watched by heraldic beasts, under the gates and into the court that would be so little different—save for the absent paint pot and the upper portion—from what it is to-day. Crafty and wheedling, he walked beside her in the gardens, sat with her in the galleries, flattering and, probably, ogling her with sighs and lowered eyelids. In the gardens where she strode briskly " to catch her a heate in the colde mornings," he was ever at her side, bowing, whispering, while her ladies watched and envied her her handsome lying Scotsman. And most of the conversation, inevitably, was on his royal mistress, for Elizabeth was more than curious about every detail of Mary's looks and appearance. She was the rival queen of Britain and one who gave small value to modesty, so that Elizabeth, the virgin, would have been no woman had she not burned with jealous dislike. Few queens have had such sentimental tushery written about them than this unfortunate Mary of Scotland —or, perhaps, fortunate when one remembers her loyal biographers— but she was a stupid, and not particularly attractive, woman imprisoned in her senses, lacking Elizabeth's brave spirit and sanity.

Yet Elizabeth, in her rustling maidenhood, was jealous, although cynically she proffered her beloved Dudley for Mary's husband— most likely realising he would be refused and wishing to humble him—and now she questioned Melville sharply and he needed all his wits to avoid insulting either lady. She wanted to see Mary, she told him one time at Hampton Court, " and because their so much, by her, desired meeting could not be so hastily brought to pass," writes Melville, " she appeared with great delight to look upon her Majesty's [Mary's] picture. She took me to her bed-chamber, and opened a little cabinet, wherein were divers little pictures wrapt within paper, and their names written with her own hand upon the papers. Upon the first that she took up was written, ' *My Lord's picture*.' I held the candle, and pressed to see that picture so named; she appeared loath to let me see it; yet my importunity prevailed for a sight thereof, and found it to be the earl of Leicester's picture."

Few scenes in history are so delightfully intimate as that candlelit vision in a panelled room in Hampton Court of the great queen, painted and jewelled, her red-capped head high against the fanning ruff, showing the courteous Scot her woman's treasures, sharply watching him while he looked on Leicester's proud face painted in miniature. It is for such moments that one almost loves Elizabeth, when one catches her without the whalebone bodice, the monstrous farthingale, unarmoured for a little time, a woman showing the portrait of the man she loves but dares not marry. Melville asked if he might take it to show his queen—the marriage then being mooted—and swiftly Elizabeth denied him. Nay! she could not part with her lord's pretty picture; it was, she said, the only likeness of him she possessed; but Melville, glimpsing Dudley himself talking with Cecil at the further end of the chamber, whispered that as she possessed the original surely she could part with the painting? But Elizabeth was still girlish, no doubt acting to Dudley as much as to Melville, and she would not give up the miniature. Then she kissed detested Mary's portrait—well might she have spat on it—and Melville kissed her hand in acknowledgment of the great love she thereby showed his queen.

There were occasions at Hampton Court when Melville—instructed by Mary who warned him that Elizabeth remained a woman under her virginal cuirass—would talk of foreign fashions, " declaring my observations of the customs of Dutchland, Poland, and Italy, the busking [boards placed from the crutch over the stomach to push up the breasts] of the women was not forgot, and what country weed I thought best becoming gentlewomen." And at chatter of weeds—strange how the word to-day is attached only to widows' dress—Elizabeth was reminded of her own wardrobe—which was notorious, no maid of honour appearing in a becoming gown without Elizabeth instantly demanding it—and assured him that she had clothes of every mode and material; thenceforward, each day he appeared she appeared in a different bejewelled gown, one day wearing English style, another day French, a third Italian, demanding to know which best suited her; and when shrewd fellow, Melville decided on the Italian, she was delighted because it showed off her curled reddish hair to perfection under caul and cap.

Conversation next coming to the mystery of women's hair, its shades and coiffure, Elizabeth asked " what colour of hair was reputed best; and whether my queen's hair or hers was best; and which of them was fairest ? " A treacherous cornering question from which Melville skipped by saying that " The fairness of them both was not their worst faults." But Elizabeth, stout woman, was not to be foiled by such masculine prevarication. In plain language she insisted on knowing which was the fairer, she or Mary. You, said the crafty Scot, are " the fairest Queen in England, and mine the fairest Queen in Scotland." But a fig for such skullduggery! how could there be comparisons when there was only one queen in either country? Elizabeth would not be cheated, she would have the apple which Melville dared not give, knowing right well that it would be reported instantly in a triumphant note carried by hard riding messengers to Scotland; but driven further and further into the trap, he at last said that each was the fairest lady in her own country but, while Elizabeth was whiter, Mary was very lovely. Unable to prod him from that cunning compromise, Elizabeth now wanted to know which was the taller, she or Mary? and to this Melville boldly answered that Mary was the taller, whereupon Elizabeth complacently remarked that then " she is too high; for I myself am neither too high nor too low."

The inquisition was not over, however Melville sweated, for Elizabeth would now be told what were Mary's amusements. Here he was on safer ground and said that when he had received his despatch, his queen had just returned from hunting in the Highlands and that, when serious matters gave her time, she read histories, although sometimes she liked to play on the lute or virginal. Did she play well? asked Elizabeth; to which Melville discreetly replied: " Reasonably for a queen."

Now was Elizabeth's chance to prove her superiority, Melville having baffled her at every other point; and that night her cousin, Lord Hunsdon, led the young Scot, hush hush, to a quiet gallery where—although Hunsdon whispered he could not be sure of it— the queen might be heard playing on the virginal—an early form of harpischord, unlike the piano in that the notes were not struck but were plucked by quills, being a development from the medieval psaltery which was a form of lute played with a plectrum. And in that quiet gallery—lost to us now for ever, with so much else— they heard the queen play, as Melville put it, " excellently well." He knew, however, that he was expected to show how ravished he was by the sound, so he lifted the tapestry hanging over the door and, seeing the queen's back was towards him, tiptoed within. There he stood " a pretty space " until Elizabeth caught sight of him and, in maidenly confusion, ceased to play. " She appeared," he writes, " to be surprised to see me, and came forward, seeming to strike me with her hand; alleging that she used not to play before men, but when she was solitary, to shun melancholy. She asked me how I came there ? I answered   As I was walking with my lord of Hunsdon, as we passed by the chamber-door I heard such melody as ravished me, whereby I was drawn in ere I knew how; excusing my fault of homeliness, as being brought up in the Court of France, where such freedom was allowed ;   declaring myself willing to endure what kind of punishment her Majesty should be pleased to inflict upon me for so great an offence.   Then she sat down low upon a cushion, and I upon my knees by her; but with her own hand she gave me a cushion, to lay under my knee; which at first I refused, but she compelled me to take it.   She then called for my lady Strafford out of the next chamber; for the Queen was alone.   She inquired whether my queen or she played best ? "   This time, Melville had the courage —or the weakness—to give her, in his own words, " the praise."

After thus proving her superiority at the virginal, Elizabeth must next contest the absent Mary at dancing and she forced Melville to delay his departure for two days purely that he might watch her.   " Which being done," he writes, " she inquired of me, whether she or my Queen danced best ?   I answered, the Queen danced not so high, and disposedly as she did."   This had been the complaint of the Spaniards at the late Mary's court, that the English conception of dancing was merely leaping.   Violent though it was, Elizabeth enjoyed dancing almost to her dying day.   Six or seven galliards each morning, apart from music and singing, were her daily exercise, writes a courtier in 1589.   And there was that awful occasion at Hampton Court when the Earl of Oxford—whom some enthusiasts, led by Dr. Looney, believe wrote Shakespeare's works—remarked: " By the blood of God, that she had the worst of voyce, and did everything with the worst grace that ever any woman did."   The insult was apparently remembered when, for no known reason, he was banished from court and locked into the Tower.

But it was not always merriment at Hampton Court.   Here Elizabeth prayed and brooded on the fate of Mary of Scotland, and to here she summoned a council in October, 1568, to argue what could best be done with that errant queen, and here were produced those notorious Casket Letters about whose authenticity historians still quarrel.   The problem was a serious one, for the queen had taken refuge in England and the Roman catholics were rallying around her while she intrigued with them through—although she knew it not—English spies who were cunningly knotting her in treachery inspired by themselves. But we must leave this fascinating episode, for it is outside our history, although many conferences were held in the palace which had become Elizabeth's favourite country home. Here at Christmas she would make merry and she added her portion to the house—her badges can be seen: you will find them, for example, with her initials and the date 1566 on the two outer turrets facing the Base Court—and she built stables adjoining Wolsey's on the Green. Probably, as Mr. Law suggests, they were made for the coaches which were now being introduced into England, for until then women had usually ridden horses, sometimes astride, but often on pillion—a soft leather pad being

The Base Court + Great Hall.

attached to the back of the saddle, with a loop fitting under the horse's tail, on which the woman sat sideways, gripping a thong from the back of the rider's belt with which to steady herself—or they would be carried on chairs or in open corracles; and it is astonishing that covered coaches should have been so late an invention. You can still see Elizabeth's initials, E.R., each side of a Tudor rose on some of the leaden water spouts against these stable walls, or the plain date above her Tudor rose.

Then again, in 1572, we hear of her falling ill of the smallpox at Hampton Court and learn that Dudley nursed her tenderly, for he " did watche with her all night. This morning thanks be to God ! she is very well. It was but a soden pang. I pray God long to preserve her. These be shrewde alarmes," as one wrote to Cecil. Elizabeth herself gives full details. " True it is," she wrote, " that we were about XIII dayes paste distempered as commonly happenith in the begynning of a fever; but after twoo or three daies, without any great inward siknes, ther began to appere certain red spotts in som parte of our face, likely to proove the small pox; but, thanked be God, contrary to the expectation of our phisycians, & all others about us, the same so soon vanished awaye as with in foure or fyve dayes passed no token almost apeered; and at this day [October 22nd] we thank God, we are so free from any token or marke of any suche disease that none can conjecture any suche thing. So as by this you may perceave what war our siknes. . . . "

But by this, I fear, we cannot perceive what was her sickness, as it is most unlikely that she would have suffered smallpox twice, the first attack usually acting as an inoculation against further attacks. It was more likely to have been mere biliousness which, to the physicians of those days, might appeared to have symptoms as terrifying as the dreaded pox.

For the remainder of Elizabeth's reign there is little to record, save Christmas festivities and the performance of masks, so popular at the time, playing of myths and symbolic tales, usually with most flattering references to the Virgin Queen. Ben Jonson was the master of this form and, with almost frightening facility, he spun them to order in beautiful verse. To-day we find them rather tedious reading, but they were not meant to be read, they were for acting, often by non-professional actors, and like all amateur theatricals they were probably a joy to the performers, however the audience may have shuffled on their stools. Not only masks, however, but plays were acted in our Great Hall. In Cunningham's work on court revels we find Hampton Court often named as the theatre. There we find references to carpenters, carvers, and joiners busy at building the stage around the screens and minstrel gallery, for the Elizabethan stage was of two floors, as can be seen in the famous sketch by John de Witt of the Swan Theatre about 1600. On the upper floor would be performed scenes such as the balcony scene in *Romeo and Juliet* and Richard III's announcement of his " usurpation," and so on.

From the accounts, we learn that the stage at Hampton Court was built of stout scaffolding, posts, rafters, and screens, " having also apt houses made of canvas, framed and painted accordingly as might serve their several purposes," such as the " painting of seven cities, one village, and one country house." The pantry at the lower end of the Hall, behind the screens, was the " tyring-room," or green room, while the Great Watching Chamber was used for rehearsals. We find mention also of the essential wardrobe for the " airing, repairing, amending, brushing, spunging, rubbing, wiping, sweeping, cleaning, putting in order, folding, laying-up and safe bestowal of the garments, vestures, apparel, disguising, properties, and furniture . . . which else would be mouldy, musty, moth-eaten and rotten"; while tailors, haberdashers, buskin-makers, upholsterers, and silk weavers were called on to make costumes and properties such as wings and wigs, vizards and wands, and counter-feit fish, fruit and flowers, and all else needed for a realistic perfor-mance.

There were no footlights to this stage, but rather toplights, for ropes were stretched across the beams from which lamps were suspended, while high on the walls burned candles in silver sconces and " candlesticks with perfumes to burn at the end of matches."

Plays and masks, dancing and singing, might make Christmas a merry season at Hampton Court, but what was of greater impor-tance to the queen were New Year Gifts, given then as we give Christmas boxes nowadays. In this exchange, inevitably, she won, for while a farthing toy from the hand of the sovereign was to be accepted with extravagant gratitude because of the giver, the reverse was also true: the most precious offering could not be considered worthy of being given the queen. Usually Elizabeth dispensed something one would not have bothered to glance at in the stalls of the Royal Exchange, some mere silver-gilt trumpery, while the gentlemen and ladies had to squander little fortunes to obtain something she would not spurn. Dresses she liked most, and jewels: anything to adorn her ageing body.

In the Presence Chamber on her jewelled throne, beneath a velvet canopy, the queen would sit with her white-garbed maids behind her. Lords, spiritual and temporal, great ministers and ambassadors, with courtiers and the officers of the household and great ladies, would each in order of precedence approach the queen, the women would curtsey and the men fall on one knee before her —one knee to royalty, two to God—while humbly they begged her to accept caskets and jewels, and pendants and rings, and bodkins to keep the hair in place, or they would give gold and silver plate; but the more cunning offered gowns, sleeves, fripperies to bedeck her.

The court physician would present her with pots of preserved fruits, the master cook would produce some culinary rarity, the yeoman of the guard a subtlety showing a military exploit, the yeoman of the pastry a fruit pie. . . . And graciously or petulantly the jewelled goddess in unbending garb would take whatever was brought, particularly clothes, even when she had become a sad, bald, scraggy creature.

See her in her broad bed in the morning when the curtains are parted and sunlight dares to glare on the yellow skin smeared with last night's cosmetics, the skull as if bound in vellum, the blue eyes dark in hollows; see her lying, almost a skeleton, in that vast sea of silk while ladies run with a flurry of skirts to the wardrobe. No mirrors but their eyes—fearful of age, she would have no mirrors in the palace —to reveal her skinnyness as they paint and dress her, lifting the creaking near-corpse out of bed to draw silk stockings up the legs to be buckled under the knees.* No underclothing, as we know it to-day, was then worn—such would have been considered indecent—nor was it necessary when skirts dragged the dust and rushes after them, great shells to keep off cold. Elizabeth would wear many skirts over the farthingale, that skeleton of wire and bone, and her breasts would be almost fully revealed above the low-cut bodice, a thin scrap of silk mayhap tossed over their up-swelling to semi-conceal them. Her hair would be elaborately frizzed and curled and padded and her face meticulously painted.

---

* It was her silk-woman, Mistress Montague, who knitted and presented Elizabeth with her first pair of silk stockings on New Year's Day, 1559. Seeing the queen's delight, Mistress Montague promised to make her some more. " Do so," urged Elizabeth, " for indeed I like silk stockings well, because they are pleasant, fine and delicate, and henceforth I shall wear no more cloth stockings."

Then this little creature who had been almost lost in the vasty bed would stand, a giantess in her garments, brave enough now to face a hundred handsome men.

But I fear this chatter of dancing and clothing might give the impression of Elizabeth continually living indoors at Hampton Court, and that is far from truth. As already remarked, she would walk every morning, even in winter, to catch a heat—to get warm, we would say—except when she noticed she was spied on, whereupon instantly she would become the queen again and would saunter queenlily. Well tended were her gardens, laid out with plants " which are trained, intertwined and trimmed in so wonderful a manner, and in such extraordinary shapes," noted one who saw them, " that the like could not be easily found," while there were " sundry towers, or rather bowers, for places of recreation and solace, and for sundry other uses."

She would go hunting, too, but this hunt was not as we know it to-day. In Bushey Park, the almost tame animals were herded into enclosures and then chased out to be slaughtered by hunters seated safely in pavilions. When Elizabeth hunted, musicians went with her and were placed in bowers of greenery—in little leafy tents under the trees—while a lady disguised as a nymph would curtsey, symbol of Diana, and offer a crossbow to the queen, she being a mere revered virgin huntress even than the moon.

When in 1592, the Duke of Wurtemberg visited Hampton Court, Elizabeth was unfortunately away and, although the duke went hunting she did not ride with him; but he gives us an enthusiastic description of the palace which is best repeated in his own words. " Now," he wrote in his diary, " this is the most splendid and most magnificent royal palace of any that may be found in England, or, indeed, in any other kingdom. It comprises ten different large courts [only five are actually large], and as many separate royal and princely residences, but all connected; together with many beautiful gardens, both for pleasure and ornament—some planted with nothing but rosemary; others laid out with various other plants. . . . In short, all the apartments and rooms in this immensely large structure are hung with rich tapestry of pure gold and fine silk, so exceedingly beautiful and royally ornamented that it would hardly be possible to find more magnificent things of the kind in any other place. In particular, there is one apartment belonging to the queen, in which she is accustomed to sit in state, costly beyond everything; the tapestries are garnished with gold, pearls, and precious stones—one table-cover alone is valued at about fifty thousand crowns—not to mention the royal throne, which is studded with very large diamonds, rubies, sapphires, and the like, that glitter amongst other precious stones and pearls as the sun among the stars. Many of the splendid large rooms are embellished with masterly paintings, writing-tables inlaid with mother-of-pearl, organs, and musical instruments, which her majesty is particularly fond of. Among other things to be seen there, are life-like portraits of the wild man and woman whom Martin Frobisher, the English captain, took in his voyage to the New World, and brought alive to England."

While glancing at the visitors' book, it might be as well here to quote the remarks of another traveller, the German Hentzner in 1598, his *Journey into England* being one of the most fascinating windows we have through which to see the Elizabethan world.

"Hampton Court," he wrote, " is a royal palace, magnificently built with brick by Cardinal Wolsey in ostentation of his wealth, where he enclosed five ample courts [as already mentioned, there were actually three large courts with three smaller ones] consisting of noble edifices in very beautiful work. Over the gate in the second area is the queen's device, a golden rose, with this motto: *Dieu et mon Droit*. On the inner side of this gate are effigies of the twelve [ten] Roman Emperors in plaster. The chief area is paved with square stone; in its centre is a fountain that throws up water, covered with a gilt crown, on the top of which is a statue of Justice, supported by columns of black and white marble."

Of this vanished fountain, the already quoted Duke of Wurtemberg informs us that it had a " waterwork, by which you can, if you like, make the water play upon the ladies and others who are standing by, and give them a thorough wetting." A schoolboy jest, yet typical of that boisterous age when Marlowe could have devils tie crackers to the singing monks in *Dr. Faustus* and thereby bring laughter from the groundlings; although it is not for us to sneer when farce is still considered superior to wit on the London stage. But to return to our guide, Hentzner:

" The Chapel of this Palace," he tells us, " is most splendid, in which the Queen's Closet is quite transparent, having its windows of crystal. We were led into two chambers, called the Presence, or Chamber of Audience, which shone with tapestry of gold, silver, and silk of different colours; under the canopy of state are these words embroidered in pearl: VIVAT REX HENRICUS OCTAVUS. Here is besides a small chapel richly hung with tapestry, where the queen performs her devotions. In her bedchamber the bed was covered with very costly coverlids of silk. At no great distance from this room we were shown a bed, the tester of which was worked by Anne Boleyn, and presented by her to her husband Henry VIII. All the other rooms, being very numerous, are adorned with tapestry of gold, silver, and velvet, in some of which were woven history pieces; in others Turkish and American dresses, all extremely natural. In the Hall are these curiosities: a very clear looking-glass, ornamented with columns and little images of alabaster;" many paintings; " the Bible curiously written up on parchment; an artificial sphere; several musical instruments; in the tapestry are represented negroes riding upon elephants; the bed in which Edward VI is said to have been born, and where his mother Jane Seymour died in childbed; in one chamber were excessively rich tapestries, which are hung up when the queen gives audience to foreign ambassadors. There are numbers of cushions ornamented with gold and silver; many counterpanes and coverlids of beds lined with ermine; in short, all the walls of the palace shine with gold and silver. Here is also a certain cabinet called *Paradise* where besides that everything glitters so with silver, gold, and jewels, as to dazzle one's eyes, there is a musical instrument made all of glass except the strings."

I care not what song the sirens sang or what tongue Achilles spoke when he lived amongst women, but I do care, I care most deeply, about the loss of those precious things. Even in Elizabeth's day, as Hentzner shows, they were so valuable as to be almost museum pieces; how doubly, nay, trebly valuable would they be to us now! That musical instrument—lute, most likely—made all of glass, save for the strings, so that one could have watched the queen's long fingers—when one knelt, as one would have knelt, at her feet—through the glass like long pearls quivering through water. Ah, to possess that to-day! To hold in our coarse hands this glass—and glass was rare and expensive in those times—which the great queen once held and breathed on to see its transparency misted with her breath: or to have that mirror from an age in which most people used metal for reflection, with its ornaments of little alabaster images—cupids, mayhap, or nymphs offering the queen of nymphs, Diana's sister, this image of herself—and to see the bed with its high tester worked by Anne Boleyn's own extra-fingered hand; and the Turkish pantaloons, stolen perhaps by a pirate from some bey's harem; and the American dresses, Aztec or Inca garments probably of feathers scumbled to pastel shades or, mayhap, just ropes of beads. Even the artificial sphere would be a treasure to hold—whatever is meant by that description: most probably a " shew-stone " such as that into which grave Dr. Dee spoke with angels in his home at Mortlake with crop-eared Kelly for interpreter; and it is likely that that cunning doctor gave this very globe to the queen, for he had cast her horoscope and given the most auspicious day for her crowning while, in later years, she had ridden to look into his crystal. " Her majestie," we are informed, " being taken down from her horse by the Earle of Leicester, Master of the Horse, at the Church wall of Mortlake, did see some of the properties of that glass [which foretold the future] to her Majestie's great contentment and delight." In the British Museum to-day you can glare into one of the great doctor's crystals, unfortunately a round one and not oval, as true divining crystals should be shaped. And then there was that cabinet called *Paradise*, and that room to which another foreigner, Justus Zinzerling, gives us a key a decade or so later—in 1610 to be exact.

It was, he writes, the most eminent room in all Hampton Court for " it captivates the eyes of all who enter, by the dazzling pearls of all kinds. It is strange that the keeper of this room," he adds with natural irritation, " is so sordid that you must bargain beforehand about his fee; yet from his dress he appears a grand gentleman ": a humiliation from which most of us even to-day have suffered. Taylor, the water-poet, called it a " most pompous room," for apparently it contained examples of needlework, amongst others, from the hands of the queen herself. And now, all vanished. . . .

She was not always at needlework, as her council well knew, for she could roll a lusty oath when it pleased her to be displeased. But it is the historian's unhappy task to face such buffets, ours merely to watch her in repose, amongst her treasures, or in the gardens of Hampton Court. Soon, most reluctantly, I must turn the page on her reign, for it is the turning from our palace's great period and my inclination is to linger. But already we have lingered too long and we must pass from her as she was soon to pass from this world, noting merely that on February 2nd, 1594, four gentlemen of the court were robbed in our palace, the chamber door in one of the five towers in the vanished Tilt Yard being broken at six o'clock in the evening " and all their trunks likewise, out of all of which the thieves took and carried away of jewels and ready money, from these four, to the value of £400, and no news heard of them since." The thief in chief, one John Randall, was eventually hanged for this dastardly prying into gentlemen's mails when under the divine protection of the queen, while his accessories were, strangely, pardoned.

Nor should we forget the interesting detail given by wise Dr. G. B. Harrison in his *Last Elizabethan Journal* of the proclamation uttered in September, 1602, against the rascals who dared fish or snare " pheasants, partridges, or fowl of the river within six miles " of our palace.

Now for the last times at Hampton Court do we watch Elizabeth, and it is a scene most appropriate to this indomitable woman. But first, one glimpse of her " dancing the Spanish Panic to a whistle and a tabourer [a small drum slung from one shoulder], none other being with her but my Lady Warwick." Thus was she glimpsed through a window when she was wellnigh seventy years of age; and now, finally, we watch her leaving the palace in 1599.

" At her majesty's returning from Hampton Court," we are told, " the day being passing foul, she would (as was her custom) go on horseback, although she is scarce able to sit upright, and my Lord Hunsdon said, ' It was not meet for one of her majesty's years to ride in such a storm.' She answered in great anger, ' My years ! Maids, to your horses quickly '; and so rode all the way, not vouchsafing any gracious countenance to him for two days. As she passed Kingston, one old man fell on his knees, praying God ' that she might live a hundred years,' which pleased her so, as it might come to pass, which I take to be the cause that some preachers pray she may last as the sun and the moon."

But even the sun and moon must set and when they rise again in similar glory mayhap there is a new goddess in the sun, a new man in the moon over Hampton Court, for Elizabeth died in terrible terror at Richmond Palace on March 24th, 1603, in the seventieth year of her age.

Chapter VII
KING JAMES THE FIRST

UNDER Elizabeth, Hampton Court was like a setting for the *Fairie Queen* where knights gathered in worship of Gloriana and were tamed to loving by her skill at the virginal or in the dance. As apotheosied in that archaic poem, there was in those splendid Elizabethan days a blend of medieval worship of womanhood with the release of a sceptical yet soaring spirit, as seen in Marlowe and Shakespeare where God has vanished from the scene and man finds man himself his own enemy or his love. Although Faustus might taunt God, then grovel to Him, Marlowe, the avowed athiest, had, like Faustus himself, a passion for earthly splendours, for dressing gaudily, a peacock to ride in triumph through Persepolis, for it is passing brave to be a king, Techelles, if only in the spirit. And it is noteworthy that Shakespeare, interested, unlike Marlowe, purely in the emotional tangles of mankind, makes but scanty references to God and almost none to Christ. It would seem that, like Ralegh* and others of his school, he was a deist or even perhaps an athiest, for this was the age of England's economic expansion when spirituality went into worship of a woman. That there were often many insulting things said about Elizabeth, and threats of rioting at her meanness, as when she would not pay the starving sailors who had defeated the Armada, she nevertheless remained a living symbol for which men strove to achieve greatness to be made worthy of her. And it is interesting that England's heroic and prosperous eras—those of Elizabeth, Anne, and Victoria—came when a woman sat on the throne. We would do well not to be supercilious about such matters and, like communists obsessed by the hocuspocus of words such as the differential calculus—which have become totems to be worshipped but never argued—to attempt to place all man's endeavours on an economic basis. This economic interpretation of history is as false as any other narrow interpretation, for the achievements of man cannot be reduced to any simple formula

---

* It is strange how Ralegh's name has been persistently misspelt. In his life of that great man, last of the Elizabethans, Stebbing notes: "From June 9, 1584, he used till his death no other signature than Ralegh. It appears in his books when the name is mentioned ... The spelling Raleigh, which posterity has preferred, happens to be the one he is not known to have ever employed."

such as greed for money or love of God or woman or even honour. The psycho-analysts, at whom it has become the correct thing to sneer—for the next generation will always raise supercilious eyebrows at the interest of the past generation—are profoundly true in stressing the importance of symbols. There is none of us not controlled by symbols usually driven into us during childhood, like the miser with his symbolic gold; and the Elizabethans had their symbol—and it would be difficult to find a more fascinating one—in a woman, the mother-wife-and-mistress of all men.

With Elizabeth's death, with the fading of this symbol, came a period of confusion, of money grabbing and cruel selfishness, for Englishmen no longer had any ideal for which to fight—we see this plainly in Shakespeare's later despairing plays—and therefore fought wholly for themselves or sought refuge in bitterness or dreams. It is true that the great works we label Elizabethan were mostly written during James I's reign, that Shakespeare, Jonson, Bull, Inigo Jones, were now to reach their flowering, but the fact that we persistently label these men, not Jacobean, but Elizabethan—the period of their youth—proves that we associate them with the queen and not the king. And, in modern idiom, one might say—what a king !

Nature seemed determined to expose kingship for what it was, deliberately smashing Elizabethan idealism, by flinging at Englishmen a diseased and ugly and cowardly monarch and thus through him to explode the myth of Gloriana. James suffered all the physical ailments that are degrading, from hæmorrhoids to catarrh. He was, a contemporary tells us, " of middle stature, more corpulent through his clothes than his body [he wore numerous garments to protect himself from assassination, of which he naturally lived in mouselike terror], yet fat enough; his eyes large, ever rolling after any stranger that came in his presence. . . . His beard very thin, his tongue too large for his mouth, which ever made him speak full in the mouth, and made him drink very uncomely. . . . His skin was as soft as taffeta sarsanet [a fine silk,] which felt so because he never washed his hands, only rubbed his fingers ends slightly with the wet end of a napkin. His legs were very weak . . . that made him ever leaning on other men's shoulders; his walk was ever circular."

Slobbering on his men favourites, it was not unnatural, as Mr. Hugh Ross Williamson in his brilliant biography of the first Duke of Buckingham remarks, that " his new subjects had never taken kindly to the dribbling, bulbous-eyed, bandy-legged king,

Hampton Court from the River—Danckerts

with his passion for young men, jewellery, and horses. Also they disliked intensely the hordes of his countrymen who had accompanied him from Scotland and on whom he showered money and honours with reckless generosity." This passion for pretty youths might have been harmless enough had not James, in his maudlin worship, given them such power as he gave to Robert Carr and later to George Villiers who, by his abuse of it, was eventually to destroy James's son, King Charles I. To steal again from Mr. Williamson: " As long as Cecil [Elizabeth's great minister] lived, James's dominance by his favourites had affected policy only indirectly, in the sense that his extravagant gifts to them had complicated his already chaotic finances and increased the tension between him and parliament. But on Cecil's death the management of state affairs passed directly into the hands of the Earl of Somerset, whose influence over the king had increased steadily since the day when, as Robert Carr, an obscure Scottish page with nothing to recommend him but his looks, he had attracted James's attention by falling off his horse in the tilt yard." Canny even in his love affairs, James was always careful to have these young men introduced to him by his wife, Anne, a charming drunken creature. What she thought of the situation may be surmised from her remark to Buckingham: " You do well in lugging the sow's ear and I thank you for it. . . ." while his relations with her can be imagined from his own statement: " I wonder not so much that women paint themselves as that when they are painted, men love them."

His main interests were disputations, hunting—" If God himself came to speak to me, I would not listen," he once said when a foreign envoy would call him from the hunt—and young men whom, Sir John Oglander reports in his *Commonplace Book*, he loved " better than women, loving them beyond the love of men to women. I never yet saw any fond husband make so much or so great dalliance over his beautiful spouse as I have seen King James over his favourites, especially the Duke of Buckingham." Openly to his council James himself confessed, while outlining his policy, that his boys came before England. " I, James," he said humbly, " am neither a god nor an angel, but a man like any other. Therefore I act like a man, and confess to loving those dear to me more than other men. You may be sure that I love the Earl of Buckingham more than anyone else, and more than you who are here assembled. I wish to speak in my own behalf, and not to have it thought to be a defect, for Jesus Christ did the same, and therefore I cannot be blamed. Christ had his John, and I have my George."

After that there is nothing further I can say.

Now this shambling slobbering king lolled with his boys in Elizabeth's chaste Hampton Court which the cardinal had built and where great Henry had plotted and lusted; and as if to degrade all that his predecessors had made noble, he sold knighthoods by the sheath-full, travelling from the manor in July, 1603, to tap the first three hundred on the shoulder with a sword that made him tremble, for he had a horror of cold steel. There is, however, one thing for which we lovers of Hampton Court must thank this wretched king, for parsimonious though he was with candles, he yet loved the mask. Although Whitehall was usually the scene of these performances, Hampton Court was, at least, honoured with the first, if by no means the best, produced in his reign. So fond was James of this miniature play that he squandered money on it to such an extent that each production was estimated to cost about £1,400—as already remarked, it is quite useless trying to translate such sums into present money, not only because money to-day is practically valueless, wealth being only in property and possessions, but because of the extreme difference between essentials like food and drink and extravagances such as jewels and clothes. It was, at any rate, a vast sum he squandered on these exquisite little plays which Jonson was to make magical. But it was money far better spent than on the backside of a Carr or a Villiers.

The mask was a combination of play and ballet, usually topical or allegorical, and later developed with an anti-mask which was often almost a parody of the mask itself and was in time to destroy it as an art-form by turning it into something like a modern pantomime. The popularity of these plays was not because of their poetry—or busybody Inigo Jones, the designer, could never have had great Ben Jonson dismissed over a petty dispute—but because of the fun in dressing-up, ladies and gentlemen taking part, the music, both vocal and instrumental, being given by the court musicians assisted by the quire boys of the Chapel Royal: in the 1606 New Year's gifts we find James giving each of his twenty-six musicians " one payre of perfumed playne gloves." The poetry was considered mainly as a relaxation, a stop-gap, while the dancers rested or changed costumes; and yet how exquisite was much of this poetry any reader of Ben Jonson knows.

By lucky chance the first mask presented at Hampton Court was pirated by one Edward Alde and the infuriated author, Samuel Daniel of the sonnets, published the authentic version with stage directions. Thus we possess not only the poetry but can see how and by whom it was acted, the queen " taking the part of Pallas, in a blue mantle, with a silver embroidery of all weapons and engines of war, with a helmet-dressing on her head, and presents a lance and target." Owing to this fortunate piracy we can examine the mask in detail and that will relieve us of the necessity of examining any of the numerous others, for in form they were all alike, save that, later, the anti-mask—the kind of parody within the mask—began to expand until it transformed the whole almost, occasionally, into slapstick.

For this occasion let us again attempt to return to the past, don ruff and padded breeches, and see Hampton Court as a gentleman of James's period would have seen it.

There was the usual plague in London this Christmas of 1604, and after a dismal progress to show the people what kind of a king they'd got from Scotland, James and Anne of Denmark settled at Hampton Court where, Sir Thomas Edmonds informs us, they "have an humour to have some masks this Christmastime." That charming if insignificant poet, Daniel, had been invited to write the words and, sadly I confess it, they are neither particularly poetical nor interesting. Nevertheless, Daniel became a dear favourite of Queen Anne's who made him a gentleman-in-waiting extraordinary and, later, a groom of her privy chamber, while he was created Master of the Queen's Children of the Revels.

Everybody with the slightest excuse crowded to Hampton Court this year to see what to make of their new majesties—" highness " died towards the end of Henry VIII's reign—and there were furious quarrels about precedence and lodgings, the gathering being so huge that the palace could not roof them all and tents had to be raised in the park. Banquets, masquerades, plays, tennis matches, and even a tournament were arranged to keep the guests from arguments; and with James's abhorrence of violent sports this last must have been a great condescension on his part.

The weather at sight of their majesties matched England's mood, for it was foul and stinking. As Sir Dudley Carleton remarks, he was " welcomed with fogs and mists, which make us march blindfold "; but there were torches and candles enough within the palace to keep the fog at bay while men and women shivered at new arrivals lest they brought plague on their garments, and there was merry-making in the Great Hall.

Now on this night of Sunday, January 8th, let us, as the hands of that astronomical clock of dead Henry's nears ten, stroll from our lodgings—I fear such humble folk as we would be given only a tent in the smoky open—and fumble through the fog towards the Great Hall. We cannot get lost, unless we turn right-about, for there are torches to show the way, crackling through the yellow mists like dissolving jewels of fire in wool, brightening garments with flickering

Doorway in
Great Hall.

colour, furring wide skirts of women and the tight-hosed legs of men, and rippling over bricks as red as Wolsey's hat or Cromwell's blood. We can hear the muffled tap on a drum and the plaintive squeak of a tightened lute-string while we lurch through opaque mists to the hall from which light rolls and tumbles in yellow-white waves into the fog, and the laughing lords and ladies scramble up into it, stumbling on the steps, rising out of dimness into the dazzle.

Seats have been raised high on either side while a mountain conceals the screens: painted to look like vegetation, this mountain swells to near the ceiling's carved and coloured pendants. Opposite us, as we push in through the crowd, stands the Temple of Peace topped with a cupola and having within it an altar tended by a Sibylla, with Somnus's cave wide-open nearby. We edge our way along, stumbling amongst those already seated, to find our seats, and find them just in time . . . for the herald in his gay tabard flings open the door beside the halpace, shouting, " The King ! " while trumpets blare as if the trumpeters would blow their brazen souls through the shining mouths as the king stumbles out with Prince Henry and the great men of the realm about him. He slouches in his ermined robes; his doublet quilted to be stiletto-proof, he clings to a man's arm because his weak legs slide under him, his eyes are roving roundly and his slack lips dribble into the thin brown beard, while he chatters— he is sure to be chattering with his over-large tongue, so vain is he of his learning. His handsome son, Prince Henry, friend of Ralegh, strides upright beside him; and we like this son far more than we like his dad: he looks a man.

Now is his royal majesty seated under the canopy of state in front of the lovely south oriel window with its painted glass of many colours. He is seated; so we, too, can sit, rustling and shuffling back, squeezing our rumps against other rumps that would usurp our place, while we watch the company. All are worth watching this night; we will not sound their names, their titles in clipped consonants and sighing vowels; we will but gaze on them, for they are brighter than the tapestries in front of which they sit, glimmering and glittering with many-coloured jewels, as if splashed in spangles, the women's great skirts folding into sensuous shadows and their painted flesh seeming ripe and edible, luscious as fruit, their eyes all black in candlelight, cats' eyes, velvet eyes, moving in lashed slots under painted lids; mouths, too, are painted, and all flesh is perfumed. The Hall seems indeed a spicery of commingling many-flavoured perfumes, as if we had been rolling in an East of musk. Great frills of lace upstand behind women's heads, as though their necks were broken and they must have support; frills are about the men's necks, too, as though they were decapitated and nodded their heads on salvers. Lace, lace, lace . . . lace clean and rustling, but rarely very stiff, for Anne Turner is only beginning her investigations into yellow starch nor knows that she'll get herself hanged in time.* Lace and jewels and silks and velvets: all along the galleries there is a rippling wave of jewels and of cloths foaming with this lace, cloths of all textures, all colours, rustling and moving as men and women whisper and titter together and strive to appear unexcited, as though every night they watched a mask with royalty.

Hush . . . there is a hole in the floor: look ! . . . there are cellars below and up from these cellars rises a lady in black. She is a-glitter with stars: therefore she must represent Night. Out of the trap she rises in the middle of the floor, then marches to the music to the cave where Sleep apparently lies sleeping. She stands above him and speaks; she says:

> *Awake dark* Sleep, *rouse thee from out this cave:*
> *Thy mother* Night *that bred thee in her womb*
> *And fed thee first with silence.* . . .

But we no longer listen, for Sleep is stirring, yawning, groaning in his grotto. He is dressed in a transparent shift over black clothes, cunningly suggesting day and night, and he has red poppies about his head, for poppies, too, mean sleep. In his right-hand is a white wand and in his left a black one, and the white is that with which he can weave you dreams to your wishing. How that woman does prate, that Night ! She gives poor Sleep no opportunity to wake, and he keeps on rolling and yawning, impatiently waiting for her to stop that he might say his lines. At last she babbles to silence and Sleep can slouch up slowly, still yawning and stretching himself while he

---

* According to Stow's *Annales* starch was introduced into England by a Dutchwoman in 1564 and she charged £4 to £5 to teach her craft. Stubbes, in his *Anatomy of Abuses*, called it " a certaine kind of liquide matter which they call Starch " made " of all colours and hewes, as White, Redde, Blewe, Purple, and the like." Yellow was the popular colour until Mrs. Turner's execution for conspiracy in the murder of Overbury when the hangman wore band and cuffs of that hue. Barnaby Rich, writing in 1622, says that before she was killed Mrs. Turner " bitterly protested against the vanity of these yellow starcht bands " and her outcry made the onlookers so ashamed that never again would they wear them.

in his turn talks Mr. Daniel's dull poetry and promises to interpret the dreams we are about to see, for he says:

> *And this white horny wand shall work the deed,*
>> *Whose powers doth figures of the light present:*
> *When from this sable* radius *doth proceed*
>> *Nought but confused shows, to no intent.*
>>> *Be this a temple; there* Sibylla *stand,*
>>> *Preparing reverent rites with holy hand.*
>>> *And so, bright visions, go, and entertain*
>>> *All round about, whilst I'll to sleep again.*

And the ill-mannered knave rolls himself up again in his cave; but look! over the screens—pray forgive me, the mountain—a wench runs down in a garment like a rainbow, as if she were on fire within a prism. She is Iris, messenger of the gods; and a dull messenger she proves herself for she declaims in prose. She is, she tells us, the daughter of Wonder, now made the messenger of Power, and she has descended to signify the coming of the goddesses. On she pipes, whirling her multi-coloured skirt, that seemingly liquid rainbow, around her shapely legs and the swell of her rump, while on and on she babbles . . . but with such a wench our eyes are preferable to our ears as she spouts tediously Mr. Daniel's prose while we watch and, fidgeting, wait for the goddesses to arrive. But instead of goddesses next comes Sibylla, a plain woman garbed in black and white, like a nun; we want no nuns at our protestant court. Now Iris has given her a perspective glass which she pushes into one eye, shutting the other, and smirkingly quizzes us with impertinent smiling.

Then she's off, too, and in prose, the devil take her. " What have I seen ? " she cries, staggering as she smites her chest, " where am I ? or do I see all ? Was this Iris (the messenger of Juno) or else but a phantasm of imagination ? Will the divine Goddesses vouchsafe to visit this poor temple ? Shall I be blest to entertain so great powers ? It can be but a dream; yet so great powers have blest as humble roofs, and use, out of no other respect than their own graciousness, to shine where they will. But what prospective is this ? Or what shall I herein see ? Oh, admirable powers ! What sights are these ? "

These be the goddesses for whom we have waited; and as Sibylla in her rainbow gown leans to show us the breadth of her beam and the arch of her bosom when the bodice falls, peering through the spyglass, the masked goddesses rise to group themselves atop of the mountain —that is to say, in the musicians' gallery. But alas, no goddesses are these, they are only the queen and her ladies. And as each of them rises into the torchlight, Sibylla, squinting through her glass, tells us which she be in rime.

First, of course, Juno—who is in truth the Lady Suffolk, that fat fireship, tangled in a sky-blue mantle embroidered with gold and figured with peacock feathers, with a golden crown on her head and a sceptre in her hand. Declaims Sibylla:

> *First here imperial* Juno *in her chair,*
> *With sceptre of command for kingdoms large,*
> *Descends all clad in colours of the air,*
> *Crown'd with bright stars, to signify her charge.*

And Lady Suffolk—'tis she, for sure—nods to our applause. While she seats herself, up strides another lady . . . the queen herself! How different from our late dear queen! She flops her flesh in a blue mantle embroidered with silver weapons of war—arrows, bows, guns, slings, and other murderous instruments—wearing a helmet crowded with jewels too big for her head and with a lance in one hand, and—O, ghost of virgin Elizabeth!—her jewelled kirtle reveals her legs in jewelled buskins to above the knees. Sibylla pipes:

> *Next war-like* Pallas *in her helmet drest,*
> *With lance of winning, target of defence,*
> *In whom both wit and courage are expressed,*
> *To get with glory, hold with providence.*

Now they all appear, each in their turn, while Sibylla declaims four lines of introduction. First, Venus—'tis my Lady Rich, and she's venerian enough for Venus—clad in a silver and grey mantle embroidered with doves which seems to fly about her at every move she makes, and with a scarf of divers colours—for some strange reason representing amity—about her waist. Next, Vesta, a virgin—and God forgive us! 'tis Lady Bedford!—wearing a white mantle with golden flames, while in one hand she holds a lighted lamp and in the other a book. Now up trips Diana, who is, indeed, my Lady Hertford in a green mantle embroidered with silver crescents and with a pearly crescent stuck on her head like horns—but more likely it is my Lord Hertford who is horned—and carrying a bow and quiver. Next Lady Derby as Prosperine, in a black mantle having gold flames for hell and wearing a crown of gold to show there is gold under the earth, if you know where to dig for it. Next Macaria, Concordia, and Astrea, goddesses of felicity, concord, and justice, who are, we knew too well, merely the Ladies Hatton, Nottingham, and Walsingham; and the Lady Hatton as Felicity has a purple and silver mantle embroidered with figures of Plenty and Wisdom and she holds a herald's staff, while Concordia wears a parti-coloured mantle of crimson and white to symbolise the union of England and Scotland—crimson for England's leopard and white for Scotland's unicorn—and it is embroidered—pretty thought—with silver hands clasping silver hands amongst parti-coloured roses, red and white, and she holds a branch of these same red and white roses in her hand. Lady Walsingham as Astrea wears a crimson mantle embroidered with silver swords and balances. Now appear three more ladies: Susan Vere, Dorothy Hastings, and Elizabeth Howard as, respectively, Flora, Ceres, and Tethys. Flora in a mantle of divers colours embroidered with flowers, holds a flowerpot in her hands; Ceres in straw colour with silver embroidery, grips a sickle; and Tethys in a sea-green mantle embroidered with silver waves and a dressing of reeds, upholds a trident.

And for the last time, Sibylla declaims:

> *Lastly comes* Tethys, Albion's *fairest love,*
> *Whom she in faithful arms doth deign t'embrace*
> *And brings the trident of her power, t'approve*
> *The kind respect she hath to do him grace.*

Then swinging towards the king, her prismatic gown swirling fierily with her and curling around her plump legs, she cries:

> *Thus have I read their shadow, but behold !*
> *In glory when they come as* Iris *told.*

While her voice lisps to silence and she stands stock-still, arm upraised, to low music in silver robes the three graces, holding white torches, stand on the mountain in front of the goddesses; then hand in hand, delicately, they step down a winding stairway to the hall, their ruffling garments pressed upwards by the knees as the dangerous descent is made. Between each rank of goddesses march three torch-bearers, pages in loose white satin gowns, their heads and garments a-glitter with stars, all walking in quick time to music from satyrs whom we see, nude to the waist, goat-bearded and horned. seated in cavities in the painted rock. Louder skirls the music.

triumphant, blood-trembling, as the stately march continues, goddesses, torch-bearers, and the graces marching—with never a blush amongst them—to the dais. Then as the goddesses walk to lay their gifts within the temple, the graces sing:

> *Dessert, Reward, and Gratitude,*
> *The* Graces *of Society,*
> *Do here with hand in hand conclude*
> *The blessed chain of amity.*
> *For we deserve, we give, we thank:*
> *Thanks, Gifts, Desserts, thus join in rank.*
> *We yield the splendant rays of light*
> *Unto these blessings that descend:*
> *The grace whereof with more delight*
> *The well disposing doth commend;*
> *Whilst Gratitude, Reward, Desserts,*
> *Please, win, draw on, and couple hearts.*
> *For worth and power and due respect,*
> *Deserves, bestows, returns with grace,*
> *The meed, reward, the kind effect,*
> *That give the world a cheerful face,*
> *And turning in this course of right,*
> *Make virtue move with true delight.*

While thus the graces sing, the goddesses, one by one, are placing their gifts within the temple; then the graces stand aside while the goddesses pull up the hems of their skirts and merrily dance to the sounds of lutes and violas.

It is a circular dance they dance until suddenly its tune shuttles them into squares, then into triangles, then again into circles in shuddering tiptoe movements to the viola's and lute's soft stringing. The goddesses pause, trembling while the music flutters their limbs, then they weave into a circle as the graces sing.

Now gentlemen dance with them. We see Pembroke, Howard, Southampton, Devonshire, Sidney, Nottingham, Monteagle, Northumberland, Knollys, Worcester, and others. Gentleman and goddesses trip it in stately measure, hands on hips, then finger-tips on finger-tips. Then they spring to a galliard as the satyrs call the tune, hopping and leaping right merrily, until suddenly, at the music's command, they move into graceful gliding coranto. Little Prince Charles, despite his weak limbs, is dancing with them and they catch him and toss him like a tennis ball from hand to hand, from crooked arm to arm, the little prince, laughing and gurgling, is tossed and caught in men's strong arms, crushed to ladies' breasts, then is tossed up again, is caught again, while all laugh and the king, laughing, dribbles in his beard.

For all his dignity, the Spanish ambassador must join the dancing, to leap and hop and spring. He is a lusty old reveller, the Spanish dog! I swear he leaped six feet that time; as if roasting on his own Armada, he felt the deck too hot for his toes, up he springs. He has a lady's little finger in his little finger, yet he prances and bounces while the English, jealous of his lusty springing, spring too. All are springing, leaping, but none leap as high as the Spanish dog. Save perhaps Pallas, the queen: she makes a nimble partner for the Spaniard while all are hopping, skirts are tossing, feet tap-tapping, so that we can scarcely hear Iris shouting her lines:

" As I was the joyful messenger . . . now the same of the departure of these divine . . . now return back again to the spheres of their own being . . . myself this much I reveal . . . these deities by the motion of the all-directing *Pallas*, the glorious patroness of this mighty monarch . . . found there the best, (and most worthily the best) of LADIES disporting . . . delighting to be the best-built temples of honour and beauty . . . no objects for mortal eyes . . . under whose beautiful coverings they have thus . . . will be pleased, the rather at their invocation . . . to grace this glorious monarchy . . . these blessings represented. . . ."

The dance is finished, back to the mountain-top trip goddesses and graces . . . and we hustle, pushing, kicking, to the banquet in the presence chamber.

Thus went this royal mask at Hampton Court and great was the stir it made. Otherwise we would not possess these details with which to reconstruct the scene. But what are black words to conjure those bright eyes and heaving breasts, the brilliant colours of the garments, the hissing, rustling of torches, or to bring back the soft music of viola and lute? And it is a pity that this mask should be by " well-languaged Daniel " and not by Jonson, for although the mask may seem to our corroded appetites a stupid play of attitudes, these lords and ladies had never seen the Sardanapalus banquets given by Hollywood and therefore they were fortunate, for we have lost the ability to be satisfied, like children, with a Christmas tree and trinkets. Nor must you despise this form because of what has been quoted here; you have only to read Ben Jonson to see how even so stilted a medium as this can become magic in a genius' hands.

But we must squander no more space on this argument. It is time we watched James in another, a scholarly role; and it is at such moments, despite his piddling passion for the letter rather than the spirit of words, that we can most admire him.

This was the great conference between anglicans and puritans in Hampton Court during January, 1604. It would be tedious here to disturb the dust of those old arguments, momentous though they were at the time, but we must remark James's surprising tolerance, his dislike of executions for religious reasons, while he attempted to reconcile the irreconcilable, the puritan creed with Roman catholicism. His wife was converted to Rome and he allowed priests to enter the country undisturbed and only when their own behaviour forced his hand did he forbid their coming. Indeed, his tolerance was such that they believed that they could convert him, an illusion which outraged James when he heard it, for his pet and preposterous idea was to make himself a kind of protestant pope, winning the warring sects to peace under his rule and thus amicably dividing the spiritual world between himself and Rome. That the idea was laughable does not detract from the nobility of the king's intentions, while from this Hampton Court conference was born a masterpiece for which all English-speaking peoples must be grateful—the authorised version of the Bible.

Of the conference itself, important though it be in history, I feel it would be wearisome to recount the arguments, quarrels, discussions on theological points of small interest to-day. James, of course, being a pedant, thoroughly enjoyed it. As he wrote to a friend in Scotland: " I have peppered thaime as soundlie as yee have done the Papists "; but we will sum up with the comments of wise Sir John Harington: " The King talked much Latin, and disputed with Dr. Reynolds [a puritan]; but he rather used upbraid-ings than arguments; and told them they wanted to strip Christ again, and bid them *away with their snivelling*. Moreover he wished those who would take away the surplice *might want linen for their own breech!* The bishops seemed much pleased and said his Majesty spoke by the power of inspiration. I wist not what they mean; but the spirit was rather foul-mouthed."

Probably, and perhaps rightly, I shall be sternly rebuked for thus dismissing this most important conference while devoting so many pages to such a carnal affair as a mask, but I confess indifference towards those theological disputations that meant so much to men of the period. Between puritan and churchman it was vastly exciting to argue the exact meaning of *Ecclesiasticus* xlviii. 10, and it gave the king rollicking joy to be able to expound it for hours and hours; but to me it is dreary stuff. Let this congress take its rightful sprawling space in church history-books and, save that it was at Hampton Court that that miracle, the revised version of the Bible, was plotted, I pass unheeding to what are, to me, more interesting matters.

The royal parties were riotous affairs, drunken, dirty, indecent debauches, of which Sir John Harington gives us a delightfully detailed description which, with reluctance, I pass over as it was enacted at Theobalds, at Cheshunt.

We pass to Prince Henry who takes far larger space than his father in the chronicles of Hampton Court, as he lived here with his household for many months, enjoying the numerous opportunities for sport in the grounds and park. To read the list of his household one realises how hemmed in was a prince, attended like a king with chamberlain, secretary, cupbearers, carvers, sewers, and such; and there is one curious rule in his ordinances commanding that " noe childe, page, scowrer, or turnebroach [turnspit], to marry." With gentlemen-ushers and waiters in his presence chamber, with pages sleeping therein at night, the lad was carefully watched, while two yeomen of the guard, with halberds, kept the gate to assist the porters in case of trouble.

But to an athletic youth like Henry this continual guard would have been little trouble and, had he wished, he could easily have eluded it. He died too young—at nineteen—for us to hazard a safe estimate of his possibilities, but I don't doubt had he ruled—instead of poor Charles with his weak legs and his stutter—there would have been no Great Rebellion, for he showed remarkable tolerance and intelligence for his age. A strong protestant, a lover of learning and the arts and, above all, of arms and horses, he should have proved a great king. He worshipped Ralegh and when James locked that great man into the Tower, he said openly that none but his father would have kept such a bird in a cage. Although his quarrel with his father was no violent one, he was contemptuous of James's catamites, and England watched him with hope that turned to such despair at his death that it was even believed that the king had poisoned him.

But Henry is now only a boy of eleven at Hampton Court and in the palace there still hangs a portrait of him that must have been painted at about this date. It shows him, appropriately enough, at the hunt. At his feet a stag lies dead while Robert Deveraux, Earl of Essex, kneels on one knee before him and grips the beast by one antler, probably to draw back the head so that the blood should flow easily, for Henry has just cut its throat and is sliding his sword back into its sheath. A greyhound and a horse are behind him, with a groom holding the horse, and his royal arms hang on the thin branch of a distant tree. Both lads wear green hunting-dress, with those ugly breeches of the period dangling loose over the knees, while on Henry's head perches a feathered hat, and Robert's hat is lying beside his knee. Henry was expert at all sports and there are prints showing him displaying his skill with pike and lance; he was also clever with the bow and was famed for his tennis; and probably it was of Hampton Court that the anecdote treats when Essex wanted to hit him with his tennis-racket, prince or no prince, for calling him the son of a traitor.

Our palace was the perfect home for such a lad, with its tilting ground, its tennis courts, its bowling alley, its river for fishing, and those broad parks for hunting; and very happy must have been those months for Henry before his fussing shambling dad returned in the autumn.

Locked into the Tower of London was Sir Walter Ralegh. With his heroic dreams, his scientific speculations, his mastery of English, his courage in action, Ralegh symbolises perfectly the age that was done, and, as though he would destroy all the greatness of Elizabeth's reign, James detested him, persecuted him, drove him to his death. Now came his opportunity of tormenting the great man further. In 1604, Cecil had promised Sherbourne Castle to Ralegh, the estate having been given to Ralegh by Elizabeth in 1592, but certain words had been carelessly omitted by the clerk who had drawn up the lease. Therefore he pleaded with Cecil to have a proper grant made out. It was not the moment to ask Cecil anything for that great statesman was almost demented by the demands of James's minions bleeding dry the exchequer, so Lady Ralegh herself appealed to the king. The king, of course, agreed to see the trouble righted but, instead, at Cecil's suggestion, gave Sherbourne to his darling Carr. But even he had to make some pretence of legality in such a theft; therefore late in 1607 the crown began proceedings to establish its claim on the estate.

Lady Ralegh was a brave woman and not one easily to be thrust aside. She went to Hampton Court and James walked past her without a word. She did not stir, she waited, and when James returned she stood before him, and he muttered that " he mun have the land, he mun have it for Carr." But " she, being a woman of a very high spirit and noble birth and breeding, fell down upon her knees, with her hands heaved up to Heaven, and in the bitterness of her spirit beseeched God Almighty to look upon the justness of her cause, and punish those who had so wrongfully exposed her and her poor children to ruin and beggary."

It seems fitting that this Elizabethan genius should be jailed for no cause by one who hated the " sight of a soldier or any valiant man," and it is also fitting that in the palace beloved of the great queen, Lady Ralegh's petition should be spurned that the catamite Carr should be enriched. The waddling king, unable to walk straight but going circular-wise while he dribbled into his beard, this man who would not change his clothes but wore them until they became rags, who never washed himself, who mouthed of God yet swore so outrageously that his blasphemies often frightened himself, this fattish drooling coward rolling his eyes at men until they blushed like girls with shame, this " modern Solomon " who robbed his subjects with a jest, telling his Scottish comrades to content themselves for " I will shortly make the English as beggarly as you," this fellow in our palace turned his padded back on Lady Ralegh. There is no need to seek reasons for his hatred of her husband. It is plain enough. Aubrey wrote it in an unfinished sentence: " Sir Walter Ralegh had that awfulness and ascendancy over other mortals that the K——.
. . ." The pen, when it stopped, had written sufficient and we can add the words ourselves.

That is a dark hour in Hampton Court but a fitting scene to make plain the new and miserly reign that set the sun of Elizabeth.

The notorious Gunpowder Plot has naught to do with Hampton Court and brave Guy Fawkes cannot enter our gallery, so while the years pass we will watch the king and prince out hunting. As already remarked, James once swore that if God himself were to call, He'd not take him from a hunt; it was therefore natural that the clamour of his people could not stay him when he had these woods of Hampton Court and Bushey Park for sport. So fierce was this passion—strange in a king with a pathological horror of steel—that an anonymous letter was once sent him, threatening to poison his hounds unless he gave more time to government and less to the sport. The threat merely spurred him to greater exertion in the field and, at home, to the writing of a " proclamation against hunters, stealers, and killers of deare, within any of the king's majesties forests, chases, or parks," which was issued from the palace on September 9th, 1609. Later came a second proclamation, in fury, because James was stared at while hunting—" bold and barbarous insolency of multitudes of vulgar people who, pressing upon us in our sports as we are hunting, do ride over our dogs, break their backs, spoil our game, run over and destroy the corn, and not without great annoyance and sometimes peril both of our own person and to the dearest son our prince, by their heedless riding and galloping . . . our will and pleasure is" that they be conveyed to the nearest jail.

Ruthless in punishing poachers, he " loved beasts," we are told, " better than men, and took more delight in them, and was more tender over the life of a stag than a man." Dressed in a suit as " green as the grass he trod on, with a feather in his cap, and a horn instead of a sword at his side," his ghost must haunt Bushey more than the palace, hallooing to the death of the animals he loved under the chestnut trees.

A visitor to England in 1613, the Duke of Saxe-Wiemar describes one of these hunts. " The huntsmen remain on the spot where the game is to be found," he writes, " with twenty or thirty hounds; if the king fancies any in particular among the herd, he causes his pleasure to be signified to the huntsmen, who forthwith proceed to mark the place where the animal stood; they then lead the hounds thither, which are taught to follow this one animal only, and accordingly away they run straight upon his track; and even should there be forty or fifty deer together, they do nothing to them, but chase only the one, and never give up till they have overtaken and brought it down. Meanwhile the king hurries incessantly after the hounds until they have caught the game. There is therefore no particular enjoyment in this sport. Two animals only were caught on this occasion. . . . His majesty now and then uses longbows and arrows; and when he is disposed he shoots the deer."

Since this observant foreigner has shown us the king at a hunt, it would be as well to follow him inside the palace, for he is a most valuable informant and tells us of the royal throne with a canopy above and the royal beds nine feet long and as many feet wide; but what interests me in his diary is his mention of that curious paradise room in the park, for in it he saw golden tapestries and royal robes and a large unicorn's horn. The unicorn's horn was a famed specific against almost any illness, particularly against poisons. Dip it in your glass, you were told, and poison was immediately neutralised. It was extraordinary the faith that was given these curling horns, parings from them—as valuable as gold—being prescribed for various ills, and men paid huge sums for one. Yet they were only the horns of the narwhal sold by rascally Scandinavian seamen, although I don't doubt they did as much good as some of our own specifics which lie, and literally lie, in ranks on many a chemist's shelf.

But we must leave our unicorn's horn, dipped most likely often into craven James's food and drink, to watch poor Frances, the daughter of Lord Chief Justice Coke, shiver before Buckingham's lunatic brother. For Buckingham—I use the title for convenience sake: he received it later—now is king of the king. This handsome rascal had usurped Carr's place in James's love and was carefully bringing his relations into positions of power and money. You can see him and his family, including the lunatic brother, in the painting of the Villiers family hanging in Hampton Court. The mad brother stands languidly behind the nurse who is seated with baby George, and his right arm hangs negligently on the back of his notorious brother's chair.

Sir John fell passionately in love with one of the beauties of the day, Frances Coke, who was then fifteen and was enamoured of—she said she was betrothed to—Henry de Vere, Earl of Oxford, then unfortunately abroad. But all her clamour about her betrothal, including a letter from de Vere which she had forged herself, could not hold back the hungry Villiers when they sniffed gold, for Frances's mother, Lady Hatton—she so hated her husband she would not use his name—was extremely wealthy. The father was soon bribed—or rather, he had to pay a bribe, being in disgrace for having protested at Buckingham's attempt to get money from the king's bench enrolment of pleas—and he agreed to help.

But his wife would not surrender, hating equally her husband and all the Villiers, and she hurried Frances to Oatlands, not far from Hampton Court, where the already mentioned letter was forged. Coke thereupon invaded the manor and carried off his daughter whom he delivered to Buckingham's mother, and Lady Hatton in fury obtained a warrant ordering her husband and daughter to appear in the Star Chamber, while Coke retorted with a summons for abduction and forgery. The council, who naturally sided with Lady Hatton, compromised by giving her custody of her daughter while allowing Buckingham's brother, the lover, John, to visit her.

King and favourite were on a progress to Scotland at the time, and on their return Lady Hatton was placed in preventive custody while Frances was given to her father who soon had her consent to the marriage, for he tied her to a bedpost and whipped her until she agreed; after that, having proved his slavish surrender to Buckingham, he was graciously readmitted to the royal council.

On September 29th, 1613, the weeping girl was driven to Hampton Court. Nine long-bodied coaches with huge painted wheels, carrying the Coke family, rattled over the drawbridge to be met by a huge gathering in festive mood. In the chapel, poor Frances stood beside the man she detested while the Bishop of Winchester performed the ceremony, the king giving her away. Afterwards, records one who was present, there was feasting and James "dronke healthe to the Bride, the Bridegroome stood behinde the Bride: the dinner and supper. The Bride and Bridegroome lay next day a bedd till past 12 a clocke, for the Kynge sent worde he wold come to see them, therefore wold they not rise. My Lord Coke looked with a merrie Countenance and sate at the dynner and supper, but my Ladie Hatton was not at the weddinge, but is still at Alderman Bennettes prisonere. The Kynge sent for her to the weddinge, but [she] desired to be excused, sayinge she was sicke."

There was, inevitably, a mask that evening in the Great Hall and more feasting in which King James, again inevitably, became drunk, drinking so often the healths of doting groom and frightened bride. All night he staggered about the palace, playing stupid japes, tying sheets together so that sleepers could not sleep, dragging off Frances's left stocking and tormenting her with bawdy jests, while he sang about the galleries, dressed only in his nightshirt. In the morning, still in his nightshirt, he ran to greet the wedded couple, jumping and rolling on their bed in lewd excitement.

Frances is a sad and pitiful memory in Hampton Court—although I am glad to add that she did eventually marry the man she loved—and if, as some say, we haunt the scenes of our deepest sufferings, her ghost must certainly walk here, sobbing and shuddering from loathed fingers, for she was martyred for the Villiers' ambitions; and even a king in his nightshirt bouncing on her double-bed could scarcely have compensated for the embrace of this creature who was later to be locked up by his own brother for insanity.

We have another melancholy event to record, the death of Queen Anne from a combination of ills including gout, liver trouble, phthisis, and dropsy.

"About twelve o'clock," we are told, " she calls for the wench [Danish Anna] that sat by her, and bids her fill some drink to wash her mouth. She brought her a glass of Rhenish wine that she drank out, and says to the woman, ' Now have I deceived the physicians.' Then she bids the woman sleep by her, and in seeing her sleep, she would sleep. But within a quarter of an hour after she again called to the woman, and bids her bring some water to wash her eyes, and with the water she brought a candle, but she did not see the light, and asked the woman for a light. She answers : ' There is one here, Madame; do you not see it ? ' ' No,' says the Queen. Then the woman called in the physicians, and they gave her a cordial, and sent for the Prince, and for the Lords and Ladies. This was about one o'clock. She laid her hand upon the Prince's head, and gave him her blessing. The Lords presented a paper to her, and she did sign it as she could, but her sight was gone, which was to leave all to the Prince, and withal her servants to be rewarded. Then the Bishop of London made a prayer, and we all sat about her bed and prayed. And when her speech was gone, the Bishop calls to her, ' Madame, make the sign that your Majesty is one with your God, and longs to be with Him.' She held up her hand, and when the one hand failed her, she held up the other, till they both failed. To the sight of all that looked on her, her heart, her eyes, her face, was fixed upon God, and her tongue, while she had breath, expressed so much; and when that failed, her hands. And when all failed, the Bishop made another prayer, and she lay so pleasantly in the bed smiling, as if she had no pain; only in the last, she gave five or six groans, and had the pleasantest going out of this world that ever anybody had; and two days after looked as well as she did at any time this two year."

Immediately began a disgusting scramble for her property, her will being ignored, and out of the booty, the king gave his dear Buckingham handfuls of her jewels with £1,200 in land and the keeping of Somerset House. It took four great carts to carry her personal property to her husband, while her servants were imprisoned on the charge of embezzling some of it; but the charge was never proved, and James, to show how deeply he felt the loss of his queen, was at the races even before she was buried.

For the remainder of his reign, Hampton Court is of small importance, save for the celebrations at the arrival of the Spanish ambassador and the disgrace of a certain Dr. Whiting because of a sermon he dared preach before the king in the chapel. What was his actual offence we do not know, but I doubt if we would be far wrong if we hazarded the guess that he questioned the divine right of kings and made some, not sufficiently flattering comparison between James and the Almighty.

So now, and not reluctantly, I confess, we leave this pedant's reign; but mention must be given of two portraits which hang in the palace, both allegedly by Vansomer. In one, James stands in royal crimson robes, lined with ermine; he is crowned and holds a sceptre in his right hand and has the orb in his left, and he looks indeed slightly awkward, as if he were already a waxwork in Madame Tussaud's immortal gallery. Behind him, through open lattice windows, we see Inigo Jones's Banqueting House, and he must therefore have been painted in his palace of Whitehall. The other portrait shows him in a less doll-like posture, fingering the insignia of an order instead, as was his embarrassing habit, of a portion of the masculine garments that is not usually toyed with in society.

Chapter VIII
CHARLES THE FIRST

THIS is a truly pathetic king who limps after his shambling father, for all those faults of Charles, which were to cost him his throne and, in the end, his life, were faults ingrained in him by an unhappy childhood. Devoid of humour, with the exaggerated dignity of a man whose body ridiculed dignity with its five feet two inches, its red nose and weak legs; with all the obstinacy and lack of imagination of one who had been humiliated by a healthy popular brother—so weak indeed had Charles been as a baby that the great ladies had refused the risk of rearing him—and with a stutter that made him savagely determined to prove his superiority and divine birth even at the cost of his head, he was a most unhappy creature. Those exquisite paintings of Van Dyck's reveal, not Charles, but the god Charles wished to appear; in the charming family group at Windsor Castle we note that the artist has made the little king sit on the edge of his chair and don high heels to give an appearance of height, while his armour in the Tower is a boy's suit; in our own Hampton Court portrait, even Van Dyck's cunning could not conceal the malformed legs as he sits astride a horse. The stammer—when he was a baby, James, with his furious curiosity, had wanted to cut the strings of the tongue, but had been fortunately restrained—was embarrassing, save when he was with friends—it is noteworthy that stammerers do not stammer when alone—and at his first parliament it is almost painful to read his apology: " Now because I am unfit for much speaking, I mean . . . to have my lord speaker speak for me. . . ."

With these handicaps in one who must always seek to over-awe his fellows, it is surprising that Charles's neuroses were not even more crippling than they did become. Particularly when we note his lonely childhood while his elder brother was considered almost a god, active and beautiful and wise, do we feel constrained to sympathise with, and even respect, the wretched king. That he had great courage is undoubted and his strong will is proved by his determination to master his body and to emulate his brother at sport; and certainly he became a magnificent horseman, for on horseback all men are equal. But the weakness that lies under bold shows of arrogance, the terror that seizes one when alone and naked before one's ego, made Charles cling for strength to two people who, being both strong and arrogant, merely dragged him deeper into ruin— Buckingham and Henrietta Maria, his queen.

It was inevitable that these two, favourite and queen, should detest each other, for both were dominant characters, and it is difficult to surmise what would have happened in the struggle between them had not the patriot Felton used his dagger. Most likely, for she had the bedroom for dominance, Charles would have abandoned Buckingham as he later abandoned his good servant, Strafford, to the axe. For in such pathological loves as Charles's for Buckingham, the love of a weak man craving another's strength, the weak man often takes revenge, if only to satisfy the secret shame within him.

There has been much sentiment written about Charles and Henrietta Maria, cartloads of volumes pulpy with tears, but I cannot pity them. Such little tolerance, such little giving was needed for them not to have suffered; but Charles had been reared by that disputatious father to dispute everything except that kingship was divinely bestowed. The teachings of James, the greedy stupidities of Buckingham and Henrietta Maria, all combined for his destruction and, as with most weak characters, it was impossible for him to give back a step once he had decided to stand. Such a man cannot compromise, for he is too conscious of his own weakness to unveil it, even to save his life.

The marriage began as no happy one. Henrietta was a garrulous vain little girl, probably aghast to see her red-nosed husband after contemplating his lovely portrait, and, like Charles, she could not compromise. Their married life was a hell of quarrelling for a time, with Buckingham ever the demon to prod the embers when there was a chance of their cooling. Religious tolerance had been promised her and her troupe, but that did not satisfy Henrietta. She not only refused to have anything to do with a coronation which included a protestant service, she outraged the country by crawling on her knees to Tyburn where Roman catholics had been martyred with, needless to say, many murderers, thieves, and such trash.

She was stupid in the way that Charles was stupid. Both had a preposterous sense of their own dignity only equalled by a scorn for the people of England. Henrietta, of course, won the private battle, for her ego was not crippled by a stutter and weak legs, and she had the good fortune to have her rival murdered before he could do irreparable damage to all chance of married happiness.

Hampton Court did not escape these squabbles.

Madame Saint-George was the principal cause of a bad beginning. She had been Henrietta's governess and guide, and *ma mie*, as Henrietta called her, was as determined as Buckingham in her own way to ruin the marriage. Uproars started when Charles, who naturally detested her, refused to let the woman push into the coach with him and his queen; and his queen was thereupon so offended that the speechless Charles abandoned her to Buckingham, for he was badly handicapped in argument, particularly with a woman who, it seems, never could stop chattering. Of course, Buckingham gleefully made trouble greater and Hampton Court echoed piercingly with a queen in continual hysterics while the tiny king bit his nails in despair, for Charles was strongly attracted by the woman and badly needed the flattery of love. He had had few opportunities for loving, his bashfulness being such that he could barely talk to a woman without blushing. It was natural that he should desire her for, as yet, we hear of no woman in Charles's life: Jane Whorwood was to come later.

This was no happy married couple the palace housed, but it had seen few happy couples since its building. Indeed, a most sardonic palace it must have become after Henry's matrimonial disasters, Mary's false pregnancy, Elizabeth's celibacy, and the homosexual titterings of James, to have now, at last, an apparently normal pair who did nothing but scream at one another, with Buckingham ever fluttering in between, stirring Henrietta to howls of protest by bullying her as though he were her husband, then playing on Charles's feeble masculinity by prompting him to act the man and keep his French bitch in her rightful place—under his foot or in his bed.

But soon they were off to Windsor, the plague sniffing close to Hampton Court, the queen still shrilly voluble, Charles in silent fury, and Buckingham smiling slyly in his beard.

Charles decided that the barrier between him and his wife was these accursed Frenchmen and -women who had followed in her suite, particularly the priests ever stiffening her with reminders that England was a land of heretics and that her husband was doomed to eternities of fire. In this decision, Charles was perfectly right. So long as Henrietta retained her French court with its hatred of England, spurring her to rebellion, he would never master her. Then there was the damned French ambassador who, against all precedent, demanded rooms at Hampton Court, and got them, being given the Water Gallery in which Elizabeth had been imprisoned. And the ambassador, of course, brought his suite with him; and a hungry suite it proved, eating deep into the king's almost empty purse. Indeed, poor Charles had become almost a prisoner in a French colony and he had only Buckingham to whom he could turn for sympathy, and Buckingham's sympathy merely inspired him to further acts of feeble rage that drove him and Henrietta yet further apart. To get rid of her household was the only solution.

In Hampton Court he set his council to draw up rules to govern the queen's new household, but Henrietta refused to sign them. " I hope," she said, " I may be suffered to order my own household." Outraged, Charles considered this an insult to his authority, and the quarrel ended like all their quarrels—in a fury of words from her while he stood, tongue-tied, blushing, defeated, but inwardly murderous. His only revenge was to send Buckingham to her and Buckingham's method of frightening her into submission was simply to remind her with sinister emphasis that " queens of England had been beheaded before now."

France sent a peacemaker, a very wise choice, the Marshal de Bassompierre, whom Henrietta gleefully welcomed, but the marshal was not to be tricked by sentimental appeals or coy arts. His mission opened badly, for on his arrival at Hampton Court on Sunday, October 11th, 1626, he found his dinner so cold that it was uneatable and, of course, Buckingham must interfere. He told the marshal that the king desired him not to discuss any business, to which Bassompierre replied with dignity that ambassadors were not commonly limited in what they had to say, and if such were his instructions, he was fully prepared to go back to France immediately. Buckingham strove to calm his justified choler by explaining that Charles could not help fuming into a passion and that that was not decent in the chair of state in front of the great persons of the realm; besides, the queen would be present and she was so furious at the dismissal of her servants that she might commit any extravagance and would at least weep before the court. Therefore, said Buckingham, the king dared not have a public meeting and would prefer not to have the audience at all than to be humiliated by a scandal, but gladly would he grant one in private.

Bassompierre, who refused to be insulted by not being openly accepted as the representative of France, agreed to compromise. Let Charles receive him in public, he suggested, then interrupt their talk by saying that the matter was too important to be discussed in a brief meeting and would need the leisure of a private audience. On these conditions, he agreed to meet the king, but he would not steal to him in private as though to some conspiracy. Upon which Buckingham embraced him, saying that he had offered his assistance, but now that he realised that the marshal was so skilled a diplomat, he withdrew the offer, for the marshal would need no assistance and could do well without him; and he left him, laughing friendlily.

The meeting, however, came to nothing. Charles, apparently offended by the ambassador's stiff dignity, met him only in public while Bassompierre had later a short interview with the queen, and then drove from the palace where he had been ill-fed and wellnigh insulted. But he was a tolerant fellow and suffered the insults with wisdom's equanimity. As himself said: " I have received condescension from the Spaniards and civility even from the Swiss, but English arrogance I have never overcome." Nevertheless he was back at Hampton Court on October 15th at the appeal of the king, who, poor wretch in the grip of his inferiority, realised too late that royal dignity was of small account compared to friendship with his wife. Bassompierre records that far from being dignified, he was in a chattering rage when they met in one of the galleries, complaining furiously about the intrigues of his wife's French household and of their insolence in setting her against all things English, including the language, which she refused to learn. Charles, indeed, became so passionate that he behaved childishly, demanding from the marshal, as though this private quarrel were an international one, why he did not execute his commission and declare war on England. Coldly, Bassompierre replied that he was not a herald to declare war but merely a soldier of France to fight should it be declared.

" I witnessed there," he wrote, " an instance of great boldness, not to say impudence, of the Duke of Buckingham, which was, that when he saw us the most warmed, he ran up suddenly and threw himself between the king and me, saying, ' I am come to keep the peace between you two.' Upon which I took off my hat, and as long as he stayed with us I would not put it on again, notwithstanding all the entreaties of the king and of himself to do so; but when he went, I put it on without the king desiring me. When I had done that, and the king could speak to me, he asked me why I would not put on my hat while he was by, and that I did so so freely when he was gone. I answered that I had done it to do him honour, because he was not covered, and that I should have been, which I could not suffer: for which he was much pleased with me, and often mentioned it in my praise. But I had also another reason for doing so, which was, that it was no longer an audience but a private conversation, since he had interrupted us, by coming in, as a third, upon us. After my last audience was over, the king brought me through several galleries to the queen's apartments, where he left me, and I her, after a long conversation, and I was brought back to London."

Impossible now to trace this gallery in which the courtly marshal showed how a Frenchman can behave before an English boor: it

Tudor
Chimneys.

has probably gone, like so much of that Stuart palace which was the Tudor palace; gone like the queen's apartments to the east, smashed down by William and Mary in their lust to be modern. How sadly little of that palace is left us now in which the kindly Frenchman tried to bring this foolish couple into each other's arms. . . .

And he succeeded: he laid the first step to the royal double-bed, although himself did not fully realise it, but after his wise counsel a new and smaller French retinue was given Henrietta, for she was to be permitted, Charles agreed, a bishop and ten priests in addition to a confessor, and ten musicians for her chapel, while her household was to consist of two ladies of the bedchamber, two physicians, an apothecary, a surgeon, a grand chamberlain, an esquire, a secretary, and two gentlemen-ushers: all from France.

For many years now, after Buckingham was assassinated and the royal couple reconciled, Hampton Court takes on small importance, for when husband and wife live quietly, happily, there is little to report. We hear only of plays acted in the Great Hall, including *Hamlet*, and of the plague approaching so that those Londoners who had property nearby or any neighbours who visited London, were commanded to remove themselves, while justices went to make certain that their homes were closed. This very silence about Hampton Court shows how contented the king and queen had become now that Buckingham was dead and the masterful Henrietta had the king her slave, for she was one of those gynarchic females prepared to use tongue, tears, or nails or any unscrupulous trick to have her own wilful way. We see this side of her plainly in later life, during her exile in France, when she lied and fought to convert her children to Rome, which, had they given way to her, would have lost them all hope of regaining England. That martyrdom of matriarchal misery was years hence, however, while now she crowed in Hampton Court with a tame king at her heels.

And, like all who loved this palace, Charles began improvements. One of these was an excellent idea, although it aroused natural indignation from those whose property chanced to be in the way, for he had a channel cut from Longford to the manor. It was two feet deep and eleven miles long, and to this day it is known as the King's or Longford River and it still supplies the ponds and ornamental waters. Statues were added to the statues already poised in the gardens and paintings added to those on the walls within; the catalogue he had drawn up lists three to four hundred pictures in his palaces, for, like Buckingham, Charles was a connoisseur, as is proved by his choice of Van Dyck for court-painter. He also attempted to open a park for red and fallow deer as far as Richmond, to the fury of those living in the proposed enclosure. So furious, indeed, were their outcries that he was strongly advised to drop the scheme, but opposition inevitably aroused all Charles's stubborness, for a weak man dare not reveal his weakness. But his ministers and even Archbishop Laud implored him to put aside this disastrous plan when his throne was so insecure, and with great reluctance he at last agreed; but it must have left a hot scar on his vanity, for he was ever intolerant of advice unless it could be twisted to appear as his own idea.

Although the threat of civil war was darkening the future and upstart squires and merchants were talking treason, Charles was in love and men in love can live blind to everything beyond the skirt-hem of the beloved. And because this is the only period of his reign when Charles can be said to have been really happy I feel justified in quoting Sir John Suckling's rimes, that we might be merry a minute or two before swords are drawn and the parliamentarians ride to desecrate our Chapel. This poem has only its title to justify its inclusion in a book such as this; but it is a gay poem and I like it, so here it is, entitled *Upon* My Lady Carlyle's *walking in Hampton Court Garden.* T.C. and J.S. discuss the desirable beauty of this lady as she strolls amongst the flowers, T.C. being Thomas Carew and J.S., of course, the poet.

> Tom. *Didst thou not find the place inspired,*
> *And flowers, as if they had desired*
> *No other sun, start from their beds,*
> *And for a sight steal out their heads ?*
> *Heardst thou not music when she talked ?*
> *And didst not find that as she walked*
> *She threw rare perfumes all about,*
> *Such as bean-blossoms newly out,*
> *Or chaféd spices give ?*
>
> J.S. *I must confess those perfumes, Tom,*
> *I did not smell; nor found that from*
> *Her passing by aught sprang up new;*
> *The flowers had all their birth from you;*
> *For I passed o'er the self-same walk,*
> *And did not find one single stalk*
> *Of anything that was to bring*
> *This unknown after-after-spring.*

Tom. *Dull and insensible, couldst see*
A thing so near a Deity
Move up and down, and feel no change ?

J.S. *None and so great were alike strange,*
I had my thoughts, but not your way;
All are not born, sir, to the bay;
Alas! Tom, I am flesh and blood,
And was consulting how I could
In spite of masks and hoods descry
The parts denied unto the eye;
I was undoing all she wore,
And had she walked but one turn more,
Eve in her first state had not been
More naked, or more plainly seen.

Tom. *'Twas well for thee she left the place,*
There is great danger in that face;
But hadst thou viewed her leg and thigh,
And upon that discovery
Searched after parts that are more dear
(As fancy seldom stops so near),
No time or age had ever seen
So lost a thing as thou hadst been.

While Suckling and Carew with lolling tongues rimed in the wake of Lady Carlyle's skirts, stripping her naked in their dreams' bed, the king in Hampton Court watched with deep content his busy-tongued wife who was now so gentle to him. Happy in his love, content to be mastered, to surrender that weak frightened will into a stronger's keeping, Charles could yet at times berate her, for she irritated him by revealing that she stood on legs. Actually, like any common mortal, this busy queen often walked instead of being carried in a chair or coach. To his kingly horror she would sometimes steal from Hampton Court to roam the town market. That, he rebuked her, was the behaviour of a young girl and not of a queen; while some argued that her using her concealed legs in such plebeian fashion was the cause of the premature birth and death of her baby.

Greater humiliations, however, were in store for him. At Hampton Court on December 1st, 1641, he was presented with the

Grand Remonstrance, the first definite prelude to the civil war, for it recapitulated all the troubles of his reign, together with parliament's good deeds, attacked Charles's councillors and demanded that in future parliament alone should appoint his advisers. Charles tried to temporise, saying that he was aghast at the harshness of the demands but would consider them; parliament, however, knowing his tortuous trickeries, forced his hand by publishing the manifesto. Now men had to take sides, to choose between loyalty to the king or to elected parliament. London, thinking purely of money, sided at first with Charles and sent a deputation to Hampton Court, imploring him to live nearer the city, for a distant court meant loss to trade. Charles knighted the deputation, thinking the empty honour sufficient to bribe them to his side.

Closer came the civil war and none could warn the king. Why did not Archbishop Laud, so proud of his prophetic dreams, dream blood those nights ? Often in his sleep he foretold the doom of others: as when he records in his diary of how " one morning between four and five of the clock, lying at Hampton Court, I dreamed that I was going out in haste and that when I came into my outer chamber there was my servant Wi. Pennell, in the same riding suit which he had on that day sevennight at Hampton Court with me. Methought I wondered to see him, for I left him sick at home, and asked him how he did and what he made there, and that he answered me, he came to receive my blessing; and with that fell on his knees: hereupon I laid my hand on his head and prayed over him, and therewith awaked. When I was up, I told this to them of my chamber and added that I should find Pennell dead or dying. My coach came; and when I came home I found him past sense and giving up the ghost. So my prayers, as they had frequently before, commended him to God." Such dreams did not come now with threats of a block in Whitehall; but neither did they warn him that his own head must fall before very long on Tower Hill.

Nobody seriously warned Charles of the dangers of his obstinacy. Henrietta, indeed, spurred him to his doom. " Go, you coward," she jeered, " and pull me these rogues out by the ears, or never see my face more." So off Charles went to parliament but, indecisive as usual he dawdled on the way, while the queen, boasting of his intentions, gave the opportunity for spies at court to send warning so that the defiant members could be smuggled out. Charles dared not pursue them, the city was rising against him in the streets, men were armed to protect their parliament's liberties and, like Louis's famous flight to Versailles, Charles fled with his family to Hampton Court, attended by Lord Digby and a guard.

They were not expected. The palace was closed and the unhappy king, with his queen and their three eldest children, had to huddle together in one room in the vast echoing manor. Tears have been distilled to ink about Charles's plight, for royalty will always find its maudlin sympathisers, and one cannot help but pity now this wretched man who merely inherited the mine laid by his father and who, because of his princely education and physical disabilities, was unable to appreciate the feelings of the people. Such characters rarely know remorse; nailed to their shrinking egos they dare not admit the possibility of themselves ever being in error; and even during this brief exile in Hampton Court, surrounded by his attendants and with a guard of some thirty or forty cavaliers, Charles would scarcely have wasted thought on rectifying his blunders; more likely he would have cursed the commons who had dared defy their king. One can see hysterical Henrietta nagging, accusing him of having brought down the disaster by his pusillanimity, while he resentfully brooded on revenge. He had abandoned the city, surrendering to his foes the armaments in the Tower, and left himself open to capture.

After a few mournful days he left with his family and attendants for the greater security of Windsor.

Next we find the parliamentarians stabled at Hampton Court after the battle of Naseby, sealing the doors of the state apartments. It is painful to write of the devastation which followed when these iron men of God strode through the palace, missionaries of their own righteousness. Much as one may sympathise with the parliamentary cause, one can feel little but helpless anger at this zealous destruction, this massacre of loveliness, for in their detestation of popery, the puritans assaulted any statue or painting which to their dark minds appeared idolatrous. With the ecstasy of a Savonarola at the Burning of the Vanities, they hacked at Hampton Court, and that is why the chapel is now no more, save for the fan-vaulted ceiling. They dragged down the altar, they pulled down the railings and levelled the steps while shivering to coloured splinters the gay glass in the windows. Images and pictures were inevitably assailed, for they were considered, not as art, but as symbols of superstition. Above the altar had hung a painting of the crucifixion: that was destroyed. Another painting of Mary Magdalene was ripped to rags, like many others. The chapel was left in ruins from which it has never recovered, and even Grinling Gibbons' delicately carved oak reredos far from compensates for that terrible loss. When we visit that chapel to-day we see it not merely denuded but, in places, degraded by ruthless restoration. Stripped naked of beauty, it was very bare under the commonwealth, as the inventory of Cromwell's goods reveals. "In the Chappell," we learn, was merely, a "pulpitt standing on a table of Deal" with "Twelve long formes," while in "the Anti-Chappell" was "A cedar plank eighte foote square lying on two formes." Nothing there now to distract the carnal eye, no paintings, no images; nothing of luxury to let the body relax, only hard forms and a cedar plank to remind the flesh that it was too too human.

It is difficult for us with our tolerance for religion to understand the prejudices of these men, but religion was then a living political question. These slashed paintings and smashed images were to these puritans not pigment on canvas or inanimate stone but satanic symbols. One can understand their intolerance while not sympathising with it. I have only to look down on the chapel to feel rage burn inside my throat to think of what it once contained. The ceiling is proof of its lost perfection, with its blue vault powdered with stars and the joyously carved and gilded pendants.

But let us shut the doors on this degraded chapel, on these men of God busy with their devil's work, for the king has been captured —or rather, has been sold by the Scots to whom he had delivered himself—and is now the prisoner of parliament. And a very awkward prisoner he proved, for parliament found itself in a position similar to the French revolutionaries when they captured their king: so long as he lived he must become the pivot of plots. Yet there can be no doubt that parliament wished to treat him with all deference, hoping only to make him realise that the days were past when the people could be used as royal personal property.

On August 24th, 1647, Cromwell escorted him to Hampton Court, as Colonel Hutchinson tells us, "rather as a guarded and attended prince than as a conquered and purchased captive." Henrietta was not with him: she was busy in France, trying to raise men or money for his rescue, but even without her railing to bolster his ego, Charles proved himself as stupidly stubborn as ever, unable to move beyond the circle of his vanity, distrusting everyone.

The Chapel from Pyne's *History of the Royal Residences*
Courtesy of the British Museum

He dined again in public in the Presence Chamber and was given every outward aspect of royalty, being permitted, on his parole, to hunt in the parks while he was allowed to receive visitors. To him returned old courtiers, and cavaliers and roundheads jostled in the Presence Chamber, smiling uneasily at one another. Evelyn was one of those who hurried to pay his respects as he recorded in his diary: "I came to Hampton Court, where I had the honour to kiss his majesty's hand, he being in the power of those execrable villains, who not long after murdered him." So leniently was he treated that those of his partisans who had been voted delinquents, and who had fled overseas, were permitted to return that they might wait on him. His children lodged nearby at Sion House and he was allowed to visit them and to have them visit him. Sir Thomas Herbert, who was present at the first meeting of Charles and his little Duke of Gloucester and Princess Elizabeth, wrote that " so soon as they saw their royal father, upon their knees they begged his blessing, who heartily gave it, and was overjoyed to see them so well in health, and so honourably regarded."

The same Sir Thomas bears witness to the king's noble treatment in our palace, writing: "Hampton Court was then made ready for the Court, and by Mr. Kinersly, Yeoman of the Wardrobe and others, prepared with what was needful for the Court. And a Court it now appeared to be, for there was a revival of that lustre it had formerly, his Majesty then having the Nobility about him, his chaplains to perform their duty, the house amply furnished, and his services in the accustomed form and state; every one of his servants permitted to attend in their respective places; nothing then appeared of discrimination; intercourse was free between King and Parliament, and the army seemed to endeavour a right understanding amongst different parties, which gave hopes of an accommodation. The Commissioners also continued their attendance upon the King, and those gentlemen that waited at Holmby, were, by his Majesty's appointment, kept in their offices and places; the General likewise and other military commanders were much at Court, and had frequent conference with the King in the Park, and others were attending him; no offence at any time passed amongst the soldiers of either party; there was an amnesty by consent, pleasing, as was thought, to all parties."

As an example of loyalty to an idea, even though it be personified by a man whom one had every reason to hate, it is interesting to note that one of Charles's attendants now was Carew Ralegh, son of the Sir Walter whom Charles's father had murdered for the sake of a promised dowry from Spain. Carew could have felt no love for the Stuarts. Not only had they robbed and killed his father, but Charles had stolen from him much of his own inheritance, being bribed with £10,000 to let a usurper keep his estate; only on Carew's promise not to sue for his own did he erase the stigma of treason from his name. James had hated the lad, groaning that he was like the ghost of his father, and Charles, according to his treatment of him, shared that dislike. Yet when rebellion came, with the idealism of his great parent, Carew sided with his oppressor—as also did his cousin, the Rev. Walter, who suffered persecution for his loyalty—and it is humbling to recall his ghost now in Hampton Court, waiting upon a master who had persecuted him, because kingship was an ideal that must, to such as him, have appeared semi-divine; and it should be recalled that, in all his terrible martyrdom, despite the prompting of spies, Sir Walter, in or out of the Tower, never spoke treason against his royal enemy.

Cromwell often came to visit the king during what Sir Thomas calls these " halcyon days," but it was noted that he would not kiss the royal hand, although otherwise he behaved with perfect respect. We do not know what took place during the many discussions between the two and it has been suggested that Cromwell intended to betray parliament, to put Charles in power while himself ruled under him, but Cromwell was largely guided by Ireton, his son-in-law—we find that he somehow lost purpose after Ireton's death—and Ireton was an exceptionally intelligent man. His object unquestionably was to restore the clipped king under a powerful parliament. One of our great difficulties in judging this period is that we think too far ahead and not sufficiently back, that we forget how close we are to the Elizabethans, and that kings' names and history-book dates do not cut a period into sections for, in many ways, Cromwell, as G. M. Young points out in his *Charles I and Cromwell*, was of " the late-Elizabethan vintage—an instinct of reverence for Parliament, very like the Royalist's sentiment for the Crown, or the Anglican's for the Church. He had known it in its great days, in '28 and '41 when it had not yet degenerated into the leaderless, cantankerous assembly which continued to sit in St. Stephen's with no visible intention of ever doing anything but sit there and distribute jobs among its friends. But still it was Parliament: even in its decay, it stood for the Cause, for order and liberty . . . for justice?—hardly; for peace?—perhaps."

Peace was certainly everyone's desire and, with a little compromise, it could easily have been sealed: but compromise was the one thing that Charles could never do. It is a pity we have no report of the conversations between him and Cromwell for, indeed, Hampton Court could never before or since have seen so ill-assorted a couple. Slovenly Cromwell, with his great laughter and God-flowering speech, striding beside the neatly garbed bandy-legged stuttering king who must have shuddered from his touch, paced these halls side by side, whispered together in the galleries or strolled together on the terraces or in the trim gardens, sat together in the presence chamber, Cromwell trying with all his cunning arguments to make the king a friend and Charles ever withdrawing within his charm and plotting how to take revenge, yet flattered by these attentions for, as he remarked to one of the officers: " You cannot do without me—you will fall to ruin if I do not sustain you." And one of his servants, amazed at this self-confidence, cried: " Sir, your majesty speaks as if you had some secret power that I do not know of." That secret power was Charles's duplicity with which at the beginning he completely deceived Cromwell who swore that he " was the uprightest and most conscientious man of his three kingdoms."

Feeling secure and, mayhap, proud of his cunning, the king now again had his portrait painted with his second son, the Duke of York. It has been argued that this painting is not by Lely, but I feel that we can accept it without question, for it is in his earlier tighter method; and besides did not the painter's friend, Richard Lovelace write verses *To My Worthy Friend Mr. Peter Lilly*: *On that excellent Picture of his Majesty and the Duke of Yorke, drawne by him at Hampton-Court* "?

> *Thou dost the things* Orientally *the same*
> *Not only paints its colour, but its* Flame:
> *Thou sorrow canst designe without a teare,*
> *And with the Man his very* Hope *or* Feare:
> *So that th' amazed world shall henceforth finde*
> *None but my* Lilly *ever drew a* Minde.

The king is shown leaning on a staff and holding a letter addressed *Au Roi Monseigneur* while the duke, hand on hip and eyeing his father, offers a penknife with which to cut the strings. Charles is growing fatter here and his hair is thinning.

He had given his promise not to escape and therefore was allowed liberty within reason with his friends about him. His nephew, Charles, Elector of Palatine, landed in England that he might, perhaps, explain why he had been so tardy with help during the actual fighting; but more precious even than friends were his children to Charles.

He kept both sly hands busy, one with parliament and the other with Cromwell, thinking to play one against the other, while he pleaded with the Scots to invade England. But he gave no hint of his schemes as he played in the tennis-court or at billiards or rode out hunting, nor did he neglect astrologers' assistance, sending his mistress, Jane Whorwood, to consult Lilly, the expert, who wrote that " When she came to the door, I told her I would not let her come in to my house, for I buried a maidservant of the plague very lately. ' I fear not the plague, but the pox,' quoth she; so up we went. . . . Away she went early next morning to Hampton Court to acquaint his Majesty [with the stars' decision] . . . While his Majesty was at Hampton Court, Alderman Adams sent his Majesty one thousand pounds in gold, five hundred whereof he gave to Madame Whorewood."

This alderman's gift was typical of the reaction that was beginning to seep through England while royalists were working both underground and in the open, and in France, Henrietta was begging the Pope to canonise a certain Father Robert " in the hope that having contributed my endeavours to render him important on earth after death, he may obtain in heaven where his soul reposes, some favour for the kingdom which he served with so much fidelity through life." The Marquis of Ormond was stirring up the Irish, the Prince of Wales was about to sail for Scotland, and the Duke of York, disguised as a woman, had escaped from St. James's, and the king was plotting while outwardly he half-agreed with Cromwell's suggestions. Soon, however, Cromwell was forced to realise that it was impossible to trust the king and he had to relinquish all hope of compromise. As Ireton said: " He gave us words, and we paid him in his own coin, when we found he had no real intention to the people's good, but to prevail by our factions, to regain by art what he had lost by fight."

At least, however, Charles had the honesty to repudiate his parole to his guardian, Colonel Whalley, nor did this repudiation apparently affect his liberty. His children still visited him and, on one occasion at least, Elizabeth stayed the night. We are uncertain exactly what the king's lodgings were like, for William tore them down and replaced them with Wren's south and east fronts, but they were probably built on the usual plan of rooms opening one into another, while his bedchamber would most likely be in the centre; at the western end, near the staircase, would be the guard-room, and at the other end, backstairs would lead down into the court. Apparently behind these apartments ran a long gallery in which two guards stood ready, and this night when Elizabeth lodged there, these guards made so much noise, she said, that she could not sleep. Her father asked to have them removed and Whalley apologised, saying that they were instructed to make as little noise as possible and he would give them even more definite instructions to make much less noise. So thin were the walls of that old palace that one could hear another whisper or a bed creak; difficult indeed must have been intrigues in such a place. For again the princess complained and Whalley told Charles that he could do no more, for the soldiers had assured him that they trod as softly as they could, but, should the king give him his parole again, he would remove the guard altogether. But this Charles would not do.

He was no coward by any means but he inherited his father's terror of assassination and it was on this that Cromwell worked now that he realised that negotiations were futile and his one hope was to compromise him. He had proof of Charles's duplicity for, found in the saddlebags of a courier off to the queen, was a letter containing these words: "He should know in time how to deal with the rogues, who instead of a silken garter should be fitted with a hempen cord." Cromwell went cunningly to work—unless, of course, the whole tale of the intercepted letter be a lie, which does not seem likely—and an anonymous letter reached Charles, signed E.R., warning him that he was to be murdered. That this note hurried Charles's preparations appears probable, for when on the following day red-headed Jane Whorwood arrived at Hampton Court she was genuinely surprised to learn of his flight, and she most certainly would have been told.

The escape was described by Whalley before the house of commons, and although here there are discrepancies with other accounts, it must have been, on the whole, truthful. He said that he asked those waiting for the king where he was, and "they told me he was writing letters in his bedchamber. I waited there without mistrust till six of the clock; I then began to doubt, and told the bed-chambermen, Mr. Maule and Mr. Murray, I wondered the king was so long a-writing; they told me he had (they thought) some extraordinary occasion. Within half an hour after I went into the next room to Mr. Oudart [the king's secretary], and told him I marvelled the king was so long a-writing. He answered, he wondered too, but withal said, the king told him he was to write letters both to the queen and the princess of Orange, which gave me some satisfaction for the present. But my fears with the time increased, so that when it was seven of the clock, I again told Mr. Maule I exceedingly wondered the king was so long before he came out. He told me he was writing, and I replied, possibly he might be ill, therefore I thought he should do well to see, and to satisfy both myself and the house, that were in fear of him. He replied, the king had given him strict commands not to molest him, therefore durst not, besides he had bolted the door to him. I was then extreme restless in my thoughts, lookt oft in at the key hole to see whether I could perceive his majesty, but could not; prest Mr. Maule to knock very oft, that I might know whether his majesty were there or not, but all to no purpose. He still plainly told me he durst not disobey his majesty's commands."

Grinning in his cheek, the Belgian secretary and others of the royal household kept the suspicious Whalley at bay until at eight o'clock he went to the keeper of the privy lodgings and asked him to go through the privy garden to the privy stairs. These would be facing the river, and from the palace here then ran many covered galleries leading to towers and turrets, similar to the one in which young Elizabeth had been locked on her visit to Mary; and beyond these flowed the river rippling over the stairs, sucking under the Water Gate at its south-east angle.

Up the privy stairs went Whalley with the keeper of the privy lodgings; then, he said, they strode " from chamber to chamber till we came to the next chamber to his majesty's bedchamber, where we saw his majesty's cloak lying on the midst of the floor, which much amazed me. I went presently back to the commissioners [of parliament] and bed-chambermen, acquainting them with it, and therefore desired Mr. Maule again to see whether his majesty was in his bedchamber or not; he again told me he durst not. I replied, that I would then command him, and that in the name of parliament, and therefore desired him to go along with me. He desired I would speak to the commissioners to go along with us.

I did. We all went. When we came into the room next the king's bedchamber, I moved Mr. Maule to go in. He said he would not, except I would stand at the door. I promised I would, and did. Mr. Maule immediately came out and said the king was gone. We all then went in, and one of the commissioners said: 'It may be the king is in his closet.' Mr. Maule presently replied and said he was gone. I then, being in a passion, told Mr. Maule I thought he was accessory to his going; for that afternoon he was come from London, it being a rare thing for him to be from court."

But Charles was now safely away, having crept down the back-stairs, hurried through the covered galleries to the river, then turned up the king's long gallery to the paradise room in the park. The gate here, being far from the palace, would not have been guarded. It appears likely that horses were waiting for him on which, with his friends, he rode to Thames Ditton, a mile from the palace, where he crossed the river. An alternative version states that they had a boat hidden near the paradise room in which they rowed to Ditton and there mounted. No matter by which route he fled, the king was soon far from Hampton Court; and as he went, in the mud of the road he dropped a book. It was a collection of contemporary tracts lent him by a bookseller, and to-day you can see the volume in the British Museum amongst the library once belonging to George III called the King's Tracts; and you will find, darkening it, a stain from the mud in which it lay when it slipped from his hand.

Whalley sent parties of horse and foot to seek the royal fugitive; but he was too late. On the king's table he found three letters, one to the parliamentary commissioners, one to the houses of parliament, and one to himself asking " the continuance of your courtesie " in looking after certain personal belongings, so assured was Charles of becoming king again, with the postscript: " I assure you it was not the letter you shewed me to-day [the threat of assassination] that made me take this resolution, nor any advertisement of that kinde. But I confess that I am loath to be made a close prisoner, under pretence of securing my life. I had almost forgot to ask you to send the black grew bitch to the Duke of Richmond."

Thus, in darkness, for the last time from Hampton Court, Charles stole to where friends awaited him under the trees. It was a stormy night and the beat of rain and howl of wind would have concealed the sound of his footsteps, tap-tapping softly down the stairs, squelching in the mud, as the volume of tracts flopped down.

While in the warmth, Whalley strode frowning before the locked door, suspicions growing each moment, Charles, with his friends, galloped through the storm towards that brief freedom which was to end, less than two years later, in death on the block.

CHAPTER IX

PROTECTOR CROMWELL

AND now a threat to Hampton Court. God-drunken puritans, as we have seen, had destroyed the chapel; now valuers came hustling to value what remained in the palace, for royal property was forfeit to the commonwealth. On July 4th, 1649, parliament decreed that this property be sold and the money thus obtained used to pay the innumerable debts of king and queen. In the British Museum amongst the Harleian MSS. you can read what is either the original or a contemporary copy of this sad inventory of things that would be to us of almost inestimable worth. Luckily, much was reserved by the lord protector, but the small intimate articles are those that move us most deeply, bringing the past so close that we can feel dead hands on the object, whether it be a ragged shoe or a drinking-cup or a button from a coat. Not the mighty tapestries and paintings by Titian or Raphael; not even those superb cartoons by Mantegna—mutilated beyond hope though they mainly are at the hands of that murderous " restorer," Louis Laguerre, in William III's reign—now reconditioned and sealed in wax under the expert hands of Mr. Kennedy North: no, not even Mantegna or Raphael or Titian could give me such joy to possess as, for example, Cardinal Wolsey's looking-glass sold by the commonwealth for a miserable £5. Yes, £5! and it was surmounted with Wolsey's arms and must often have had its surface dulled beneath the sour breath of that dominant man. It has vanished, we know not whither; vanished with Henry VIII's stick on which he leaned his heroic bulk when he lumbered through the palace and which these parliamentarians sold for, not pounds, but five silver shillings! I fear even the sacred silence of the British Museum reading-room must be disturbed by the angry pounding of my heart as I read. Great Henry's own stick gone for five shillings, a florin, a coin you toss with, to-day not worth four pints of beer or two double whiskies or two packets of twenty cigarettes, with which you could not buy a walking-stick you would bother to discard in the lost property office: five shillings which, with tip, would barely cover a meal or, with your wife, an afternoon in the cinema, a miserable sum that even a pawnbroker would shy from offering for a broken umbrella:

five shillings ! a piece not even milled these days and which would purchase us, should we be lucky, a second-hand book or a sack of coal, forty boxes of matches, a pair of plainly imitation silk stockings, or less than an half-an-hour on a merry-go-round on Hampstead Heath. Do not tell me that we must multiply and multiply to bring the sum to modern values. I know it . . . yet, five shillings for the walking-stick of His Most Royal Highness King Henry VIII ! And his highness's gloves, valued at 6d. ! sold for 1s.; while six of the royal comb-cases reached but 7s. . . .

Let us flee from this catalogue—I can quote no further—to examine briefly: *A Survey of the Mansion Howse commonly called Hampton Court in the County of Middx, with the Barnes, Stables, Outhouses, Gardens, Orchards, Yards, Courts, and Backsydes belonging unto or used and enjoyed with the sayd Mansion Howse; togeather with the Parke, comonly called* Howse Parke, *The* Course, *and* Meadows, *thereto adjoyning, the* Hare Warren, *with Two other Parkes, the one comonly called* The Middle Parke *and the other* Bushie Parke. . . .

In this volume we have set out in full detail the palace and grounds. Unfortunately, it is impossible to quote from it without quoting the whole, but as one reads through the mounting list so calmly penned by the commonwealth's surveyors, the ghosts flee and the bricks become but bricks to be weighed against gold. Yet how can gold balance beauty and age, memories and royal splendour, loves and hates of the past ? According to this dull document, the " Totall of the annual values in this survey doe amount unto . . . An.120, lix, 00 04. Totall of the grosse values is Gr.10765 19 09." We know not the value in coins of the ghosts, for these busy men of government were too aware of the grace within themselves to see with other but material eyes. From this document, it remains uncertain whether the palace were to be demolished, but it seems unlikely that it would have been. Apparently the idea was to split the grounds into allotments for auctioning. At any rate, luckily the council of state advised that, with Whitehall, Westminster, and certain other palaces, our palace be retained for public use, together with much of the furniture, etc. Later it was presented to Cromwell to be used as kings and queens had used it, as a country house.

Yet there were many further arguments, in parliament and out of it, about selling the palace. It was given to Cromwell, then snatched back when protests sounded; it was offered to him in exchange for

New Hall, one of Buckingham's estates in Essex which he had bought, but Cromwell demurred, made pretence that it would be best to sell the place; and much of the grounds actually were sold. Later, they were bought back when, on December 16th, 1653, Cromwell was proclaimed lord protector and had no further need to mask his lusts with modesty. Hampton Court now was his.

And Cromwell loved Hampton Court; he was continually returning there, either for long or brief visits. So frequently, indeed, did he travel back and forth that royalist plots were woven to snare and kill him, for the future Charles II, in exile, had given free leave, in the king's name, for any man to murder Cromwell with pistol, sword, or poison, under the promise of a pension of £500 a year for him who dared the deed. Not only royalists, but disappointed presbyterians cocked their pistols and muttered against this new man of blood who would not build the world again according to their plan. Some in their hatred even accused him of satanism and said he met the devil in Hyde Park: a charge actually believed to-day by certain reactionary writers.* For, as in every revolution, idealists are impatient and as merciless as the defeated in attempting to destroy those who do not act as their fanaticism demands. It would have been impossible for Cromwell to have satisfied every sect and he was himself a tolerant kindly man continually badgered and threatened because the promises given to many different parties could not all be redeemed.

But, as so often, we are sliding into the nation's history and must race back to our palace in which this charming, rather boisterous, laughing, and coarsely jesting Cromwell is installed. We must, however, pause to glance at the man who, to this day, is detested by many who think in symbols only and see him as a fanatical puritan, hypocritical and treacherous. He was not that. An honest yeoman, a sincere Christian, a brave warrior, and a rather muddled thinker with a genius for speaking in splendid prose, Cromwell was a very typical Englishman of his time. He had no patience for vanities and it is worth remembering the famous anecdote of when Lely was painting his portrait: " Mr. Lely," said he, " I desire you would use all your skill to paint my picture truly like me, and not flatter me at all; but remark all these roughnesses, pimples, warts, and everything, otherwise I never will pay a farthing

---

* See S. Everard's article, *Oliver Cromwell and Black Magic*, in *The Occult Review* for April, 1936. Also the Rev. Montague Summers' *The Geography of Witchcraft*, 1927, and his *A Popular History of Witchcraft*, 1937 (both Kegan Paul, Trench, Trubner).

for it." Such was his fundamental honesty save when he babbled into mysticism; and as a soldier it is impossible to rate him too highly. The only really black smear on his biography is the ruthless massacre at Drogheda, but he was only carrying on the policy of previous rulers and was no more brutal than most invaders. He is judged harshly, however, because people will persist in seeing him through modern spectacles, divorcing him from his age. As already remarked, he was a near-Elizabethan, often thinking and acting in Elizabethan fashion. Nevertheless the Drogheda massacre was brutal even for those days, although it cannot compare with the treachery of St. Bartholomew's Night against which it would be more correct to judge it than against a modern battle, as his critics will do. And when we see it near the almost contemporary brutalities of Europe's Thirty Years' War, immortalised in the frightening etchings of Callot, it shifts into perspective.

Apart from Drogheda, there are no marks of brutality to be scored against Cromwell. As his steward, John Maidston, recorded: " His body was well compact and strong, his stature under six feet (I believe about two inches), his head so shaped as you might see it a storehouse or shop both of a vast treasury of natural parts. His temper exceeding fiery, as I have known, but the flame of it kept down for the most part, or soon allayed with those moral endowments he had. He was naturally compassionate towards objects in distress, even to an effeminate measure; though God had made him a heart, wherein was left little room for fear but what was due to himself, of which there was a large proportion, yet did he exceed in tenderness towards sufferers. A larger soul I think hath seldom dwelt in house of clay than his was. I believe if his story were impartially transmitted, and the unprejudiced world well possessed with it, she would add him to her nine worthies."

Very much the family man, even royalist pamphleteers could find little mud to sling at his private life, save at his wife's parsimony. From her portraits, Elizabeth appears a fattish sharp-eyed matron, but we know little about her, apart from royalists' insults. Mrs. Lucy Hutchinson, who knew her well, calls her and her daughters " insolent fools " and accuses them of overplaying their parts which, said she, suited them no better than would scarlet on an ape. Most likely there is truth in this charge, for while Oliver remained a typical English squire, he yet was sufficiently dizzied by his semi-royalty that men uncovered when he passed them in the park, and when foreign ambassadors arrived, he greeted them with all the pomp of a king. But he loved best, as the Venetian ambassador noted, to drive " often to Hampton Court, a pleasuance of the former kings in the country."

Here he could unbuckle himself like a warrior home from the war, rid of the fear of assassination, and could make merry with his friends. When not trying to break his neck out hunting, he would scribble verses with comrades, each trying to out-verse the other, while calling for tobacco, pipes, and a candle, so that there should be no time wasted fiddling with flint and steel to keep bowls hot. His shadow looms gigantic on the walls and towers to the carved ceiling as I see him there in one of those many chambers. Above and around him are signs of past royalty, the arms of Henry and his wives and of Elizabeth, as he laughs and sings, his coat unbuttoned and his plump friendly face wrinkled with grinning.   .

Often he would call for music, of which he was extremely fond. In Hampton Court he had two organs and, for organist, John Hingston, a pupil of Orlando Gibbons, and he liked singing glees and part-songs; while whenever he gave a dinner, there were always musicians present to soothe the savage pleasures of the table. And next to music and

The West Gate.

hunting, he liked sermons, and some of those sermons took three hours to preach. To call him a hypocrite merely because such a pastime would bore you, as it would most definitely bore me to a tavern, is absurd. To Cromwell and to most men of those days the Bible was a living voice uttering mysteries which must be wrestled with, word by word.

After Cromwell died, parliament made a careful inventory of Hampton Court which is luckily preserved in the Public Record Office, and those who conceive those puritan times as drab and miserable would be surprised on examining it to find that they would be unable to tell which were Cromwell's effects and which Charles I's—if any of royalty's possessions had been left beyond the tapestries and paintings which Cromwell rescued from the sale. Here, for example, are the contents of Cromwell's bedchamber: " Five pieces of fine Tapestry hangings of Vulcan and Venus. Two wyndow courtines—one of scarlet bayes, th' other of sarge; " then all " of sky collour damaske and cased with watchet Bayes," the following: " One small couch, Two elbow chaires, Fower back stooles, One carpet." Then: " One black Table with a turned frame. One paire of Andirons with double brasses. One paire of creepers with fire shovell and Tongs. One paire of bellowes." In his dressing-room were " One old Coberd. One Spanish Table. Two small Turkey Carpets. One paire of Andirons with double brasses. One paire of creepers and fire shovell, Tongs and Bellows. Fower back-stooles of Turkeyworke." In this inventory we also find mention of the Paradise Room which stood apart from the palace towards the river and are conducted to all its most disappointing contents after the lure of such a name, for it held merely " seven pieces of rich hangings of Arras, of the Tryumphs of the Capitall Sinns. One piece of the like Arras of Meleager. One chimney-piece of Arras of Tobias, Fower Courtines of watchet Bayes. Two paire of Andirons. One paire of Creepers."

Such luxury inevitably brought down the fury of the pamphleteers who vacillated between insults at Lady Cromwell's meanness and her ostentation. Her meanness, I regret, we must accept, as it seems the general opinion of the time; and we learn of her interfering with the cook—but what housewife has not had that accusation mumbled at her ?—and having trapdoors made through which she could spy on the servants. Also, without the faintest suggestion of truth that I can find, she was denounced as a drunkard and a whore to Cromwell's soldiers. But much dirt was inevitably slung when the royalist pamphleteers got to work. They called her "old Joan," but there is one thing for which her memory should be honoured: her interest in painting, for she was continually begging foreign ambassadors to send her portraits of the great men of their various countries: but that again might have been miserliness and snobbery, the desire to get for nothing portraits of the rulers who honoured her husband.

Naturally, her daughters also came in for spiteful comments as being haughty upstarts—"insolent fools," says Lucy Hutchinson—and again, there is probably truth in the accusation, for women are notoriously less able than men to accept the unexpected riches of life with the casualness they deserve. Altogether, however, it would seem that it was a homely family, a little puffed up by its glory, which now settled in our palace.

Of equal delight as sermons and music was the hunt to Cromwell, for he had the typical English squire's love of horses and dogs, with the lust to murder most other animals. The hunt was his joy and Queen Christina of Sweden sent him a small herd of reindeer to kill, but the lucky beasts died a less horrible death before reaching England, unfortunately for us, as some might have escaped and bred, and I would like to meet reindeer with the stags in Bushey park.

His coach-teams were carefully matched, reddish-grey and snow-white, while his agents were ever bargaining with Turks for arabs in Aleppo and barbs in Tripoli. So great was Cromwell's love of horses that once, when an important parliamentary deputation arrived, he kept it waiting for hours while he inspected a barb in the garden.

Hawking, too, was a sport he enjoyed, but he rarely had time, once he became lord protector, to spare for long on amusements. It is natural, if unfortunate, that most details of his private life come from enemies, and of these, the most interesting is James Heath in his *Flagellum; or the Life and Death of Oliver Cromwell*. Eager as he was to throw every muddy stone he could at the man he hated, Heath actually, when stripped of his malice, reveals Cromwell as a charming, jovial, kindly, artistic sportsman, while to expose his cruelty he can produce only his lust for hunting, details of which he naturally exaggerates.

"His custom," he wrote, "was now to divert himself frequently at *Hampton-Court* (which he had saved from Sale, with other Houses of the Kings, for his own greatnesse), whither he went and came in post, with his Guards behind and before, as not yet secure of his Life from the justice of some avenging hand; Here he used to hunt, and at the fall of a Deer, where he would be sure to be present, embrue his hands in the blood of it, and therewith asperse and sprinkle his Attendants: and sometimes to cokes [coax] the neighbouring Rusticks, give them a Buck he hunted, and money to drink with it." Such was surely the manners of any country squire—generously to give his capture to the poor with a gift of money? As for his alleged habit of sprinkling blood on his attendants, this, I believe, is still actually done in England, the neophyte at a hunt having his cheeks wiped with the still warm blood of the kill.

" His own Diet," continued Heath, " was very spare, and not so curious, except in publique Treatments, which were constantly given every Monday in the week to all the Officers of the Army not below a Captain, where he dined with them, and shewed a hundred Antick Tricks, as throwing of Cushions, and putting live Coals into their Pockets and Boots; a Table being likewise spread every day of the week for such Officers as should casually come to Court . . . With these Officers while he seemed to disport himself, taking off his Drink freely, and opening himself every way to the most free familiarity, He did meerly lye at the Catch of what should incogitantly and with unsuspected provocation fall from their Mouths, which he would be sure to record and lay up against his occasion of reducing them to the Speakers memory, who were never likely to forget the prejudice and damage they had incurred by such loose discoveries of their minds and inclinations. He was a great Lover of Musick, and entertained the most skillfulest in that Science in his pay, who when the evil Spirit was upon him, thought to lay and still him with those Harmonious charms; but generally he respected or at least pretended a Love to all ingenious and eximious persons in any Arts, whom he procured to be sent or brought to him; but the niggardlinesse and incompetence of his reward, shewed that this man was a personated Act of Greatness, and that private *Cromwell* yet governed Prince *Oliver* . . . He had twenty other freaks in his head, for sometimes before he had half dined, he would give order for a Drum to beat, and call in his Foot Guards, like a Kennel of Hounds, to snatch off the meat from his Table, and tear it in pieces; the like Joco's and Frisks he would have with other Company; even with some of the Nobility, when he would not stick to tell them what Company they had lately kept; when and where they had drank the King's health and the Royal Families, bidding them when they did it again, to do it more privately, and this without any passion, and as Festivous Droll Discourse."

Indeed, Cromwell rises remarkably clean out of this mud, for even Heath dared do no more than hint that he betrayed the confidences of the table: obviously he did nothing of the sort, but merely wished to warn these hotheads that others might not be so tolerant as himself, while his calling for the soldiers to eat what was left was again typical of a country gentleman, for he can scarcely be charged with the men's habit of guzzling like dogs—if that habit be not merely a maggot from Heath's brain. And although Heath might sneer, he cannot ignore Cromwell's love of music and, indeed, of all the arts. Whether he were actually mean in paying for what he liked we cannot say, but it is probable that he is here blackly reflecting some of his wife's reputation. Certainly, his jests were not to our tastes, but one has merely to read the popular literature of the period to realise that, were we suddenly to return to the seventeenth century, we would have to clip pegs on our noses and often keep our eyes shut. Such crude fun as Heath recounts, the putting of live coals in men's pockets and boots with the throwing of cushions, would not then have been uncommon, and, in truth, is far from impossible to-day amongst simple folk. And Cromwell, for all the bravura of his talk, his genius in battle and love of justice, was a simple fellow.

Like any good country squire, he took a proprietorial interest in his estate and arranged to have the bridges and banks of the New or Longford river, which Charles had dug, repaired to fill again the palace ponds and fountains. Immediately, there was outcry. The neighbours, hating this artificial river which was often overflowing and rotting their crops and drowning their sheep, had, with the exuberance of the levellers, filled it with stones and gravel after the revolution and had demolished bridges, thinking in their simple fashion that liberty had come at last. Like a king, Cromwell ignored the protests and even made matters worse by diverting the river to the Hare-warren in Bushey Park, north of the road from Kingston to the manor, where he dug two pools now called the Heron or Herring Ponds, both words being corruptions of Hare-warren Ponds. He also royally raised palings across the people's right-of-way through this Hare-warren from the manor to Hampton Wick, and the inhabitants of Wick dared do nothing but brood on these thefts by an upstart who treated them no more humanly than had the late Charles.

If often he acted thus like a king, Cromwell was also to suffer a kingly phobia—the terror of assassination which had haunted both James and Charles. There was reason enough for this, for not only was he menaced by royalists but by revolutionaries enraged to find that the new world of which they had dreamed remained only a dream. We find mention of one Captain Thomas Gardiner who petitioned Charles II for relief after he was king, boasting that in 1657 he had attempted to assassinate Cromwell in one of the galleries at Hampton Court with two loaded pistols and a dagger and, on being taken, had been given the surprisingly mild sentence of twelve months' jail. As he adds that he would have been sentenced to death but for lack of evidence, we may doubt the rascal, for if two loaded pistols and a dagger are not evidence of the intention of doing something rather dangerous, we had best close our law-courts.

But all those who watched Cromwell were not liars like Gardiner; many were determined men waiting their chance, and it was therefore natural that he should walk warily and keep a guard about him. The British redcoat, that flaming uniform of romance, was first used by these guards who, the virulent Heath informs us, were ever behind and before him, riding full gallop about his coach, when he drove abroad.

And now sorrows fell heavily upon him. His beloved daughter, Elizabeth Claypole, became desperately ill at Hampton Court from some internal trouble at which we can only guess. So worried grew Cromwell that he refused to leave the palace and there received messengers and ambassadors. Himself was far from well. The stone was dragging him to his grave and the gout was hobbling him from the exercises he loved. As usual, the doctors did their best to kill him with specifics, and he was in a nervous state owing to a bad accident when the coach in which he was travelling had been smashed to pieces. And the army was imploring him to name his successor.

The house of Cromwell was nearing its end and soon Hampton Court was to be rid of these commoners to open wide its gates again to royalty. The whole family, except Henry—then in Ireland—and Bridget Fleetwood, gathered about the dying girl's bed. Frances, whose husband had just died, was in purple mourning while Richard came hurrying from Bath. Dr. Bates was in attendance and with the usual pomposity of his profession, to hide ignorance, said that Elizabeth had an " inward impostume of the loins." On August 6th she died and the royalists sharpened their pens to scribble pamphlets retailing with relish a ghastly deathbed scene in which the dying girl had shrieked at her father for a regicide and had implored him to make atonement. That there was truth in the tale seems likely, as it is corroborated by Dr. Bates, but it was probably much exaggerated, although snobbish Elizabeth may have been infected with love of royalty and a bad conscience that she, a commoner, should die under a prince's ceiling. That she had some such failing is suggested by the fact that when Charles II came to England and had dragged from their graves the stinking corpses of Elizabeth's father and brother-in-law to rot at Tyburn, with Admiral Blake's and others, hers was left at peace in the abbey. But Charles, of course, always had a softness for the ladies.

" We have been a family of much sorrow all this summer and therefore we deserve not the envy of the world," wrote Richard Cromwell to his brother, realising the simple truth that happiness is more essential than power to a contented life; but he added bravely: " We shall still truste in God whoe is our rocke, upon whome as a sure foundation I recommend your feete."

Now, soon after his daughter, the great Oliver was to be struck down in Hampton Court, as though the ghosts of kings were breathing death upon his family.* But first, Elizabeth was given a splendid funeral down the river from the palace to the abbey, although it was practically a rehearsal for Cromwell's own. He lay in bed, fingering his Bible, having it expounded to him. He asked to hear Phil. 4, II, 12, 13, the words of wisdom counselling content, no matter how threatening was misfortune, and telling one to keep good heart for all things could be done through the strengthening of Christ. " Which read, said he (to use his own words as near as I can remember them): ' This Scripture did once save my life, when my eldest son died, which went as a dagger to my heart, indeed it did'. "

Soon he rallied a little and was considered strong enough to take exercise. George Fox, carrying a petition from the Quakers, saw

---

* There is a legend about Cromwell's death repeated by John Timbs and Alexander Gunn in the *South* volume of their *Abbeys, Castles, and Ancient Halls of England and Wales.* They write: " There is a singular anecdote of the King [Charles] traditional at Hampton Court. He was one day standing at a window of the palace, surrounded by his children, when a gipsy came up and asked for charity. Her appearance excited ridicule, and probably threats, which so enraged the gipsy, that she took out of her basket a looking-glass, and presented it to the King: he saw in it his own head decollated. Probably, with a natural wish to propitiate so prophetical a beggar, or for some other reason, money was given her. She then said that the death of a dog, in the room the King was then in, would precede the restoration of the kingdom to his family; which the King was about to lose. It is supposed that Oliver Cromwell afterwards slept in the room referred to. He was constantly attended by a faithful dog, who guarded his bedchamber door. On awakening one morning he found the dog dead, on which he exclaimed, in allusion to the gipsy's prophecy which he had previously heard, ' The kingdom is departed from me.' Cromwell died soon afterwards."

him riding in Hampton Court Park " at the head of his Life Guards, I saw and felt a waft of death go forth against him," he wrote, " and when I came to him he looked like a dead man." Yet he and his friends remained remarkably cheerful, having been given, they believed, some divine sign that he would recover. When doctors tiptoed about his bed, Cromwell complacently informed them that he knew they thought he was going to die but, said he, " I declare to you I shall not die by this illness: of this I am certain." Incredulously they looked at him, and he added: " Don't think me crazed. I am telling you what is true; and I have a better authority than your Galen or Hippocrates. God Himself has vouchsafed this answer to our prayers —not to mine alone, but those of others who have a closer intercourse and greater familiarity with Him than I have. Be cheerful; banish all grief from your faces; and act towards me as though I was a mere servant. You are able to do much by your scientific knowledge, but nature is more potent than all the physicians in the world; and God surpasses nature in a still greater degree."

How stout the heart, how firm the faith, of this strong man grinning at his doctors while already the bones were showing sharp on his broad cheeks and his eyes were sunken! In a darkened chamber in our palace he lay, scorning the physic for the Bible, and he felt no headless ghost of Charles part his bed-curtains and breathe that cold breath which all who meet ghosts feel piercing skin and icing bones. Unafraid he lay, his assurance reassuring even the doctors, and when a friend chanced to remark that the lord protector would soon become light-headed, one of these doctors turned sharply on him, saying: " You are certainly a stranger in this house! Don't you know what was done last night? The chaplain, and all who are dear to God, dispersed in several parts of the Palace, had prayed God for his health, and all brought this answer: ' He shall recover'. "

But God's message, as so very often happens, had been misinterpreted by man's desire to hear *Yes*. Cromwell never recovered. He grew worse, fell into delirium, sweating in pain; and for some reason, apparently for a change of air, he was transported to Whitehall to linger a little before he died. " It is a fearful thing," he said when he felt death close, " to fall into the hands of the living God." Gales swept through England, the worst storm known for a hundred years came, tearing off roofs and tumbling chimneys, plucking church spires and uprooting John Evelyn's orchards. " It is not my design to drink of sleep," said Cromwell waving aside a sleeping draught, " but my design is to make what haste I can to be gone."

On September 3rd, 1660, this design was completed; on the anniversaries of the decisive battles of Dunbar and Worcester, Cromwell died, at peace with God.

As Marvell sang:

> *No part of him but bare his mark away,*
> *Of honour—all the year was Cromwell's day:*
> *But this, of all the most auspicious found,*
> *Thrice had in open field him victor crowned.*
> *When up the armoured mountains of Dunbar*
> *He marched, and through deep Severn, ending war;*
> *What day should him eternise, but the same,*
> *That had before immortalised his name?*

CHAPTER X
CHARLES THE SECOND

And Richard yet, where his great parent led,
Beats on the rugged track: he virtue dead
Revives, and by his milder beams assures:
And yet how much of them his griefe obscures.
He, as his father, long was kept from sight
In private, to be view'd by better light:
But open'd once, what splendour does he throw !
A Cromwell in an houre a prince will grow . . .
Cease not our griefs, calm peace succeeds a war,
Rainbows to storms, Richard to Oliver.

THUS Marvell sang with more optimism than perspicacity;
for although Oliver's son, Richard, may not have been merely
a " peasant in his nature," as Lucy Hutchinson jeered, he
was certainly no great man. He was an ordinary country gentleman,
very fond of riding, hunting and hawking, like his father; a little
careless with money, being of a generous and virtuous nature, but
without ambition save to force that haggling parliament to pay
his debts. In the history of Hampton Court his place is slight and
therefore we dismiss him in a page as prelude to the entry of Charles
II, for he does not deserve the dignity of a chapter.

After his father's death, he rarely visited Hampton Court, as
parliament had reverted to its original intention of selling the manor
and now drew up that detailed inventory from which I have already
quoted. Ludlow, however, used his wise influence to have it retained
as a summer residence for government officials, although others
protested that to keep it whole was a provocation to ambitious men
and contrary to the interest of the commonwealth from which all
symbols of royalty should be outlawed. But as Ludlow sensibly
argued, lust for power was a far greater incentive than lust for
palaces, and should a king return, lack of palaces would not restrain
him from wasting money to build further palaces; and luckily his
commonsense prevailed. Hampton Court was again reprieved.

But the Cromwells had to decamp while Mrs. Cromwell was caught
trying to conceal crown property in a fruiterer's warehouse and

forced to surrender it. Occasionally, Richard visited the palace, but once when he rode to shoot deer in the park, he had barely succeeded in potting one before word came from parliament that none were to be killed; so he shot no more.

That rascally opportunist, General Monck, appears as the next possible owner, for parliament, having decided not to sell, offered him and his heirs, palace, contents, and parks; but he saw the offer for what it was—an attempt to bind him to the commonwealth—and he refused, taking instead a vast sum of money with the custody and stewardship of palace and park for life, an honour in which Charles confirmed him on his accession.

Now Charles II arrives, this swarthy giant with his gracious smile and his wit as substitute for honesty, to chase the parliamentary ghosts from our manor with the babble of his whores and the yapping of his lapdogs. Attractively ugly, " a tall, black man, six feet two inches high," he had such charm that few could resist him when he was intent on winning them, although he inherited his father's stutter. As himself once remarked on seeing his countenance in a mirror—" Oddsfish! I am an ugly fellow! " and a man who can thus jest against himself is rare and lovable. But one could cram a fat jest-book with Charles's remarks and, indeed, many such a book has already been made, for misfortune, far from embittering him, had merely made him scornful of the world's gifts.

A man who can treat life with such smiling contempt, turning pain and love and hatred into mockery, is a great, a lovable creature, but the tragedy of Charles as a ruler is that he could not take the job seriously, save in spasms, and then it was to consolidate the throne against the people's rights; nor can we blame him for his lack of love for the country when it had chopped off his father's head and banned the religion in which he secretly believed. Nor must we forget that his English blood was infinitesimal, descending from that sister of Henry VIII's, Margaret, grandmother of James I. Henry VIII himself, of course, had been only half-English, his father being Welsh; but as with his two children, Edward and Elizabeth, the mother at least had been English. After Elizabeth, the English blood almost vanishes from royalty, and as Mr. Hilaire Belloc triumphantly points out, even Charles's appearance was that of the Medicis, through his mother. " That unmistakable concavity of outline," he writes in *The Last Rally*, " as if the profile were modelled on a crescent moon, that extreme swarthiness of hair and skin, those deep furrows running across the hollow cheeks and framing the corners of the mouth, that peculiar length of the nose and that strong narrow chin—all these features in Vasari's portrait [of Lorenzo de Medici] forcibly recall the Stuarts of the later seventeenth century. We feel as we look on it, especially if we be unprepared, a sort of shock at such resemblance."

Fortunately, the resemblance was mostly facial, for Charles, although as lecherous as the Medicis, was not so ruthless, so brutal, so cunning. Indeed, he was most tolerant and, although a Roman catholic, concealed the fact for the sake of the monarchy while he sickened at the slaughter of parliament-men—" I must confess I am weary of hanging," he said when urged to continue taking revenge, " let it sleep,"—and his cunning consisted mainly in his ability to charm his enemies that he might destroy liberty.* His throne was insecure, and he knew it, for the tragedy was that he, father of many, had no legitimate heir, while the boy he loved, the Duke of Monmouth, was a chuckle-headed rebellious fool urged by vanity later to revolt.

" I am weary of travelling," said Charles, " I am resolved to go abroad no more." And being thus resolved, he was prepared to compromise, even to the extent of allowing the wicked Popish Plot to intoxicate bigots, but he was helpless against the popular hatred and terror of Rome and might have lost his crown had he tried to reason; for the mob knows no reason when it smells blood. " I cannot pardon," he confessed, " because I dare not." Yet when the frenzy touched his queen, he stood bravely, nobly by her whom he did not love, this pathetic Portuguese who was not only tiresome but barren. " It would be a horrid thing to abandon her," he said and would not throw her to the mob. Against this nobility must be scored his detestation of parliament, although it was natural enough, for had not parliament slain his father and did it not now try to rope him, too, from becoming an autocrat? " I care just that!" he cried, tossing his hat into the air, " for parliament." But he had cunning and knew better than to outrage the monster he feared and loathed, for he had his father's example before him; and although he hated presbyterianism—it was not, he said, a religion for gentlemen—he was yet sensible enough to have his stupid brother's

---

* He could, however, be callous enough. It was from Hampton Court that he wrote to Clarendon the day before the patriot Sir Harry Vane's trial in 1662: " Certainly he is too dangerous a man to let live, if we can honestly put him out of the way. Think of this, and give me some account of it tomorrow."

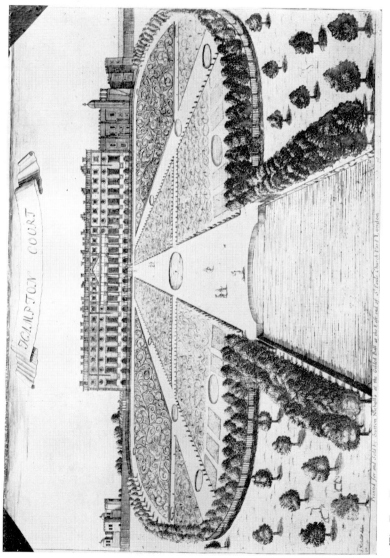

Courtesy of the British Museum

The East Front of William III's Palace

children reared by strict protestants so that when later they reigned as Mary and Anne their thrones were solid and safe.

The greatest of the Stuarts, it is sad to think that his penniless youth had made of him a man who cared more for the throne than for England, so that he could take bribes from France without even the intention of fulfilling his promised treachery, being determined only that there should not be a second revolution which, of course, there was the moment his bungling brother got the crown. And Charles knew it. " When I am dead and gone, I know not what my brother will do," he said. " I am afraid much that when he comes to the crown he will be obliged to travel again. And yet will I take care to leave my kingdoms to him in peace, wishing he may long keep them so. But this hath all my fears, little of my hope, and less of my reason."

With such a king at Hampton Court we may expect a little merriment.

Yet his household ordinances surprise us by beginning—after a brief flourish against " tipling-houses; selling or takeing tobacco, hott waters," and " beggars, idle and loose people," and " stragling and masterlesse men "—with a solemnity more worthy of a bishop's palace.

" If any of Our Court," they snarl, " shall be noysed to be a prophane person, an outrageous riotter, a ribald, a notorious drunkard, swearer, rayler, or quarrellor, a fugitive from his master, a bankrupt, suspected for a pilferer or a theefe, or be otherwise so vitious and unmannerly that he be unfit to live in vertuous and civill company, he shall be convened before his superior officer to be examined, and thereupon admonished or punished as cause shall require."

Had the puritan who drew up this regulation attempted to carry it into effect, one of the first persons he would have had to admonish would have been the king himself; but it is unlikely that Charles ever read one word of the ordinances while his household officers could scarcely have obeyed most of them. And there were other ordinances that must have proved very wearisome to so light hearted and amorous a fellow, if he permitted them to come into effect. At the same time he was very consciously a king and it is unlikely that his court was quite so casual as it is usually depicted, while such regulations as the following would most likely have been obeyed: " when Wee goe to walk abroad a gentleman usher daily wayter and a gentleman usher assistant shall goe next before Us, and a gentleman usher daily wayter, or gentleman usher assistant and a gentleman usher quarter wayter shall goe behind Us, unless there be no gentleman usher daily wayter, or gentleman usher assistant. And the same orders shall bee observed when Wee goe into Our barges, or any where by water."

Royalty must never be alone is the theme of these regulations; even when it retires to bed, it must walk there in procession; and a ritual must be followed in turning down the sheets, although, particularly with such a bed-hopper as Charles, one wonders how strictly, at this date, such rules were kept. Indeed, from other sources we find a very different picture. For example, Hamilton in his life of de Gramont—I quote from the charming 1714 translation—wrote that the court was " the Seat and Fountain of *Sports*, *Pleasures*, *Enjoyments*, and all the *Polite* and *Magnificent* Entertainments, which are generally inspir'd by the Inclinations of a *tender*, *amorous*, and *indulgent* Prince. The *Beauties* studied to *charm*, the *Men* to *please*: And all, in short, improv'd their Talents the best they could. Some distinguish'd themselves by *Dancing*, others by *Shew* and *Magnificence*; some by their *Wit*; many by their *Amours*, but very few by their constancy."

Charles loved Hampton Court and continually travelled there to oversee the workers he had set to redecorate and rebuild the palace. Not only did he take these almost daily journeys, but on one occasion, at least, he walked the full distance from London—in February, 1673—beside the coach of his adored Louise de Queroalle, a Breton spy from France and his wife's lady-in-waiting. But he was a powerful fellow, expert at games, from fishing to hunting, and particularly delighted in tennis—all to be had at the palace— while he altered Henry VIII's tennis play, modernising it after the style he had seen abroad, and on many morning, before six o'clock, he would be found there with ball and racket.

We have details of his restorations and the full account of masons fitting the stones for the tambours—projecting portion of the main wall to give variety to the strokes*—and " sawing part of the blacke

* Antonio Scaino da Salò (1524-1612), quoted by Julian Marshall in his *Annals of Tennis*, 1878, describes it thus: " The main wall is plain, but thicker in one part, where it begins to project further over the floor, forming a figure called by the French *tambour* (*tamburino*); and this coming out obliquely, is the occasion of a variety of bounds which the ball, encountering it, makes with many and various effects, at the hands of good players, and very beautiful to see."

Although the present court retains the original dimensions—Charles II used it as the pattern for the one he built at Whitehall—it has been four times altered, practically rebuilt, marble for the line Crosse the Courte," "squaring & working of ffre stone for the Tumber [sic]," and "working black marble for the Line to goe on crosse the Tennis Court, making the grill by the Tambor"; of carpenters "plateing all that side of the Tennis Courte next the Garden new plancking both side of the sd. courte upon the wall," "taking down the gallery at the Tennis Court, and the roofe of the end gallery where the hazard is, planning all the timbers and seting them up again," "plaining and shooting of deale boords to cover the galleries at the Tennis Court over the side gallery and both the ends . . . fastening of peeces to the wall to lay the joysts upon & pinning them all down; boarding the gallery over head, making of frames for the nets to catch the balls"; bricklayers "huinge [hewing], rubbing, squareing, peeringe [making piers, or pillars], and scimonting [cementing] of tiles for to pave the Tennis Court"; sawyers "in cutting out of new & old timbers into several scantlings for rafters for ye Tennis Courte"; plasterers "imployed in burning of plaister of Paris, & laying of a great part of the walls of the Tennis Court therewith"; and masons "working black marble for the Line to goe on crosse the Tennis Court, making the grill by the Tambor."

Nor did Charles confine his energies wholly to the tennis court: he raised a guardhouse for foot soldiers in the Tilt Yard, for which we may well be angry; although the building yet stands, it stands on something of far greater interest and is, indeed, a flat ugly building. From France he lured gardeners, hoping to make Hampton Court the equal of those pleasure grounds he had visited abroad when often he had not pennies enough with which to buy a rose for his mistress. The dwarf yew trees he later raised with the skill of his head gardener, Rose, became famous and were quite show pieces; and he set to at the park, planting that noble avenue of limes arching from the east front, while he had dug the great canal running for three-quarters

since Henry erected it. Robert Long, the marker, was twice sent to our palace by Charles to get the measurements exact. He was, to quote again from Julian Marshall, appointed on December 24th, 1660, "'Marker in his Maties Tennis Courts, on the death of Mr. Timothy Phesaunt'; and on the 14th of the following January 'John Dynan ye younger, after the Decease of John Dynan his ffather,' was appointed 'Rackett Maker.' Robert Long continued to fill his office for nine years, and was paid for providing 'Battellors long Paulims Shuttlecocks lynes Tennis shoes and also for his Expences and attendance in supervising the Workemen in his Maties Tennis Court at Hampton Court' and elsewhere, and also for 'the providing the long paulims after a rate of twenty pence the day the antient settlement when his Matie was prince,' on March 14th, 1661-2, and on other occasions, too numerous to quote here. About the same time occur several warrants for providing seats covered with velvet, cushions, and other necessaries for the Court at Hampton Court, where the King often played."

Quite irrelevantly, may I ask when the pretentious spelling "racquet" is to give way to the English racket? Those other painful corruptions, "rhyme" for rime and "choir" for quire, are, I fear, with us for ever; but, for purity's sake, why "racquet"?

of a mile. With all these alterations and additions, however, Charles
—apart from the attack on the Tilt Yard—did no harm like his
successors, and left the palace even more beautiful than it had been.

The Kitchen Chimneys

Almost every day, as we have said, he would gallop to Hampton
Court to watch the work progressing, then would gallop back to
London to meet his nuisance of a council at noon. He was preparing
the home for his future bride, the Portuguese Katherine of Braganza.

Katherine might have been a pretty girl had she not obstinately
insisted on wearing her country's fashions which, to English eyes,
were dowdy and ugly, while she kept with her a pack of dirty friars
most offensive to a gallant court like Charles's. Charles himself
seemed content with her at first, although in no great hurry for the
bedding, as he told Clarendon. Being sleepy after his journey to
greet her, he wrote, " I can only give you an account of what I have
seen in bedd, which in shorte is her face is not so exact as to be called
a beuty, though her eyes are excellent good, and not anything in her
face that in the least degree can shoque one. On the contrary she

hath as much agreeableness in her looks altogether as ever I saw, and if I have any skill in visiognimy, which I think I have, she must be as good a woman as ever was born."

We have also his alleged remark as reported to a friend of the Duke of York's that he believed they had brought him a bat, not a woman. The general opinion, as courtiers eyed her, seems to have been approving, although not enthusiastic. Mr. Pepys, of course, being the slave of Lady Castlemaine, was relieved to find that the royal whore had not here a dangerous rival, for the queen was too lean to stand beside my lady's curves. Lord Chesterfield considered her extremely devout, extremely discreet, exactly shaped, with lovely hands, a good countenance, a pleasing voice and, indeed, said he, all that a man could ask for in a wife. Evelyn, although appalled by her ladies, thought the queen the handsomest among them, which was small praise, and added that her teeth stuck out too far, that she was of low stature, although prettily shaped, with languishing and excellent eyes. De Gramont, of course, sneered, saying that she added no brilliancy to the court, either in her person or her retinue which consisted, said he, " of six frights, who called themselves maids of honour, and a duenna, another monster who took the title of governess to these extraordinary beauties." The beauties were also, perhaps inevitably, chaste; so very chaste, in fact, that they would not " lye in any bed wherein any man has ever laine before." Nevertheless, one was shortly to cause a great scandal at Hampton Court by, as Pepys puts it, " dropping a child "; but Charles had the gallantry to have the woman's name suppressed so that even to-day we do not know it, while the father was one of the English mission that had been sent to Portugal and he was made to compensate the lady's honour with £1,500.

Poor Katherine had been badly instructed. The Portuguese court considered the English barbarous Lutherans and both her mother and brother, the king, ordered her to remain Portuguese in every way, to dress and act in the dignified fashion of her land and to speak its language, believing that the English ladies would be certain to imitate their queen. But the English ladies—and alas ! the gentlemen, too—merely laughed at her and her women. Charles, who had been warned what to expect, had despatched an English tailor to Lisbon but the tailor had been spurned and Katherine, who was apparently attractive, if no great beauty, arrived in dresses of a cut that had gone out with Queen Elizabeth. She wore that monstrous tub, the farthingale, all wire and whalebone, which made women look as though they were animated busts atop of drapery. Her women, of course, maintained her in her folly and this appearance of anachronistic females—as if a woman to-day were to dress in Edwardian, or even earlier, fashions—set the whole court tittering, and Charles joined in the mockery.

That, perhaps, was natural enough, but his behaviour in trying to force his mistress on to Katherine as a lady of her bedchamber was not so natural, was, indeed, callous. But of that we will speak later. At the moment, Charles has just met his queen and is conducting her to Hampton Court.

When Katherine had neared England she had had the good sense not to wear her farthingale. Against the arguments of her duennas, she chose from the wardrobe sent by Charles a gown of white satin trimmed with silver lace, cut in the English mode. James, Charles's brother, who had been sent to welcome her, did a wicked thing. Having heard tales of her hoops and feathers, he asked her to wear them so that he might see what she looked like, and the rogue insisted that she looked charming. Therefore to the delight of Charles's mistresses, she was wearing them when she landed. Being short-legged, she appeared dwarfish in this broad skirt which gave to her ungraceful walk a duck-like waddle.

Lady Castlemaine was having her second child by the king when Katherine reached England, and reluctantly Charles left his mistress to greet his wife. They were quickly married at Portsmouth on the morning of May 29th, 1662, the anniversary of both the king's birthday and his restoration; then they travelled to Hampton Court.

In the British Museum is a set of seven etchings by the Dutch artist, Dirk Stoop, who had been ordered to accompany the princess from Lisbon so that he might make a pictorial record of her progress, and one of these etchings shows " The Comming of ye King's Matie: and ye Queenes from Portsmouth to Hampton Court." The great palace, more splendid then than now with its tall towers later to be lopped by Dutch William, is shown in the background as the cavalcade winds towards it. Carriages and cavaliers, flanked by pikemen, with dogs racing beside them, turn at right-angles towards the bridge while in the foreground we see drawn by six horses the royal chariot in which sit the king and queen. Charles wears a tall black hat, for the curtains are pulled apart that we may peep inside, and beside him, Katherine leans a little forward, peering upon us and the artist. Around them ride and saunter courtiers, while carriages and pikemen follow with greyhounds and, in the bottom right-hand corner, a groom is leashing a pair of dogs while another dog, half on its back, with one leg lifted, is about to lick itself in the manner of dogs. Carriages and carts are following; they had to delay at Portsmouth to hire sufficient carts to carry those monstrous farthingales —or *guarde-infantas*, as they were then called—but in this etching we cannot see the queen's gown clearly, although undoubtedly she wore one of the clumsy things, but her hair is curled in clusters about her dark face, in the mode, while Charles wears his garter robes.

Over the moat rumbled the bridal-coach, under the Great Gateway, through the Base Court to the Great Hall stairs. Up between two lines of guards the king and queen walked, their household following, under the screens and into the Great Hall where the mighty men of the realm waited to welcome them. This ceremony over, they passed through the Hall and the Great Watching Chamber to the Presence Chamber to be congratulated by the foreign ambassadors. Next followed the introduction of the nobility, lords and ladies, who bowed or curtsied as the queen, graciously bowing, continued wearily in her huge bouncing skirt through the state rooms to her own apartments where she could unlose the draw-string and step from out the wire shell, a slim little girl again with stumpy legs.

That night the Duchess of York was rowed in her barge from London to pay her respects to the new queen. This was Anne Hyde, a frog-faced woman whom James had married to the great scandal of the court, for she was a commoner, daughter of his brother's chancellor, and by no means beautiful. James's peculiar taste in women, however, was one of the jests of the time, as de Gramont— or rather, his biographer and brother-in-law, Anthony Hamilton— tells when he pursued the unattractive Mrs. Churchill. The reason for his infatuation was, however, soon revealed for, riding one day, Mrs. Churchill " stagger'd, cry'd out, and fell off her Horse. Her Fall, in so rapid a Motion, could not but be *violent*; and yet it proved *favourable* to her, upon all Accounts; for without receiving the least *Hurt*, she gave the Lye to all the *false guesses* her *Face* had occasion'd, about the rest of her Person. The D[uk]e alighted in order to help her, while she was so stunn'd, that all her Thoughts and Senses were otherwise employ'd than about *Decency*; and therefore they, who first crowded about her, found her in a pretty careless Posture. They could hardly believe their Eyes, or imagine that such beautiful Limbs belonged to Mrs. Ch[urchi]ll's Face."

Perhaps Anne also had some secret beauty, for there seems to have been little on her face, and one may have laughed at this marriage had not Anne been a Roman catholic with all the fury of a convert, for she must share largely in the blame of making James accept her faith and thereby eventually to lose his throne.

She was received this night at the privy garden gate by the river, Charles himself greeting her, for Anne had all an upstart's lust for the externals of rank and was notorious for her ceremonial pageantry. In a huge barge rowed by scarlet-clad watermen she had lain on cushions of royal red and gold until, at the water-steps, Charles took her hand as she alighted and led her through the gardens, sweet in May, to his queen's bedchamber. Curtseying low, Anne offered to kiss Katherine's hand but the queen prevented her, raising her up and kissing her. Then she sat close beside the bed while the royal family drew up their chairs to chatter and get to know one another.

The ceremonies continued. By eleven the next morning, Katherine was up and dressed and ready to receive several ladies. All the day she was meeting people; and the next day the judges arrived with their compliments; while the day after the lord mayor and aldermen of London came: but they brought gifts more acceptable than words—although words went with it: the recorder reading an oration in Spanish—a cup of gold containing £1,000.

Peered at by these curious Englishmen who looked boldly into a woman's eyes and coarsely inspected a woman's figure as though they were about to buy her—for in Portugal women were herded aside in almost oriental fashion—the poor queen bravely went through the ritual of meeting, meeting, meeting people, not even flinching before John Evelyn's critical appraisal or Samuel Pepy's triumphant leer at finding her not the equal of Lady Castlemaine.

Like an auctioneer, Evelyn examined the palace when he finished inspecting the queen. " Hampton Court," he informed his diary, " is as noble and uniform a pile, and as capacious as any Gothic architecture can have made it. There is incomparable furniture in it, especially hangings designed by Raphael, very rich with gold; also many rare pictures, especially the Cæsarean Triumphs of Andrea Mantegna, formerly the Duke of Mantua's [Charles I had bought them]; of the tapestries, I believe the world can show nothing nobler of the kind than the stories of Abraham and Tobit. The gallery of horns is very particular for the vast beams of stags, elks, antelopes, &c. The Queen's bed was an embroidery of silver on crimson velvet, and cost 8000*l*., being a present made by the States of Holland when his Majesty returned, and had formerly been given by them to our King's sister, the Princess of Orange, and, being bought of her again, was now presented to the King. The great looking-glass and toilet, of beaten and massive gold, was given by the Queen-Mother. The Queen brought over with her from Portugal such Indian cabinets as had never been seen here. The great hall is a most magnificent room. The chapel roof excellently fretted and gilt. I was also curious to visit the wardrobe and tents, and other furniture of state."

Being a passionate royalist, if dull diarist, Evelyn inspected everything, including the gardens where, he tells us, " is a rich and noble fountain, with Sirens, statues, &c., cast in copper by Fanelli; but no plenty of water. The cradle walk of horn beam [actually of wych elm] in the garden is, for the perplexed twining of the trees, very observable. There is a parterre which they call Paradise, in which is a pretty banqueting-house set over a cave, or cellar. All these gardens might be exceedingly improved, as being too narrow for such a palace."

That inspired journalist, Tom Brown, was later to translate a description by a French visitor, a far less respectful observer than the flunkey-minded Evelyn. That the palace also impressed Brown himself, despite his mask of rowdy cynicism, we know by his comment in *New Maxims of Conversation* where he takes it as an example of expensive splendour, writing that for a man to promise too much was " as if a gentleman of 200*l*. a year should affect to live in *Hampton-Court*, where the very repairs would exceed the income." The Frenchman's visit, however, to inspect the queen he translates briskly: " We likewise went to see *Hampton-Court*, where the court is at present, and which is the *Fountainbleau* of *England*. We had the honour of seeing their majesties there: The young queen is low, and of a brown complexion; and, by her face, 'tis easy to discover that she has a great deal of goodness and sweetness in her nature. She has brought some four or five *Portuguese* ladies with her, that are the most deform'd, ill-look'd devils, that ever bore the name of women. When a man sees them among the *English* maids of honour that attend her, he would be apt to swear that heaven and hell were jumbled together, and that angels and furies were lately reconcil'd to one another. But this is not all the trumpery which the queen has brought with her out of her own country; for her majesty has a concert, as 'tis call'd, of citterns, harps, and the lord knows what instruments, that make the most wretched harmony that ever was heard. Going to hear mass, we were oblig'd to suffer this vile persecution; and tho' I have none of the nicest ears, I never heard such hideous musick since I was born. As for *Hampton-Court*, 'tis a magnificent pile of building; but, upon my word, comes not up either to our *St. Germain's*, or *Fountainbleau*, no more than *Whitehall* is to be put in the same scale with the *Louvre*, or *St. James's* house with *Luxemburgh* palace."

Pepys also records his arrival, but he came about a fortnight before the king and queen, when, with his wife and friends, he was shown the treasures by the housekeeper, Mr. Marriott. All, he wrote, was "nobly furnished, particularly the Queen's bed, given her by the States of Holland; a looking-glass sent by the Queen-mother from France, hanging in the Queen's chamber, and many brave pictures. So to Mr. Marriott's, and there we rested ourselves and drank. And so to barge again, and there we had good victuals and wine, and were very merry."

For June, 1662, he wrote in his diary: "The King and his new Queen minding their pleasures at Hampton Court. All people discontented . . ."

And so it seemed at first: the king had pleasure in his bride and was merry with her in our palace, being charmed and amused by her simplicity—rare thing for that rake to find an innocent—and he would whisper lewdly in her ear for the delight of watching her blush; but his love was the love for novelty, of having so sweet and unspoiled a thing to fondle; but unfortunately, the love he took so lightly bit deep into Katherine's heart. Soon, as between his mother and father years ago in this same palace, conflict parted them and there were shoutings and tears in the chambers which before had echoed only with their laughter and kisses; but while one sympathises with Charles I faced with a vixen, on this occasion one sympathises with the queen. The trouble, inevitably, was about women—or rather, a woman: the Lady Castlemaine.

She had been determined to be confined at Hampton Court, but that was more than even Charles would tolerate—to have his bastard born in the house in which he was honeymooning—and now she was even more determined to be presented at court and acknowledged openly before the queen as his favourite. Somebody, of course, had tattled to the queen, so that when one morning Charles presented her with a list of his suggested appointments to her household, she accepted them all save the name at the top, that of Barbara Villiers, Countess of Castlemaine. That name she pricked out and, for the first time, Charles realised that Katherine was not a toy but a woman with a woman's pride and jealousy.

To his expostulations she refused to listen, and once again the palace watched a newly married king and queen glare at one another; and although after a day of sulking, Charles pretended to agree with Katherine, he thought to succeed with a sudden blow. When one day she sat in her presence chamber amongst her court, he entered with Castlemaine and presented her. All caught their breath and stiffened while Katherine graciously received the royal mistress and even permitted her to kiss her hand. But one of the Portuguese duennas recognised the haughty woman—or perhaps she knew English which the queen did not—for she whispered to Katherine that there stood her rival. It was a cruel cheat of Charles and it was like a physical blow to his wife that she had not only permitted her enemy to enter her apartments but had allowed her to kiss her hand, after all her husband's lies of reformation. She flushed and bit her lip, trying to restrain her tears, but her shame and fury could not be controlled however stiff she held her body: blood gushed from her nostrils and, almost swooning, she was carried from the room.

Now was Katherine very much alone, save for her farthingaled guard, for naturally the cynical court took Charles's side and she became a jest, an object of scorn, not of pity. And Charles was enraged, insisting that Lady Castlemaine had been insulted and that now the only hope of patching her hopeless reputation was for her to be accepted in the queen's bedchamber, while the queen's retort was to weep and wail and refuse to have the creature near her.

Clarendon attempted nobly to remonstrate with Charles who was usually respectful to this appointed keeper of his conscience and took his lectures with good humour, but now he would not listen. Angrily, he wrote that should he give way the whole country would believe him still in his pupilage and both he and Lady Castlemaine would appear ridiculous. It had grown from a question of morals to one of dignity and self-respect and, being not only king, but a Stuart, Charles was determined that the queen should obey him. He ordered Clarendon to visit her and to force her to accept Castlemaine as one of her ladies, threatening to take from him his seals of office should he not obey. Poor Clarendon, having interfered, had no alternative. He had always been a meddler and now he had meddled himself into an embarrassing position.

He went to Katherine and spoke to her with such surprising tactlessness that she burst into tears and told him, which was true enough, that the fault was not hers, but her husband's. Clarendon backed out, saying he would wait on her again at a more fitting hour, when she might be prepared to listen to humble advice from one who only wished her well. Next day he returned and this time Katherine remained dry-eyed, hurt perhaps to find him whom she had thought her friend ranked with her enemies. She asked him to forgive her recent tears but hoped he would not wonder at them, nor blame her for having greater misfortunes than most women of her condition had to suffer; she could not help giving way to her passion, she said, which was ready to break her heart. Like a true courtier, he answered that his devotion to her was such that he must loyally say what was best for her own sake, although it might neither please her nor make him gracious in her eyes. Of course she assured him that she was only too delighted to learn her faults, and he instantly informed her that she had been badly educated, having been reared in a convent where she could have learned little about the follies and iniquities of mankind; yet the climate of her country, he added, might have given her better examples than colder England, although, he was forced to confess, at the moment it was very hot, being summer. Otherwise, said he, she would not have thought herself so miserable nor her position so insupportable.

Having blamed her ignorance of man's depravity for the poor girl's horror at sharing her husband, he probably rested as satisfied as Lord Jeffries when he had some criminal hooked on a word. In some confusion, blushing and weeping a little, Katherine confessed that she knew such things did exist but that she had scarcely expected to find her husband's affections already engaged to another lady. . . . And there she had to stop, being unable to speak further through her tears, while Clarendon triumphantly informed her that that was proof she had little acquaintance with the world. For, said he, he had not expected her to be so utterly ignorant as to believe that the king, her husband, in the full strength and vigour of his youth, would have reserved himself for her, a woman he had never even seen, and to have had no experience with others of her sex. And did she, he asked, believe that when it pleased God to send a queen to Portugal that that queen would find in the court only chaste affections?

At that reminder of her country, memories made Katherine smile, but she suggested that all this talk was, after all, a little away from the point, which angered the keeper of the king's conscience; he told her that he came with a message from the king which, if she would receive it as she should, and as he hoped she would, ought to make her the happiest queen in the world. She must, said he, forget the past, forget the ladies her husband had loved, for he now dedicated himself wholly to her, without reserve; and if she met his affection with the same warmth and spirit and good humour which she knew well how to express, she would live a life of the greatest imaginable delight.

As this was her whole desire, Katherine begged him to give thanks to his majesty and to implore his pardon for any passion or peevishness of which she had been guilty, while she swore that in future she would be obedient and dutiful. But Clarendon had been concealing a bomb which he now exploded. In return for the king's good resolutions, Katherine must, he said, submit and resign herself to anything his majesty might desire: in other words, she must agree to have Castlemaine one of the ladies of her bedchamber. Too outraged even to weep, save tears of anger, her eyes seeming on fire with fury, Katherine swore that here now was proof that the king must hate her person to desire thus to expose her to the contempt of the world which would believe her deserving of such an affront should she submit to it; and rather than do that, she cried, she would board the first ship and sail direct for Lisbon.

She had not the disposal of her own person, retorted Clarendon coldly: she could not even leave this house, he said, without the king's permission, and therefore he advised her to talk no more of Portugal while there were sufficient people who would like to see her turn her back and go there. And he warned her to be careful to show no such temper to the king. But as she still bravely, stubbornly refused to have her husband's mistress in a place of honour, Clarendon left, after giving her the shrewd advice not to be too outspoken: if she thought proper to deny a thing, said he, do it by evasion but not by refusal, for if she refused the king, she would merely provoke him and would get the worst of it.

Having failed with the queen, Clarendon thought to succeed with the king by repeating, with elaborations, all Katherine's most flattering and dutiful remarks, saying that it was his entire belief that it was only her great love for his majesty that made her disobedient. He suggested that Charles wait and let time do its work. But Charles would not wait. Not only had he Castlemaine nagging at him, but he felt that his dignity was at stake, and he had his father's stubbornness in many things; to give in now, he felt, would betray him to the court as a weakling and therefore he had to have the queen surrender. That night, courtiers smirked while they heard voices shrill with fury echoing from the royal apartments: the king and queen were indulging in a very human marital squabble. Katherine wept and reviled Charles, Charles threatened her and damned her stubborn nature. Through the locked doors and out of the windows, open on the warm night, their voices carried and the gentlemen-in-waiting ceased their cards and dice to listen and wink at one another. She swore that she'd go back to Portugal and he told her she'd better first find out whether her mother wanted her back. He blamed her servants, as his father had blamed his wife's servants: he would, he swore, pack them all back to Portugal; he would give orders for it immediately, since they behaved themselves so ill, their counsel being the cause of all the trouble.

The one consolation, said Clarendon, was that the quarrel was waged in distant Hampton Court and not nearer the city, so that there were fewer witnesses to tattle. But such a scandal could not be concealed while Katherine kept to her apartments, weeping, save when tears were driven off by a paroxysm of fury, and the king made merry in his kingly fashion. He thought next to win her with tenderness and told her that since her coming to England there had been nothing between him and Castlemaine and he swore that there never would be again. But Katherine, stiffened by the encouragement of her ladies, refused to listen, answering him with tears and anger. Charles's pride was hurt; as he said, her foolish extravagancy in talking of going back to Portugal enraged him more than anything.

He ordered the keeper of his conscience to carry on again as himself had failed and poor Clarendon returned to the attack. He talked to Katherine like a lawyer, which is not the way in which to talk to a jealous woman, and he blamed her for her obstinacy, which is no way to talk to any woman. Weeping, she agreed that she had said things for which she was sorry, but her husband had treated her in such an unexpected, so unbelievable a fashion, that she had lost control of herself and she hoped that she would never again be guilty of such display of fury. She prayed God, she said, to give her patience. Clarendon prayed, too; then he argued that as a husband could not impose a servant against whom just exceptions could be made, no wife should refuse a servant commended by her husband. But Katherine shook her head. The king might do what he pleased, said she, but she would never consent to receive Lady Castlemaine as a lady of her bedchamber. Not even Clarendon's flattery could move her from that determination, although he swore that she had too poor an opinion of her own charms to think it could ever be in the power of any lady to rival her.

As she remained firm, Charles abandoned all further negotiations and turned his broad back on Katherine while he played with the ladies in the gardens of Hampton Court; and from her window secretly often must she have watched him, half-blind with tears. With petty spite he sought revenge, insulting the Portuguese ambassador and throwing the Jewish factor, Diego Silvas, into jail because the dowry had not been paid. If he ever met Katherine, it was only to upbraid her about this unpaid dowry or to laugh the louder with his courtiers. Clarendon, who was no fool, saw that through this callousness, Charles stood in danger of losing his people's love, for such a quarrel could not be kept in a palace with hundreds of servants. Naturally, popular opinion was with the queen, but Charles was too hurt and angry to listen, although he confessed he had been foolish not to have followed Clarendon's advice from the beginning. But Katherine's unhidden love, her passionate desire to please him, her apparent foolishness of innocence, had misled him into under-estimating her strength of will and her pride. Now, however, it was too late to turn back time. The quarrel was twisted into a knot, hanging noose of so many marital arguments, which could not be untied, which tautened daily. Neither dared give way to the other lest they surrender their spirit, their ego. Innumerable marriages have been destroyed because of a similar situation, even with people who love each other deeply—perhaps often when they love most deeply—when pride supplants affection and assumes preposterous proportions. And Charles was half in love with Katherine while she adored him; and she suffered more than he, having to keep to her apartments while unable to seek distractions in the way a man could seek them. Her Portuguese followers were taken from her and returned to their country with neither reward nor explanation, and only on her earnest entreaties did Charles permit her to retain her cook and two of the kitchen staff, the priests of her chapel, and one old lady so blind and ill she rarely left her chamber. Katherine was now utterly alone, religion her one refuge in this bawdy court, and her loneliness was stressed by the laughter of Charles with his friends and ladies. When she appeared amongst them, she was ignored and walked like a ghost, seemingly invisible. Even her attendants neglected her.

And she broke beneath the strain and loneliness. Had she held out longer she might have won: so strong was popular feeling on her side that Charles might have been forced to surrender; and by giving in she destroyed all hope of future happiness, for she lost Charles's respect and therefore his love by, on her initiative, speaking to the detested Castlemaine, becoming merry with her in public and, even in private, treating her as a precious friend. Therefore she lost both the people's respect and her husband's admiration of her spirit. Clarendon tells of his own disgust at this sudden downfall from her peak of dignity. This " total abandoning of her own greatness," he wrote, " this low demeanour to a person she had justly abhorred and worthily condemned, made all men conclude that it was a hard matter to know her, and consequently to serve her. And the King himself was so far from being reconciled by it, that the esteem which he could not hitherto but retain in his heart for her grew much less. He concluded that all her former aversion expressed in those lively passions, which seemed not capable of dissimulation, was all fiction, and purely acted to the life by a nature crafy, perverse, and inconsistent."

So blind are even the most intelligent of men at times. Can we blame this girl, fresh from a convent to a marriage-bed, if, having failed to win her husband by remaining firm, she thought she might succeed by obeying him? Unhappy child, her own love destroyed her, weakened and humiliated her; and from now she almost vanishes from the stage when it was realised she could not bear a child. She has no longer importance in this history; yet when in the palace I try to recall those days, it is not the many merry ladies who return to me: it is that pitiful ghost of a girl who loved and, in her ignorance, could not hold her love.

The Queen-Mother, old Henrietta Maria, arrived from Paris and although she saw at once the failure of her son's marriage, boldly she lied: " I have the joy," she said, " of seeing Katherine and the king love each other exceedingly." With tears must she have looked on these brick walls that had watched and heard her own quarrel with her husband, so similiar to Katherine's yet with so different an ending, for her husband had been weak while her son was strong.

At the bottom of the stairs leading to the Great Hall, Charles received her, then led her into the hall where Katherine embraced her. Then in the Presence Chamber the two queens sat side by side, while Charles and James acted as interpreters, for Katherine knew little, if any, English. Later they dined in private together and although king and queen might appear sweet friends, the love was broken between them, at least on Charles's part.

He was always to treat her with respect in later years and he protected her during the Popish Plot mania, but she was only a marionette at his board and was never, or very rarely, in his bed again.

There were ladies enough at Hampton Court and other palaces to take her place, for Charles was not only a king, but a fascinating man. But it would seem that the quarrel with its empty ending wearied him of our palace, for he began to prefer Whitehall near the park where he could play pall mall or wander with his wits and wenches amongst the trees and by the pond. He did not entirely neglect Hampton Court: apartments there were always ready aired for him, open, like his wife, and as rarely visited, while special rooms were prepared for Castlemaine who, naturally, expected all the luxuries she was entitled to as the king's chief mistress.

Yet he would ride over now and then for hunting and hawking, and in the summer of 1662 he was visited by the Earl of Bedford. I mention this visit for the delight of quoting from Miss Thomson's fascinating book about that noble family.* She notes that, although the king's guest, the earl had nevertheless to pay, not only for the

---

* *Life in a Noble Household*, 1641-1700, by Gladys Scott Thomson (Jonathan Cape), 1937. This is an invaluable work for social historians of the period.

Visits to royal palaces were always expensive and it is interesting to compare the above with the account given by the envoy of Duke Frederick of Württemberg and Teck on his visit to Queen Elizabeth in 1595:

" At Hampton Court a gratuity to the usher, 2 crowns.

" In the garden, 7s.

" The gatekeeper, 12 batzen [German coin].

" Slept the night in Oatlands, a hunting-box, in a deer-park and for meals, 14s."

board of his retinue, but for his birds and beasts as well. Here is
his accounting for January, 1669/70:

	£	s.	d.
Two grooms' board wages at Hampton Court for five days	0	15	0
Horses' hay and corn for five nights	2	0	0
For my diet five days at Hampton Court, with other expenses	1	0	0
For the falconers and their two horses for seven days	2	2	0
For carriage of pigeons from London to Hampton Court for the hawks	0	0	8
For hogs' hearts for the hawks	0	0	8

If Charles neglected his palace, foreigners did not, and no visit
to England by anyone of importance passed without Hampton Court
being included in his itinerary; but such reports became monotonous
catalogues of wonder. It is of more interest to learn that on June 29th,
1665, the court fled Whitehall for Hampton Court because of the
democratic plague which snatched its food from high or low, from
young and old, but more from among men than women. Charles
did not cut himself so entirely from the world as did the chatterers
in the *Decameron:* he still carried on with state affairs, and Pepys
drove from the distressed city on Sunday, July 23rd, "to Hampton
Court, where I followed the King to chapel and there heard a good
sermon; and after sermon with my Lord Arlington, Sir Thomas
Ingram, and others, spoke to the Duke about Tangier [there was
continual war with the pirates], but not to much purpose. I was
not invited anywhere to dinner, though a stranger, which did also
trouble me; but yet I must remember it is a Court, and indeed
where most are strangers; but, however, Cutler carried me to
Mr. Marriott's, the housekeeper, and there we had a very good
dinner and good company, amongst others Lilly, the painter."

Peter Lely was the fashionable portrait-painter and his skill had
far advanced since he had painted Charles I in the already mentioned
picture. As de Gramont tells us: "there was in *London* a *Painter*
celebrated for Face-drawing, call'd Sir *Peter Lillie*, who had much
improv'd himself by the great Number of the famous *Vandyke's*
Pictures, dispers'd over all *England;* for Sir *Peter*, of all the Moderns,
imitated the best *Vandyke's* Manner and came up the nearest to him.

The Duchess of Y[or]k being desirous of the Pictures of the most handsom Persons about the Court, *Lillie* drew 'em, and employ'd all his skill in the Performance: Nor could he exert himself upon more beautiful Subjects."

These portraits can be seen to-day in their rightful setting at Hampton Court in the Communication Gallery. Here is a little gallery of what we—or rather, the newspapers—might call the " glamour girls " of the restoration, and they hold themselves with greater dignity than our more wolfish-looking modern wenches with whom, judging by photographs of many " beauties," thin legs and long teeth seem the stamp of perfection. They are plump and languorous-eyed, these painted ladies of Hampton Court, their hair in careful curls, their heavy-lidded eyes lazily, speculatively amorous, while they expose breasts and shoulders with the smug self-satisfaction of tradeswomen with good ware to sell.

Good ware, indeed, they seem, warm from Lely's brush, those dimpled shoulders offered for biting, those solid breasts highlit as though polished. In every age, woman has exaggerated certain portions of her person, what psycho-analysts would call the erogenic zones but which we might name the flesh of our desire, as James Laver has so brilliantly explained in his *Taste and Fashion*. In the fifteenth century, in imitation of the Virgin, the stomach was padded to make even small girls appear enciente; later periods experimented with other areas of female anatomy, even to the posterior in Edwardian times with the bustle, following the crinoline's cult of the ankle, until recently when the leg became the zone in what is probably the ugliest of all cults, the cut-off line of the short skirt bisecting grace. During Charles's reign, shoulders apparently were the Thing: sloping shoulders, their smooth plumpness accentuated by the curls trembling darkly to them, while breasts, too, were exposed. An age of curves it was; one of the most unattractive for men with their steeple hats and those stiff pantaloons cut off below the knees, showing legs seeming sticks, but for women it was very beautiful; and as we look through this little gallery at Hampton Court we can only sigh regret that utilities of modernity, the motor cars, the buses, the active work of women, have lost her the long skirt for ever and seem robbing her of femininity as well.

These restoration ladies in their frames smile rarely; they seem rather to smirk, ogling, haughty, yet promising unlocked bedrooms. There is a birdlike hardness in their eyes which frightens one. Little love, one feels, could have been got from them without cash down, while they hold the draperies to their bosoms and watch us speculatively as though bargaining what we'd pay to have that hand removed that the cloth might fall. Visit this room, I implore you, spend a parthenophagian hour or two in this adorable company, for then you will be transported straight to Charles's days. Lely may not have been a great painter and there is a certain monotony in his treatment, but these women live for us as no collection of photographs of modern screen ladies lives. There is blood here, and expensive flesh, and healthy bodies ripe for all pleasures, whether of eating or drinking, of dancing or love; but never, thank the Lord, of strenuous exercise to turn the contours masculine.

Not all these paintings are by Lely, but his work dominates the others, although, to my thinking, the loveliest of all is by Verelst, that of the lewd Duchess of Portsmouth enticing one with a wreath of bright flowers, but more by the subtle suggestion of her smile, the black curl trembling on her shoulder and the golden knee pressed forward as though asking to be handled, at a price. But it is difficult to choose amongst such loveliness. See the Lady Castlemaine and understand why Pepys was ever pushing for a glimpse of her. A tall woman with reddish hair and blue eyes, a whore from fifteen to fifty, and plainly proud of it: you can read it in her sleepy face as, with a certain disdain, she offers her shoulders for you to admire, the lips almost sneering that we should be such fools to peep like this. There, too, is the adorable Frances Stewart, " the prettiest girl in the world "—and that is Charles's sister speaking—with her little Roman nose, whose beauty with trident and helmet was stamped on the coinage as Britannia; and although she was usually spoken of as foolish, perhaps because she blushed so readily, she was clever enough to evade all Charles's tricks. To-day she stands in Hampton Court before a stormy landscape, her breasts, pushed up by the corsage, welling high, her sleeves drooping to show the exquisite curve of shoulders. In fashionable ringlets falls her hair and her huge eyes are wary, watchful. Lady Falmouth is rosy cheeked, but she, too, was continually blushing, perhaps because of the great revenues she got from the mooring of all vessels and lighters in London Pool or because of the splendid apartments she had at Whitehall—all these Charles gave her for her love.

Here, too, we see the Misses Brookes and dreaming Mrs. Hyde and Belle Hamilton whom Gramont almost forgot to marry. And there is Jane Middleton with fruit and corn in a dish, her right breast, ripest fruit of all, carefully covered to nipple-point. The poet Waller chose her—and who would contest a poet's chart of beauty?—to represent England in his *Triple Combat* when Louise de Querouaille threatened to oust the Duchess of Mazarin from the royal bed. He sang—rather weakly, one must confess:—

> *Her matchless form made all the English glad;*
> *And foreign beauties less assurance had.*

She was one of the beauties of the day and her etched face and body were for sale in every print-shop; a kind of Miss England fighting for the king against those foreign devils.

So many ladies . . . so much loveliness. . . . Even the Duchess of York becomes beautiful here, safe in her frame. And all the others, all lovely and once living. The sneering Countess of Northumberland making stiff suggestive gesture as though to say: Meet me behind the trees and I will toss off my gown; proud Cleveland with the silently screaming Gorgon's head on her shield—symbol of her love's tyranny—while she leers and lures us; the Countess of Rochester, looking slightly drunk as though about to hiccup, yellow-haired, and daring you to slide her blue gown a little lower; fat-shouldered Countess of Sunderland attempting, and succeeding, in looking a whore. . . .

Stay awhile, I say, in this cool chamber in Hampton Court and you will feel these beauties live about you. Indeed, one needs to be but a little drowsy with good wine and you will see these ladies beckon you. There is no surer way, should you desire it, to slip back in time than to visit an art gallery; but galleries are commonly crowded and the mind grows confused with the different styles of painting, but here in this restoration chamber, facing these ladies, one can so easily slip into the painters' mood and live in Charles's days again. The very uniformity of the painting and the poses and costumes, the same uncapped and ringleted heads, the same plump shoulders and rosy breasts, the same tumble of draperies in artful disarray, make them seem sisters in some brothel in Cytherea. It appears true that faces change shape in different periods, both men's and women's, and even if stripped of their costumes one could place many portraits in their rightful age by the expression of eyes and mouth. One has only to glance through a bundle of old theatrical photographs to see how extraordinarily different the women appear from those of our own time, and it is more than the dressing of the hair. Bodies seem to shape themselves according to the owners' desire. These are spiritual sisters in Lely's room—and he did not paint them all—all wanton, all sly, all as calculating as Shylocks for their pounds of flesh; but they are also desirable, and that is much; and it is more than can be said to-day after flipping the pages of a society journal or even a cinema magazine.*

That is my restoration chamber in Hampton Court, more typical than the tennis court that Charles rebuilt—which remains still Tudor—or the trees he planted or the two firebacks of cast-iron showing an oak tree with three branches bearing three crowns with the legend *The Royal Oak* on a scroll about the trunk between the initials *C.R.*

This chapter should close on that room for there is little left to tell of the remainder of Charles II's reign. But we must not forget that Mr. Pepys of the Navy Office took coach to the palace on January 28th, 1666, and that the king greeted him delightedly, saying: " Mr. Pepys, I give you thanks for your good service all this year, and I assure you I am very sensible of it." Evelyn, too, must be recalled, for the day after Pepys he also arrived to see the king, and the king, he tells us, " ran towards me, and in a most gracious manner gave me his hand to kiss, with many thanks for my care and faithfulness in his service in a time of such great danger [the plague], when everybody fled their employments; he told me he was much obliged to me, and said he was several times concerned for me, and the peril I underwent, and did receive my service most acceptably, though in truth I did but do my duty, and O that I had performed it as I ought ! After this his Majesty was pleased to talk with me alone, near an hour, of several particulars of my employment. . . ."

Reading that, it is easily understood why Charles was so loved by those who knew him.

There is perhaps one other detail to recall, that Judge Jeffries at Hampton Court laid before the king and privy council the first hint of the Rye House plot to assassinate both king and Duke of York. It is well that that lean rogue, wriggling on the bench in agony with the stone—which explains if it does not excuse his brutality with witnesses —should be mentioned. He is so very typical of old-time justice— although his ill-fame rests more on his political persecutions in the

---

* For reproductions of the portraits and details of the ladies' histories I warmly recommend James Lavers' *The Ladies of Hampton Court* (Collins), 1942.

next reign than on his ordinary administration of the law—and until almost modern days such as he sent wretched men and women to Tyburn by the dozens. In our peaceful Hampton Court, this country refuge, we too easily forget the unhappiness there was in those good old times.

But we will turn from the tarred corpses to look once more into that room of beauty's daughters. It were best to close this reign on that gallery, so typical of this era at Hampton Court when, never before or since, have these halls and chambers known such massed loveliness, heard such laughter, such wit, such wicked whisperings. . ·. . Gay ghosts beside the darker ghosts of Tudor times: can they mingle in the palace, laughing easy women with poor Kate Howard and tragic Anne Boleyn and sad Queen Mary and the bold dignity of Queen Elizabeth ? Can one see those two giants, Henry VIII and Charles II, blinking at one another when they meet, Charles with his courtesy and sharp wit, Henry with his arrogance and bull's rage ? . . . That would prove a battlefield from which we little creatures must run, run quickly to the protection of the ladies in Lely's room, although, most plainly, they would scorn us for it.

CHAPTER XI
KING WILLIAM III AND QUEEN MARY II

WITH Hampton Court, James II has practically no associations, save for a fireback with the royal initials and the date 1687 and the exhibition in the palace of the canopy under which, to the rage of his subjects, he received the papal nuncio. In nearby Bushey Park his army was encamped, but he dared not use it when the threat of rebellion sent him scurrying abroad. Therefore can we turn the page on his reign to meet his daughter, Queen Mary II, and her Dutch husband, King William III—for he insisted on his own crowning, sensibly refusing to be merely a consort.

These two names are weighty ones in our history and we who love the Tudor world had well bring out our handkerchiefs when we see the destruction they wrought so that they might raise a Versailles or a Fontainebleau in England. Luckily for us, William died before all the rich Tudor could vanish in dust and, although much that he and Mary built is beautiful, it is not to my taste as is the intimate beauty of Wolsey's and Henry's foundations.

Like any good housewife, soon after her arrival, Mary explored her future homes and she and William took, alas, particular interest in Hampton Court and were often there, Mary walking five or six miles a day to gloat over her possessions. Every room was examined by her, the beds were prodded and shaken, and she slept all night where her stepmother had slept. The Duchess of Marlborough who followed, puffing, in her wake, records that she even turned over the quilts on every bed, as people do on visiting an inn.

The nearby country was to William reminiscent of his beloved Holland, so they decided to make our palace their more or less permanent residence; and thereupon, paid vandals spat on their hands as with picks and axes they charged the Tudor bricks with their autumnal colouring, their homely patina, to uprear bloodless bricks and stone in their place. Down go the queen's apartments, the rooms in which so many queens had lived and where Kate Howard had babbled to Cranmer; down they go in dust, crumbling and breaking; and the dust is musty like history, like the dead brought from the walls they had loved; down go the bricks and down go the ghosts; spirits of Wolsey and Henry and Mary and Elizabeth crumbled to reddish grains as the iron-studded boots of workmen trample them to powder. All the east side has fallen; here had stood those galleries with coloured glass in jalousied windows, such as the one in which Elizabeth had played the virginal and coquetted with Melville over Leicester's portrait. The royal nursery where Edward VI had played and where the cradle had stood empty for Mary's baby: that is no more; no more the cardinal's apartments, save for a few chambers to the south; no more so much beauty, so much history . . . for what cared William and Mary for England's history?—he a Dutchman and she a muddle of races with one thin strand of royal England in her bones from the grandmother of James I.

Great Sir Christopher Wren was given the task of building the new palace, and if it had to be done—against which I violently protest —no better man could have been found; but unfortunately, William was one of those fussy fellows who must tell artists how to paint, writers how to write, and architects how to build. That Sir Christopher succeeded so brilliantly as he did in reconciling turreted Tudor with debased renascence remains almost a miracle; and perhaps we should be grateful that his original plans, which mightily pleased the queen, were discarded. Had they been accepted, probably no Tudor whatsoever would have been left and I, at least, would have lost one of my deepest happinesses—to wander about the old palace and seek new angles from which to view it. I can but mope to think that William's first idea of building an entirely new home about half a mile from the river at the west end of Hampton village had not been carried out, for he was warned that the building would take too long; and the selfish rascal thinking, not of us, the future, wanted a place to live in. So he tore down and rebuilt, the devil clutch him.

In this feeling I am probably in a minority, for it seems the fashion to-day to prefer Wren and Vanbrugh and English baroque above earlier styles; but others, too, have protested. Horace Walpole, for example, when answering Wren's grandson on August 9th, 1764, wrote: " I will not defend myself on the distinction I might fairly make, that Sir Christopher Wren was a genius in some respects and wanted taste in others, which yet I presume is all I have said in effect; but it seems to me as if there was a sobriety in taste which would be a shackle on genius. That there has been now and then a genius (for genius itself is a curiosity) without taste, and often taste without genius, is evident from example. One of the greatest geniuses that ever existed, Shakespeare, undoubtedly wanted taste. In the very class which is the subject of this letter—I mean architecture—Inigo Jones seems to me to have had more taste than genius. Genius is original, invents, and taste selects, perhaps copies, with judgement. If I am right, have I wronged your ancestor? You impute to King William, Sir, the want of taste in Hampton Court— you therefore allow there was want of taste. Was I to blame when observing that want of taste? I imputed it to the architect. . . . The truth is the fault was the age, and to that I have already imputed it, not to your grandfather."

This same argument we find repeated as late as 1899 by W. H. Pyne in his beautifully produced *History of the Royal Residences;* when writing of Hampton Court he states: " It is painful to detract the merits of a great and good man: but the two illustrious architects, Inigo Jones and Sir Christopher Wren, with all their knowledge, entertained unjust prejudices against the Gothic style; and those structures which they were employed to design in the Gothic, are evidences of their want of knowledge of its general character, and of their entire ignorance of the lightness and beauty of its parts."

Queen Elizabeth's
Building.

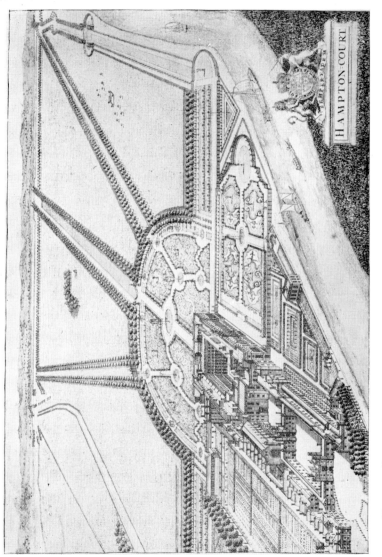

Hampton Court as finished by William III. From Kip's *Nouveau Théâtre de la Grande Brétagne*
Courtesy of the British Museum

"Lightness and beauty" appear to me the sum of the matter, for Wren's façades seem heavy beside the Tudor, seem sunk to the earth, they lack the airy delicacy of Henry's bricks. If you want dignity, spaciousness, cold impersonality, go to the Wren portion and you will see the palace of an age when monarchs were withdrawn from the people and built themselves homes to house heartless gods; but turn to the Tudor if you would reach an age when kings, although divine, were yet able to meet their councillors as human beings, able to laugh and drink with them, and to curse them and kill them if they wished.

While the terrible destruction continued, this murder of beauty, this smashing of bricks that never could be baked again, William and Mary resided in the, as yet, unharmed portions of the palace, and to them came Mary's sister, Anne. There had been some rather disgusting public arguments about Anne's allowance. William had suggested that he support her out of his revenues, but the tories—the whigs were his supporters—insisted that she have a separate allowance. There followed almost an auctioneering act between the tories and William, so suspiciously eager was he to handle Anne's money; but Anne was determined that the tories should win, as they did. She got her separate allowance and this may explain William's peculiar attitude towards her. But he was indeed, a very peculiar and haughty man with little time for women, preferring men's love—if we may believe Bishop Burnet, who knew him—and his silent morose habits must often have been very distressing to Anne.

The Duchess of Marlborough, that frightening lady who said what she thought to many people's discomfort, became furious at his callous treatment of Anne. She could, she wrote, fill many sheets with records of his brutalities to his sister-in-law, for he was no gentleman and was ill-mannered. "I give an instance," she wrote, "of his worse than vulgar behaviour at his own table, when the Princess dined with him. It was in the beginning of his reign, and some weeks before the Princess was put to bed of the Duke of Gloucester. There happened to be just before her a plate of green peas, the first that had been seen that year. The king, without offering the Princess the least share of them, drew the plate before him and devoured them all. Whether he offered any to the Queen I cannot say, but he might have done that safely enough, for he knew she durst not touch one. The Princess Anne confessed, when she came home, that she had so much mind for the peas that she was afraid to look at them, and yet could hardly keep her eyes off them."

In the already often mentioned book of household ordinances, we have details of William and Mary's meals which usually comprised ten dishes for dinner and eight for supper. Here is the dinner:—

> Pottage of Capons i, or Pulletts ii, or Chickens
>   iiii, or Partridges iii.
> or Beef boiled 24lb.
> Mutton rosted,
> Turky or Goose large, or Capons fatt ii.
> Chickens fatt vi. or
> Pigeons tame, viii. or
> Pheasants ii. or Partridges vi. or
> Cocks vi, or Quails viii, or
> Buck baked quarter or Hen Pye,
> Tarts of Sorts,

with for dessert:

> Morelles [an edible fungus], or Trouffles,
> Jelly, or
> Asparagus.

And here is the supper:—

> Pidgeons tame iiii., or
> Mutton roast or Veale,
> Capons fatt ii. or Pullets gra' iii. or
> Plovers viii. or Snites viii. or
> Pidgeons field xii. or Larks ii. doz.
> Runners vi. or Ducklings vi.
> Lamb quar' or
> Tarts of Sorts,

and dessert:

> Ragou of Sweet Bread, or
> Pistachio Cream, or
> Hartichokes, or Pease.

Even with guests, surely sufficient, one might think, for William not to steal all the peas?

This royal passion for Hampton Court was strongly objected to, for it kept both king and queen from London and not only did tradesmen suffer by the loss of custom, but affairs of state could not be quickly sealed. Bishop Burnet, although a whig and therefore pro-William, sadly records that " the King, a very few days after he was set on the throne, went out to Hampton Court, and from that palace came into town only on council days: so that the face of a court and the rendezvous, usual in the public rooms, was now quite broken. This gave an early and general disgust. The gaiety and diversions of a court disappeared."

When pressed to leave the palace, William would cry: " Do you wish to see me dead ? " for he had suffered much while resident at Whitehall. The river fogs, the stink of smoke from sea-coal fires, the rotting refuse in the streets with muck that flowed into the palace courts, had combined to make him persistently ill; for apart from weak lungs, he was one of those unfortunates hypersensitive to smells; and that was no age for people with sensitive nostrils when they shaved their heads and wore wigs to keep off lice. Those good old days in London were too much for asthmatic William after the cleanliness of Holland; for then, even in Versailles, gentlemen used any corner of the palace as a lavatory, and one may be certain the English were no more sanitary than the French in this respect.

The stinks of London and Westminster were such that they knocked poor William into bed, and his physicians decided that he could not live for a year; so ghastly yellow had become his countenance that one could barely recognise him. He was, wrote Evelyn, slothful and sickly; but the " slothful " was a tory lie, for William was a man who loved exercise and business. He was merely sick, which Evelyn, inured to these plague-stricken surroundings, could not understand; and perhaps William's taciturnity, combined with his ignorance of English—he was no expert linguist—brought on him the contempt of these insular folk. But he made no attempt to be pleasant to his new subjects, never visiting the theatre, and would remain in long silences, brooding, while men talked to him, and they could not help comparing his dull court disparagingly to Charles's, or even to James's. Particularly did women dislike him, for there were no longer amorous games at Hampton Court with a king on the throne who scorned their sex and who treated his wife like a negligent servant. Yet William, behind his mask, was very fond of Mary and his sorrow at her death seems almost excessive, but such was the mould of his humour that he could not be polite even to those for whom he cared. Mary made up for his unpopularity, for although as moral-minded as he, refusing even to listen to gossip, she was gentle and generous, and even the Stuart pamphleteers and versifiers could find no dirt to throw at her.

William rejected the pageantry of kingship, such as the laying on of hands to cure scrofula, which he called a silly superstition—as Dr. Johnson's experience proved it to be, if proof be needed—and he gave the sufferers money instead of his touch. Also he kept his hat on in church, such being the Dutch custom, and it maddened English divines who recalled the insolent quakers who kept on their hats, not only in church, but even in the law courts. William, however, was a humourless man reared in the more democratic atmosphere of Holland, and with his landing, all the outward splendours of Stuart days were gone.

At the first sight of its lovely brick, he itched to pull down Hampton Court. Work was begun almost immediately and the dust and dirt so swept into the palace that there was talk of a temporary move to Windsor, and he did for the winter of 1689 lodge in Holland House. Shortly after his going, a part of a newly erected wall fell down—was pushed down perhaps by some outraged ghost—and the palace took its revenge by killing three or four workmen and injuring others, as though demanding foundation sacrifices for the new building.

There was an immediate inquiry and Wren appeared before the lords of the treasury on December 19th, 1690, for a brisk exchange of insults between himself and Mr. William Talman, comptroller of the works. A certain Mr. Latham, whose opinion was strongly against him, Wren denounced as a madman and he swore that his own work was sound, for it had withstood the hurricane of January 11th. Mr. Talman retorted that " my lord Chamberlain's lodgings kept the wind absolutely from his building, and that Mr. Latham is not madd." Then a member of the board of works said that there were twenty-four piers near the garden and that only four of the stones were cracked, and those cracks were no bigger than a hair's breadth: indeed, said this sensible gentleman—whose verdict has since proved correct— every day the building stands it grows stronger and lighter. " Not at all," retorted the obdurate Mr. Talman, " every pier is crackt, that one may put his finger in." Another interjected that none of Mr. Talman's masons were capable of understanding such good work as this, whereupon Mr. Talman pointed out that the three masons he had used were all in Sir Christopher's employ. " The piers are all crackt," he insisted, " and hollow, and crampt with iron to keep them together. " What was done for greater caution," said Sir Christopher,

" should not be maliciously misinterpreted." Weary of the argument, seeing that he was getting the worst of it, Talman suggested that a committee be chosen; " let 6 be chosen by mee," he said, " and 6 by you " to decide the truth. Quite rightly, however, the lords refused, pointing out that such a jury would never agree. Then cried Sir Christopher: " I'le putt it on this, a man cannot putt his finger in ye cracks." " No," retorted Talman, " because you've had them stopt."

But Wren was in the right. Unbiased umpires were sent to view the building and it was then ordered that he carry on with all despatch. He could not use despatch enough to satisfy the king and queen who watched impatiently the new walls rise and the old and beautiful walls tumble down in billows of expiring mortar. They decided to live meanwhile in the Water Gallery, that in which Elizabeth had been lodged while under Mary's displeasure: it stood beside the landing-place and was detached from the palace. Decorators and furnishers soon turned it, in Defoe's words, into " the pleasantest little Thing within Doors that could possibly be made." Sir Christopher super-vised the decorations and he had the ceiling painted while he called on that genius, Grinling Gibbons, to carve the woodwork.

Mary stuffed all with fashionable bric-à-brac. This was the beginning of the bric-à-brac craze for cabinets holding china and porcelain, not for use, but as decorations. There was a special " Delft-ware Closett " made at Hampton Court for Mary's pretty pieces; and amongst other named rooms we find a " Bathing-Room " where, again Defoe tells us in his *Tour through Great Britain*, there was a white marble bath " made very fine, suited either to hot or cold Bathing as the Season should invite; also a Dairy, with all its Con-veniences, in which her Majesty took great Delight," for she was a homely creature with none of the Stuart regal vanities. " In all those hours," wrote Bishop Burnet, " that were not given to better employ-ment, she wrought with her own hands; and sometimes with so con-stant a diligence, as if she had been to earn her bread by it. It was a new thing, and looked like a sight, to see a Queen work so many hours a day." It was, indeed, a new thing for royalty to behave like common folk, and, in particular, for a Stuart to declare that she " could live in a dairy."

Nor did Mary neglect art. Sir Godfrey Kneller was commissioned to out-paint that chamber of Charles's wantons by producing what Defoe called her " Gallery of Beauties, being the Pictures, at full

Length, of the principal Ladies attending upon her Majesty, or who were frequently in her Retinue; and this was the more beautiful sight, because the Originals were all in Being, and often to be compar'd with their pictures." Not unfavourably, we hope: for this gallery in no possible way equals, for all its size in frames, the beauties whom the Duchess of York had gathered at Charles's court, but Kneller had not the flourishing brush of Lely nor his joy in feminine flesh. " Of the Beauties of Hampton Court," Horace Walpole wrote in his *Anecdotes of Painting*, " the thought was the Queen's during one of the King's absences; and contributed much to render her unpopular, as I have heard from the authority of the Duchess of Carlisle, who remembered the event. She added, that the famous Lady Dorchester advised the Queen against it, saying: ' Madame, if the King was to ask for the portraits of all the wits in his court, would not the rest think he called them fools '? "

Mary, however, refused to be put off her fancy and you can see the result to-day in the Queen's Presence Chamber. Originally there were twelve but four of the paintings have vanished; those remaining are of little value and one senses Sir Godfrey's lack of interest in the commission. They are all full-length figures against conventional landscapes with pillars and balustrades and the ladies stand in strained poses, staring boredly at you, although they do not wear the fashionable head-dress of the day, but are bareheaded. There is a heaviness in this large and lovely room, a brooding boredom as though the sitters had been reluctant to stand, and none of the ladies has that vital lure of Charles's women.

There peers the Countess of Essex, childlike and petulant yet, strangely, with a wistful air, a kind of eagerness to please, as though she wished she were only in Lely's chamber and Charles's arms. Then the Countess of Dorset, a dark hoyden trying hard to appear demure for Mary's sake: with hardness in her eyes, she almost seems prepared to drop her ermine-hemmed blue mantle if only Mary were not by. Haughtily, the dark Duchess of Grafton screens herself behind the varnish; pretty Miss Pett, wetting her fingers at a fountain, seems about to cry; while the sad-eyed and lovely Duchess of St. Albans looks as though she were eager to rid herself of ceremonial garments that she might romp with other little girls. Imprisoned there, all appear clamped in their clothes, bored with the court and envious of freer ladies.

This is no gallery in which to linger and it reveals how swiftly a period can stamp those living in it with its personality, for, after all, Charles was but recently dead and these ladies in their hearts could not have been so different from those who had rolled lewd eyes at the tall king. Had William been another Charles they, too, would have leered and frolicked; but William cared not for women and his wife was a placid if talkative matron: therefore the ladies reflected their surroundings and became mere spectres of the queen.

Gardening was another of Mary's passions and she sent experts as far as Virginia to gather plants for her Hampton Court ; and, of course, in honour of her husband, she planted orange trees, some brought from Holland, that William might feel at home. On the south front still stands this Orangery with its tall doors. One hundred and fifty feet long, with oak panelled walls, it contained during the winter months the orange trees in tubs, to be moved, when the sun returned, on to the terrace. The British Museum possesses three catalogues of Mary's botanical collections and a description of the stoves for the hothouse.

Ever busy about her new home, in *Parentalia* Wren's son remarks that she " pleased herself from time to time in examining and sur- veying the Drawings, Contrivances, and whole Progress of the *Works*, and to give thereon her own Judgment, which was exquisite; for there were few Arts, or Sciences, in which *her Majesty* had not only an elegant Taste but a Knowledge much superior to any of her Sex, in that, or (it may be) any former Age. This is not said as a Panegyrick, but a plain and well-known Truth, which *the Surveyor* had frequent experience of, when (by that Favour and Esteem *the Queen* was graciously pleased publickly to shew him, upon a Discernment and Trial of his Worth) he had many Opportunities of a free Conversation with *her Majesty*, not only on the subject of Architecture, but other Branches of Mathematicks, and *useful Learning*." Wren, indeed, was a skilful courtier.

It is not, however, my intention to enumerate all the architectural works of Wren, the decorations of Gibbons, or the gardens of Mary. Full details of these will be found in Mr. Law's great work and the guidebook tells excellently whatever a visitor might wish to know. Besides, it is truly painful to me to recall the loss of the Tudor palace; and we will speak no further of it here but will, briefly, later note many of the alterations. That such an opinion is in ill-accord with the opinion of William and Mary's time, I know full well, and also perhaps in the opinion of many to-day who, in natural revulsion from the modern architectural box, recoil with passion to the baroque. For those who love this French renascence style, let them listen to the enthusiasm of Defoe, for I would rather repeat his description than write my own.

" When *Hampton Court*," he wrote, " will find such another favourable Juncture as in King *William's* Time, when the remainder of her Ashes shall be swept away, and her compleat Fabric, as designed by King *William*, shall be finish'd, I cannot tell; but if ever that shall be, I know no Palace in *Europe*, *Versailles* excepted, which can come up to her, either for Beauty or Magnificence, or for Extent of Building, and the Ornaments attending it."

Nor will we trouble yet with the interior decorations and will mention Verrio's fuzzy paintings—recently and beautifully cleaned —only to recall Pope's lines:

> *On painted ceilings you devoutly stare,*
> *Where sprawl the saints of Verrio and Laguerre.*

You can crick your neck if such be you inclinations; I prefer to bow my head, and not in reverence. You can lose yourself in William's maze, the walks of which extend to nearly half a mile in area, and I'll not go seek you.

Let us turn back a few pages to when Princess Anne saw to her anguish the peas vanish into William's mouth.

As already remarked, she was no popular guest in Hampton Court since she insisted on having her own allowance instead of existing on William's doubtful bounty. Yet it was here, at four o'clock in the morning of July 24th, 1689, that she was brought to bed of a son who, like all her many births, was not to live. Mary forgot the family squabble in her care for her sister in her three hours' labour. Bells rang and bonfires were lit at the arrival at last, it seemed, of a protestant heir, and whatever his private opinion of Anne, William stood sponsor when the baby was baptised in the rebuilt Chapel and created him Duke of Gloucester, a name considered of ill omen. The child was very sickly and a succession of wet-nurses came to feed him, but either he was particularly greedy or they over-estimated their maternal glands, for there were many changes before a Mrs. Wanley got the job. Mary behaved like a loving sister, for as she wrote to a friend, " with my sister's confinement taking place, I have had a great deal to do—the first fortnight being constantly in her room or in the child's or surrounded by people who came on this occasion, so that you must rather blame me than any lack of news."

But for all Mary's care, for all the milk of all the wet-nurses—at five guineas a time—brought from towns and villages, little William showed small hope of survival until " Mrs Pack, the wife of a Quaker, came from Kingston Wick, with a young child in her arms of a month old, to speak of a remedy which had restored her children. As she sat in the Presence Room, Prince George of Denmark [the father] happened to pass by, and observing her to be a strong, healthy woman, he ordered her to go to the young Prince, who soon suckled her, and mended that night, continuing well while she suckled him."

Anne, having had enough of her brother-in-law—she called him Mr. Caliban—as soon as she was strong enough, packed and left Hampton Court for Kensington.

The royal couple did little entertaining but lived quietly while the people protested that they were never seen and that they kept too far out of affairs in their country home; for what use is it to pay vast sums to a couple who do not do their duty and expose themselves to insults or to cheers, according to the mood of the mob ?

All the while there was demolition and building going on at Hampton Court, all the while that voluptuous brick was being dragged down. There is a curious vicious pleasure in destruction, as I realise, having worked at demolition during the recent war. But my delight in dragging down walls papered with roses and parrots in choking dust-storms was explicable, for the buildings were mainly slums and, save for the loss of life, one would often have been grateful to the Germans. Thank the Lord I never had to destroy anything beautiful, yet I can understand the zest of dragging houses over, the exultation when the wall sways to the tug of the ropes, sways and jerks and thunders down in a blinding swirl of filthy-tasting mortar and dirt. But these workmen now hacking at Wolsey's home might well have shuddered to see Wren's cold façade rise from the ashes of a once Tudor phœnix.

Mary died of smallpox in Kensington Palace before she could live in her new apartments at Hampton Court and, for a time, work ceased. There was hope that the remainder of the old manor might remain, when unluckily Whitehall was burnt down. This was a tragedy difficult to appreciate to-day, for the treasures of that palace are forgotten, the Holbein frescoes and Wolsey's chapel, and it is remembered mainly because Charles I stepped from it to the scaffold. With Whitehall gone, William was more or less forced to return to Hampton Court with its memories of Mary, of her plans, her gardens.

Work began again. Wren and Gibbons got busy, and at least we should be grateful that lesser men were not posted to the spoiling. We have lost much, indeed, but we have gained those exquisite carvings in limewood, the lovely mantelpiece of musical instruments with musical score, and the wooden garlands, and fruit and flowers and game in the King's State Apartments. For these we can almost forgive Verrio's paintings which are so rigidly conventional that Horace Walpole thought he must have spoiled those on the walls and ceilings of the King's Great Staircase of deliberate purpose,* although Evelyn gaped at them in wonder, thinking the design, colouring and " exuberance " equal to the greatest old master or— please note—anything in France. For that was the key continually struck. France. Versailles. England must out-build, out-paint, out-decorate, out-garden France, and the only way the artists could think of doing it was by imitation and by destroying old and lovely English things.

See these Verrio paintings around the King's Staircase, the muddle of formless gods and goddesses, bad Rubens, heroes of ancient Rome, all in flat bright colours, depthless, dead. Charles II brought this artist to England: why I cannot tell. But on this staircase there is a work of intricate loveliness, the iron balustrade designed by that French genius, Jean Tijou, whom we have also to thank for those noble iron gates, over ten feet high, beside the Barge Walk near the river, which had been designed for the Great Fountain Court. Here is iron that seems as soft as feathers, beautifully wrought into beautiful designs, a dark tracery through which to watch the Thames flow by as through a magic screen. The Lion Gates, opening

---

* Walpole suggests that, being a cavalier at heart, Verrio "spoiled his work on principle," but this seems rather far-fetched, although apparently he accepted the commission with reluctance. Walpole also, in his *Anecdotes of Painting*, gives an amusing picture of Verrio coming to Hampton Court for money, having spent the advance of £1,000 Charles II had given him. Finding it impossible to approach the king, he shouted, " Sire, I desire the favour of speaking to your Majesty." " Well, Verrio," said the king, " what is your request ? " " Money, Sir, money," replied the artist; " I am so short of cash, that I am not able to pay my workmen; and your Majesty and I have learnt by experience, that pedlars and painters cannot give long credit." Smiling, Charles reminded him that he had recently been given £1,000. " Yes, Sir," said he, " but that was soon paid away, and I have no gold left." " At that rate," said Charles, " you would spend more than I do to maintain my family." " True," said Verrio, " but does your Majesty keep an open table as I do? "

on to the Wilderness, are also his work, but they seem dwarfed by the huge stone piers on either side.*

The Lion Gates.

But Verrio is a different matter with his splodges of colour shaped to figures. In the Queen's Drawing Room, in the east range, we find on the ceiling Queen Anne—for we leap here a little ahead of time—as Justice, while on the wall facing the windows she smugly

* These railings of twelve elaborately foliated panels, no two alike, are, I am pleased to say, kept in excellent repair. For years they were in exile, in museums, hidden in store-rooms, but now they are in place again. They suffered from their exile, being crudely repaired with copper and rusted in places, but Mr. T. M. J. Minns, head blacksmith—or rather, art-metal smith—at Hampton Court has been working on them since 1937, save during the war when he was at the London Docks, and is bringing them back to their original perfection. As it takes about two days to make one small leaf, we can have some idea of the length of the task, for there are some six hundred leafs in Tijou's work, not to speak of acorns and nuts and oak-apples and Scotland's thistle, Ireland's harp, the Order of the Garter, and all the other exquisitely hammered details.

receives homage from the four quarters of the globe; on the north wall, Danish George, Lord High Admiral of England, points to the fleet; and on the south wall the British fleet rides at anchor while, drawn by sea-horses, Cupid sails over the waves. . . . For these vast pink figures, these empty coloured spaces, must the Tudor bricks tumble down?

While detesting the destruction, we can at least accept with pleasure the faded furniture that remains: William's tall four-poster—a bed for a ghost, with its dusty plumes and crimson velvet hangings—and the other beds and knick-knacks, while it is interesting here to note how royal apartments were then arranged. The king's side faces south on to the Privy Garden while the Queen's faces east on to the Great Fountain Court. Facing inwards, parallel to these chambers, are the communicating galleries and the private apartments where royalty could escape the continual ceremonial, could throw off the god-like masks and snort and loll and drink and spit and do things human again. A state staircase leads up to each set of apartments and smaller staircases lead to other rooms and different floors. By one direction you approached the king's apartments, by another the queen's, entering hers from behind the Chair of State under its embroidered canopy. To visit the king you walked up the staircase surrounded by Verrio's gods and goddess, holding, if you wished, Tijou's delicate iron balustrade, and then entered the Guard Room where the guard would be standing, watching, around the walls on which the three thousand pieces of arms, arranged in sprays, in circles, in formal designs are yet to be seen, placed there by Williams' gunsmith, a man named Harris. Passing the yeoman of the guard, you would enter the large doorway on your left to the First Presence Chamber.

Before, however, visiting William, let us linger in this vasty room, for on our right is a little doorway, and this opens on to one of the few remaining Wolsey's chambers. It is well to enter its cosy quiet, to look at the arched fireplace and see the linenfold panelling of the walls, for we are back in that vital dangerous Tudor world. Luckily, this room has been saved and here we can breathe again, out of the lofty blankness of the Guard Room with its glittering metal. Here we are home, when we turn our backs on that unforgivable eighteenth century partition which cuts the chamber into two tiny rooms. Beyond is a second chamber with fine panelling and a carved ceiling of Wolsey's date. We are fortunate to have even this little left, but

The Guard Room from Pyne's *History of the Royal Residences*
Courtesy of the British Museum

in the eighteenth century sash windows were actually inserted and when recently the plaster was scraped off, merely a part of Wolsey's ceiling showing Wolsey's badges was recovered. But that is something for we can feel here again the intimate warm Tudor world before we return to the slippery ceremony of William's day when kings thought heighth and breadth of rooms gave majesty, not trusting to themselves, it seems, to awe their courtiers.

Sighing, we return to the Guard Room and enter the First Presence Chamber with the Gibbons' carvings of fruit and flowers. Facing you as you entered would have stood the chair of state ; next comes the Second Presence Chamber, a little smaller, then the Audience Chamber from the windows of which we can see the Privy Garden. For the decorations of these rooms we must forget the paintings now hanging there. When the king was in residence, tapestries would have been hooked against the walls, and for that reason I make no mention of what hangs there to-day. The King's Drawing Room follows, with its Gibbons' cherub-heads; then the King's State Bedroom, followed by the King's Dressing-room or Little Bedroom with Verrio's ceiling of Mars on the lap of Venus, singularly inappropriate when we remember the kings and queens who have slept under it. From this opens the Writing Closet. These were the private rooms into which royalty could escape while courtiers crowded the rooms through which we have passed almost to the bedroom door. Out of the Writing Closet, should the king wish to avoid his followers, there runs a private staircase to the ground floor and the garden.

It is really here that William's building ends, for Mary's death put an end to finishing her apartments, but it would be as well to continue rather than to connect the different rooms in the succeeding reign. Eighty feet long stretches the Queen's Gallery with its Gibbons' cornice and John Nost's marble chimneypiece, exquisitely carved. Then comes the Queen's Bedroom—for her apartments stretch from the king's, meeting here, so that bedrooms at least should not be far apart—decorated in the next reign by Sir John Thornhill with a ceiling of Aurora rising in her chariot out of the sea with Night and Sleep below her; and this, although disappointing, is certainly finer work than Verrio's. The Queen's Drawing Room follows with the Queen by Verrio as Justice on the ceiling, of which we have already spoken. This opens on to her Audience Chamber used mainly by the early Georges for state receptions and it has in one corner a door which leads to a private staircase down to the rooms facing the

Fountain Court. Next we reach the Public Dining Room—so-called in the days of George II—with William Kent's decorations, while to the north stands the suite given to Frederick, Prince of Wales, of which we will have much to say later.

This inspection is hurried because I wish you to visit these rooms yourselves and should I describe them in detail this book would become merely a catalogue. So let us continue from the Public Dining Room, through a small lobby to the Queen's Presence Chamber and Guard Chamber, which would be for the queen what the Guard Room was to the king, where her courtiers waited to be summoned to the presence. The Queen's Bathing Closet follows with its tall arched marble bath still remaining in the wall. Most uncomfortable it must have been to wash there, impossible to bathe in; but, after all, one

washed so rarely in those days when rice powder was plentiful and wigs were on your head. Next the Private Dining Room and the Little Closet opening on to the Queen's Private Chamber or dressing-room with a second bath.

These were the chambers designed for William and Mary and used by Anne and the Georges. They seem to us to lack privacy, being a series of boxes running one into another, but that is because we are not kings and queens. They had little privacy. They shut themselves in the centre of outer-rooms, like queen bees, and remained there, prisoners of ceremony. That they did not resent this public life is proved by the tenacity with which they clung to their thrones and, when pushed off them, intrigued and battled to regain them. But even for little people there was small privacy in those times with multitudes of servants, while the poor lived dozens in a room in tenements. When they wished it, the king and queen could at least retire to the centre of their honeycomb and take off their wigs and know the pleasure of keeping others waiting while they dozed. And truly when I see these lofty beds I envy them. They look so comfortable and, with the curtains shut, would be so cosy, rooms within a room.

Amidst the continual rebuilding, William, after Mary's death, lived quietly at Hampton Court. There is little worthy of record in a social history such as this, for council meetings are for constitutional histories, but we might mention that William was initiated by Wren into the mysteries of freemasonry and that he often presided over a lodge in the palace; that in the parks he hunted; and that in the palace he met ambassadors, while in the chapel he held a chapter of the knights of the garter during which he infuriated the nobility and lost many friends by bestowing the garter on his favourite, the Earl of Pembroke.

Even Hampton Court, however, with its lawns and parks and avenues and flower beds was to William no substitute for Holland. He was ever pining to go home and, it would seem, the only way his subjects could keep him in England was by crippling and practically murdering him with medicines, so that he was never well enough to travel. At least, that is the impression one receives from reading the terrifying accounts of his treatment, for medicine in this period was probably at its lowest ebb, even the knowledge of the middle ages of valuable herbs being rejected and left to wise women often to be burnt for their skill as witches. Luckily, the doctors usually quarrelled so much amongst themselves that one's main hope of survival was to call in as many as possible so that in their wrangling, their countermanding one another's remedies, one might recover by nature's help alone. Three of the most pompous medical muddleheads of the time, Sir Thomas Millington, Dr. Radcliffe, and Dr. Lawrence, came to argue over William's body.

Radcliffe and Millington fought a brave battle in Latinity. Radcliffe said that the royal swollen legs were the result of dropsy and prescribed purging and asses' milk, while Millington argued that such remedies were contrary to the royal constitution and he prescribed garlic. " That," sneered Radcliffe, " will destroy such weak lungs as the king's." " Weak lungs ! " cried Millington, "why his lungs are the soundest part about him ! " Next they quarrelled over the king's projected journey, whether the sea would be good for him or not, and having more or less amicably settled this question, Millington rashly suggested that Dr. Hatton be called in for consultation as he had been the king's first physician and therefore knew more about the patient's weaknesses than they, whereupon " Radcliffe, as if he were frightened at the name, flung out of the room in a passion; and so they broke up, resolving nothing," luckily for the patient.

When they met again on the night of June 26th, 1700, William took a pill containing long Latin ingredients and was prescribed " 20 drops of the tincture of the Salt of Tartar to be taken every day; and the juice of 30 Hog-lice at six o'clock at night." By a miracle, this potion revived him: it probably so shocked him that he thought it better to perish naturally than disgustingly and therefore forced his sour features into cheerfulness. Millington, however, was not satisfied and loudly insisted on garlic being the sovereign remedy. But what most likely brought life back into William was the approach of the day of escape, for he was determined to go back to Holland.

Now the philosopher, John Locke, tried his hand at medicine and agreed with Millington that the royal dropsy was not dropsy, for his complexion, said he, was too fresh for that complaint. Whereupon, encouraged, Millington gave William " 2 grains of Scammony sulphurated, with 26 grains of the Stomachic pills, to be taken at night going to bed." Small wonder that William, groaning in Hampton Court, on being asked by a friend if he were out of sorts, sorrowfully replied that " he should be very well, if they would leave off giving him remedies. He had taken something that had put his stomach out of order."

He managed, however, to get out of England alive, and during his absence work continued at the palace under Wren's supervision. William, however, returned on October 20th, 1700, and soon had to struggle with Louis XIV's ambitions and English apathy about the troubles on the continent. The ensuing discussions and meetings of ambassadors are for history books of a different shape from this; suffice it that politics were argued and reargued continually within the palace while still the damned workmen toiled and Tudor bricks were trampled to rusty dust.

Then again the physicians settled on their prey. " His Majesty is not very well," we learn with a premonitory shudder, " his appetite abates, and his legs are more swelled; but it chiefly arises from his great thoughtfulness in relation to the public. Physicians have been consulted and have prescribed remedies." The awful list of these remedies is too painful to repeat, drugs and poisons and doctors alone know what were all tried out on that patient gentleman, but here are a few of the things he swallowed: spa water, gentian, tartar virtiolated, salt of wormwood, salt of steel, balsamic syrup, Epsom salts in chicken broth, crabs' eyes, steel prepared with sulphur, hog's lice, chalybeate pills, elder flowers. . . .

The following year these determined, undaunted physicians returned to the assault with " four spoonfuls a day of the juices of garden scurvygrass, water-cresses, Brooke-lime, and oranges, with Rhenish wine and wormwood-water compound, with some drops of the Tincture of Steel." And we cannot wonder that William became a secret drinker and that again he fled from Hampton Court to Holland on June 30th, 1701, to return on November 3rd.

He returned to find himself surprisingly popular, for James II had died and France had acknowledged his son as the rightful King of England. Terror of popery made the country welcome William as though it loved him: bells were rung and bonfires lit while London and Westminster pulled back all curtains and let the lights illumine the streets. It was November 5th, so with William's return went the anti-papal ritual of burning Guy Fawkes, while deputation after deputation waited on the king in those newly built apartments in Hampton Court. William was ill, dropsical and consumptive, but he was delighted that the English people had at last recognised the danger of France's ambitious militarism.

Ill though he was, he insisted on going out of doors and even rode to the hunt—or rather, to what we to-day would call coursing, one of the vilest of English blood-sports. " I am hunting the hare every day in the Park," he wrote to a friend, " with your hounds and mine. The rabbits are almost all killed, and their burrows will soon be stopped up. The day before yesterday I took a stag at rest with the Prince of Denmark's pack, and had a pretty good run, as far as this villainous country will permit." Refusing to listen to the doctors advising rest, he said that when he stopped hunting he almost stopped breathing and the swelling in his legs grew worse. " At this rate," said he to his advisers, " I must always have a doctor to tend me. I'll do what I have a mind to. I am very well acquainted with my own constitution. All the doctors would have me take hot things, and lead a sedentary life: but they are mistaken. Every one that is above 30 or 40 years ought to be his own physician. From my infancy I have all along lov'd shooting and have often times been wet up to the knees, after which I always fed heartily, without shifting myself, and then slept in a chair, being very tired. Now my legs being always cold, I believe that has occasioned the swelling of my feet; but so long as I eat well, I am of the opinion 'twill do me no harm."

When they attempted to wrap him in " Warm Bags of the Power of Cummin-seed, Mint, Roses, and Lavender to be applied to his leg," he kicked off the bags after two attempts, for they broke his rest, and as he said: " I must sleep; I had rather have swelled legs than not sleep."

Having had his fill of English physicians he had brought from Holland a Dr. Govard Bidloo who prescribed " Forty drops of the Tincture of the Salt of Tartar, morning and evening in a draught of medicinal wine," and the result was surprising. Yet William was a doomed man. They placed his legs in a stove to make them sweat. " How can that succeed ? " asked his naturally puzzled majesty. " 'Twill heat me; besides that, no force can make me sweat. I have often been told that if I could sweat I was cured. But as soon as I take a suporifick medicine, I become thirsty, and then I cannot sleep, and am oppressed in my breathing."

Although the physicians were finally to kill him, what delivered William into their hands was a fall near Hampton Court. The incident is a muddle of contradictions and the full facts are not known. William himself said: " I was riding in the park at noon and while I endeavoured to make the horse change his walking into a gallop, he fell upon his knees. Upon that I meant to raise him with the bridle, but he fell forward to one side, and so I fell on my right shoulder upon the ground. 'Tis a strange thing, for it happened upon a smooth level ground." Apparently he had not noticed the mole hill which Vernon, one of his closest attendants, mentions in a letter to a friend; and because of this accident, the jacobites were always to toast the mole as the little gentleman in black velvet.

William III's Palace

William did not die in Hampton Court. He was driven to Kensington Palace and there put to bed, helpless to the doctors, with a broken shoulder that must have suffered badly in a seventeenth century coach. There, while the doctors fought one another for the honour of killing a king, he died on the morning of Sunday, March 8th, 1702, before he could smash down the whole of Tudor Hampton Court—that being his expressed intention, as Defoe warns us.

" I have been assur'd," he wrote, " that had the Peace continu'd, and the King liv'd to enjoy the Continuance of it, his Majesty had resolv'd to have pull'd down all the Remains of the old Building: such as the Chapel, and the large Court with the first Gate, and to have built up the whole Palace after the manner of those two Fronts already done. In these would have been an entire Sett of Rooms of State for the receiving, and, if Need had been, the Lodging, and entertaining any foreign Prince, with his Retinue; also for Offices for all the Secretaries of State, Lords of the Treasury, and of Trade; and to have repair'd for the Dispatch of such Business, as it might be necessary to have done there upon the King's longer Residence there than ordinary; as also Apartments for all the great Officers of the Household; so that had the House had two great Squares added, as was design'd, there would have been no Room to spare, or that would not have been very well fill'd.   But the King's death put an End to all these Things."

After that, even I will turn jacobite in their toast to the little gentleman in black velvet who, by killing so great a king, saved for us so much of my Tudor Hampton Court.

Chapter XII
QUEEN ANNE

FORTUNATELY, Queen Anne did not care for Hampton Court, preferring draughty Windsor or cosy Kensington Palace. I say "fortunately" because had she shared her brother-in-law's passion she might have continued his work of vandalism. As it was, she was satisfied to complete what he left unfinished and then try to shift from the costs. For the costs of William's building were huge and unpaid bills were ever reaching Anne, including Verrio's. She paid him something, then employed him for further decorations until, going blind, he retired on a pension, probably remaining in the palace. She also added her own building debts to William's with various alterations, particularly for Wren's restoration of the Chapel to practically what we see to-day; but on the whole, except for a few council meetings, the palace takes small place in her reign, save for a poem and a murder, although the murder was neither conceived nor committed actually within the walls: it started nearby, in the Toy Tavern which was pulled down in 1852 and stood at the western entrance, to your right as you enter.

Anne was a pleasant but not particularly intelligent woman with a sweet voice that charmed even her enemies, and she was so little a Stuart at heart that she actually doubted the divinity of kingship. But she revived with zest the Stuart custom which William had let lapse of touching for the King's Evil; on one day alone, in March, 1712, she in "diamonds and a black hood" touched two hundred scrofulous heads which included little Sam Johnson's. Perhaps, however, this faith in royalty's magic fingers was more lust for the piece of gold Anne tied around each child's neck.

> *King William thinks all,*
> *Queen Mary takes all,*
> *Prince George drinks all,*
> *And Princess Anne eats all,*

they sang while she was princess, and there was truth in the rime, for George would drink anything while Anne certainly liked her belly. But she had few other pleasures, being practically crippled with dropsy and gout and often appearing covered with bandages "in extreme pain and agony, everything about her in much the same disorder as about the meanest of her subjects"; while she had sorrows sufficient for any woman in the birth and death of at least fifteen children.* A simple creature, she had at least that rare consolation of royalty, a happy marriage; although George was usually drunk, he was amiable, and she loved him. Nor did scandal pass her by, calling her " Brandy-faced Nan," for it seemed she liked a nip or two in the tea that was her favourite tipple: for tea she loved, as witness Pope:

> *Close by these meads, for ever crown'd with flow'rs,*
> *Where Thames with pride surveys his rising tow'rs,*
> *There stands a structure of majestic frame,*
> *Which from the neighb'ring Hampton takes its name.*
> *Here Britain's statesmen of the fall foredoom*
> *Of foreign Tyrants, and of Nymphs at home;*
> *Here thou, great ANNA! whom three realms obey,*
> *Dost sometimes counsel take—and sometimes Tea.*

But whether there was, as was whispered, brandy in the tea she sipped so often within these walls which from neighbouring Hampton took their name, we cannot argue for certain. If there were, there is no blame to be thrown. Anne's life was no happy one.

Crippled though she was, she yet would not always stay indoors but would drive her *chaise roulante*, with two gentlemen to hold the reins and to walk either side of the horse's head as she trundled along the eight or so miles of shaded drive. When she felt sufficiently well,

---

* In his scholarly and fascinating biography of *Anne The Last Stuart Monarch* (Thornton Butterworth), 1937, Neville Connell writes that " Anne is variously stated to have had seventeen, eighteen, or nineteen children; but this confusion arose through counting as children, miscarriages that occurred at some state of pregnancy. Treating the matter broadly, Anne had six children—two sons and four daughters . . . So far as I am able to trace, she had twelve miscarriages . . . The frequent miscarriages from which Anne suffered, and the deaths of her children at such tender ages, there is little doubt, were the result of venereal disease. In the rollicking days of the Restoration, syphilis was very common. Pepys records in his diary: ' He [Mr. Pickering] tells me plainly of the vices of the Court, and how the pox [syphilis] is so common there, and so I hear on all hands that it is as common as eating and swearing.' . . . Burnet openly suggests that ' the miscarriages of both Anne Hyde and Mary of Modena were the direct result of James II's lechery ' and wrote that ' Anne Hyde was tainted with it.' This statement is, as far as I know, uncontradicted. The papers of the Rev. Thomas Woodstock contain a similar statement . . . Burnet's statements are often coloured by his own personal prejudices, and the same may be true of Woodcock. The latter was ejected from the living of St. Andrew's Undershaft and left his mark in the history of non-conformity, so that he may easily have been prejudiced against a Roman Catholic Duchess of York. Whatever may be the truth of this, Anne undoubtedly suffered from hereditary syphilis, or had herself been infected. The affection of her eyes, her frequent miscarriages, the early deaths of her infants, and the hydrocephalus from which Gloucester suffered, are frequently the results of hereditary syphilis. Another symptom is the loss of juvenile expression, so that children come to look like little old men and women. This is certainly borne out by the picture of the Duke and Duchess of York with their two daughters, where the artist has depicted these symptoms in the six-year-old Anne. There is the possibility that Prince George may have suffered from this disease, but this seems improbable. So far, there is no evidence to support this. Prince George was a faithful husband, no hint has been made that he ever had a mistress, and with the exception of drunkenness and stupidity, no aspersion has ever been cast on his character."

The Queen's Gallery from Pyne's *History of the Royal Residences*
Courtesy of the British Museum

she would hunt in this same chaise, drawn by one horse, as Swift records in his *Journal to Stella*, " which she drives herself and drives furiously like Jehu, and is a mighty hunter like Nimrod." On one occasion, he told Stella, she hunted a stag until four in the afternoon, careering in her chaise no less than forty miles.

Diana's Fountain
Bushey Park

He also records a levee in her bedchamber at Hampton Court when " we made our bows, and stood, about twenty of us, round the room, while the Queen looked at us with her fan in her mouth, and once in a minute said about three words to some that were nearest to her; and then she was told dinner was ready, and went out. . . . I dined at her Majesty's board of green cloth. It is much the best table in England, and costs the Queen £1,000 a month while she is at Windsor or Hampton Court, and is the only mark of magnificence or royal hospitality that I can see in the Royal household. . . . I walked in the gardens, saw the carto[o]ns of Raphael and other things and with great difficulty got from Lord Halifax, who would have kept me to show me to-morrow his house and park and improvements [at Bushey]. We left Hampton Court at sunset." Swift was always avoiding dinner invitations because of the vails, the appalling tips which guests had to give; as he said of this same Lord Halifax : it would " cost me a guinea to his servants and twelve shillings coach hire; and he shall be hanged first."

But poetry's association with the palace during Anne's reign is not so much with Swift as with Swift's dear comrade, Alexander Pope, who wrote his exquisite *Rape of the Lock* at a friend's request, in the hope of patching a stupid little quarrel that occurred here at some unspecified date in 1711.

Four Roman catholic friends were rowed one day to the palace: Lord Petrie, "the Baron," Sir George Brown, "Sir Plume," Mrs. Morley, "Thalestris," and Miss Arabella Fermor, the "Belinda" who

> . . . . *to the destruction of mankind,*
> *Nourish'd two Locks, which graceful hung behind*
> *In equal curls, and well conspir'd to deck*
> *With shining ringlets the smooth iv'ry neck.*
> *Love in these labyrinths his slaves detains,*
> *And mighty hearts are held in slender chains.*
> *With hairy springes we the birds betray,*
> *Slight lines of hair surprise the finny prey,*
> *Fair tresses man's imperial race insnare,*
> *And beauty draws us by a single hair.*

The actual tale on which Pope based his masterpiece appears so slight that one suspects a deeper meaning because of the resultant uproar. The four had dinner somewhere in the palace and then sat down to play cards. After the fashionable game of ombre was finished, coffee, as Pope so delightfully tells us, was made, the ladies roasting and grinding the berries and boiling the water. Then Petrie, borrowing scissors from Mrs. Morley, clipped a lock from Miss Fermor's hair as she bent over her cup. At this outrage, the din became so tremendous that it echoes, in perfect poetry, to this day. Why there should have been such agitation at a foolish prank, or a lover's gesture, we do not know, but Pope was brought in to try to soothe it with rimes; and for some inexplicable reason, his poem brought even more furious outcries, although why any lady should object to being made immortal in words so delicate and yet so powerful, I certainly cannot tell.

There is now little but the murder to mention before we close this brief chapter of Anne who cared so strangely little for our palace. Nor should the murder rightfully enter this book for, as already remarked, it occurred outside the grounds, but this chapter is so slight I feel I can be forgiven its inclusion, if only for dark contrast to the petty squabbling of *The Rape of the Lock;* it is a sprinkle of blood after a snip of scissors snipping at a curl.

As remarked, the Toy Tavern is no more, but it stood roughly opposite the present Mitre Hotel, south of the Trophy Gates. It was a popular drinking resort for visitors to the palace, and on the night of April 27th, 1711, eighteen gentlemen were gathered there. Amongst them were Sir Cholmondeley Deering, M.P. for Kent, and Mr. Richard Thornhill. Between these two rose a drunken quarrel and, words becoming insufficient, they fell to with their fists, smashing the wainscot and, according to Swift, no less than seven of Thornhill's teeth, Sir Cholmondeley stamping on his face when he was down. Satisfied, his antagonist bloody and spitting teeth, Sir Cholmondeley was handsome enough to admit that he had been in the wrong and to offer to be friends again. But Thornhill, and who can blame him? rejected the apology, for, said he, it was not sufficient recompense for battering a man's teeth out of his head. Sir Cholmondeley then spoke the grossest insult, he said that he did not know where to find him, which was tantamount to calling him a coward, whereupon Thornhill howled: " That is a lie ! "

When Thornhill had been put to bed, some time later Sir Cholmondeley again apologised and again his apology was rejected, and a meeting was appointed at Tothill Fields—Hyde Park, "this time of the year being full of company." On the morning of May 9th, Sir Cholmondeley appeared at Thornhill's lodgings with a brace of pistols and was offered " a Dish of Tea, which he refused, but drank a glass of small beer." Thirst quenched, they set out for Tothill and there " they came up like Two lions with their Pistols advanced, and when, within four yards of each other discharged so equally together, that it could not be discovered who shot first." Another account reports that they ran so close together that the muzzles of their pistols met.

Sir Cholmondeley fell and Thornhill, " after lamenting the unhappy catastrophe," was tried at the Old Bailey, and little else but the duel and trial was discussed in coffee-houses, taverns, newspapers or drawing-rooms until he was acquitted of murder but, being found guilty of manslaughter, was burnt in the hand. His release only sent him to his death at the swords of assassins. Three months later he quarrelled again at Hampton Court, this time with two men who hastened after him, caught up with him at Turnham Green, and stabbed him before he could either gallop off or even scramble from his horse.

As already remarked, Anne had small love for our palace, perhaps because of William's churlish treatment of her there; she preferred Kensington where she added to the grounds and finished the gardens begun by her sister, and Windsor where she enlarged the Royal Park that she might hunt, when gout and other ailments permitted, in her *chaise roulante*. Her other recreations, apart from drinking, were, when her wretched body allowed, beagling and dancing, but she had usually to console herself with the spectator's part at cock-fights or races, or she gambled indoors or listened to music. Rarely, however, were these pleasures indulged in at Hampton Court; but she was living there during the peace-agitations of 1710.

At that time, she was hard pressed for money, all gold being bled in battle, and was worried because the pensions of her husband's servants were already five quarters in arrears. Gout nipped her to add physical agony to mental stress and she became so ill that in November " there came a fellow booted and spurred to a coffee house in the City " who announced that he had just left Hampton Court and that the queen's life was despaired of. But mental worries, more even than the gout, drove Anne now to her sick-bed. Not only was she distressed about money, but there was the war to be reckoned with and Marlborough to be faced. He came to Hampton Court in mid-November and strongly pleaded with her not to give way now that the enemy was beaten; but Anne was a stubborn woman, no longer under Sarah's influence, and others now guided her. No arguments could shift her from her purpose and Marlborough was doomed with his victories.

There is little else to record, but perhaps we should mention that that meddlesome Act of November 13th, 1712, forbidding disorders or indecencies on the stage was drafted here, while the custom of gentlemen sitting on the stage itself was forbidden, or even of their going behind the scenes, while those who disobeyed were threatened with action as " contemners of the Royal authority and disturbers of the public peace."

So far had royalty and public opinion travelled in the short span from the merry reign of Queen Anne's uncle.

Chapter XIII
KING GEORGE THE FIRST

UNDER the first two Georges, Hampton Court to me seems always bathed in that luminous dawn, or twilight, of a Watteau or a Fragonard painting. Reading the letters and records of that time, however, soon claws that romantic scenery aside and we see the lewd dull kings and their wearisome court-life of which the ladies in waiting were continually, quite naturally, lamenting. But shut the records, the many volumes of correspondence—and correspondence was then indeed voluminous—and at once the illusion returns when I walk in Hampton Court. Moonlight falls, softening the stone of Wren's façades, scumbling the bricks with violet, great purple skies mist with violet clouds, and the terraces are clear-cut with shadows. From under the trees sounds a harp or a mandoline, a girl is singing exquisitely, her voice rippling like a bird's song, while ladies move lithely in belling skirts that cling about them like familiar pets, and men with three-cornered hats tucked under their arms, powdered wigs on their heads, and patches on their powdered cheeks, lean to whisper to divine Mary Bellenden or sweet Molly Lepell:

> So powerful her charms, and so moving,
>   They would warm an old monk in his cell;
> Should the Pope himself ever go roaming,
>   He would follow dear Molly Lepell. . .
> Or were I the King of Great Britain,
>   To choose a minister well,
> And support the throne that I sit on,
>   I'd have under me Molly Lepell. . .
> Should Venus now rise from the ocean
>   And naked appear in her shell,
> She would not cause half the emotion,
>   That we feel from dear Molly Lepell. . .
> In a bed you have seen pinks and roses;
>   Would you know a more delicate smell?
> Ask the fortunate man who reposes
>   On the bosom of Molly Lepell. . .

There is both truth and mockery in that song. Under this moonlight the voice sings, playfully tender, for we move in that sophisticated yet pastoral world so popular with the versifiers of the time when Corydon had no beard and Phyllis, while tending sheep and cows, had yet every clean ribbon in place; when the death of two peasants-lovers struck by lightning could inspire Pope to writing three different epitaphs, the first running:

> *When Eastern lovers feed the funer'l fire,*
> *On the same pile the faithful fair expire:*
> *Here pitying Heav'n that virtue mutual found,*
> *And blasted both, that it might neither wound.*
> *Hearts so sincere th' Almighty saw well pleas'd,*
> *Sent his own lightning, and the victims seiz'd.*

Even the merry common-sense of Lady Mary Wortley Montagu cannot explode the sentimental fantasy of a cynic, for she, too, must speak in rime:

> *Who knows if 'twas not kindly done ?*
> *For had they seen the next year's sun,*
> *A beaten wife and cuckold swain*
> *Had jointly curs'd the marriage chain:*
> *Now they are happy in their doom,*
> *For Pope has writ upon their tomb.*

Through the age runs this blend of sentiment and hardness, romance and realism, idealism and bitterness. It is the period of Tristram Shandy who knows not himself whether he be laughing or weeping; when men thought nature was to be improved and the word " picturesque " spelt, not something quaint, but a view that looked like a painting, applauding nature for almost equalling art.

Hampton Court is now, to me, set in fairyland, and that is probably because of this same goblin, Alexander Pope. That *The Rape of the Lock* was written during Queen Anne's reign does not deter me from placing it during the period of the early Georges', for homely Anne, plump and bandaged, sipping tea with mayhap something in it, was no Titania; while about the Princess of Wales, later Queen Caroline, there is such good humoured charm, although she may have been no beauty, such good sense and such kindliness, that she may well sit for our fairy queen. And she had such adorable imps about her, such dear and lovely ladies made even more lovely by the wit of Pope, Swift, Gay, Peterborough, and Arbuthnot.

Let them proclaim with bleeding pens the tedium of their existence: I do not believe it. Why! even while they complain, my blood stirs with longing to be with them. Listen to Mr. Pope repeating their laments: " I went by water to Hampton Court, unattended by all but my own virtues, which were not of so modest a nature as to keep themselves, or me, concealed; for I met the Prince with all his ladies, on horseback, coming from hunting, Mrs. B[ellenden] and Mrs. L[epell] took me into protection, contrary to the laws against harbouring papists, and gave me a dinner, with something I liked better, an opportunity of conversing with Mrs. H[oward]. We all agreed that the life of a Maid of Honour was of all things the most miserable: and wished that every woman who envied had a specimen of it. To eat Westphalia ham in a morning, ride over hedges and ditches on borrowed hacks, come home in the heat of the day with a fever, and (what is worse a thousand times) with a red mark on the forehead from an uneasy hat! all this may qualify them to make excellent wives for foxhunters, and bear abundance of ruddy complexioned children. As soon as they can wipe off the sweat of the day, they must simper an hour and catch cold in the Princess's apartment; from thence (as Shakespeare has it) to dinner, with what appetite they may;—and after that, till midnight, walk, work, or think, which they please. I can easily believe no lone house in Wales, with a mountain and a rookery, is more contemplative than this Court; and as proof of it, I need only tell you Miss L[epell] walked with me three or four hours by moonlight, and we met no creature of any quality, but the King, who gave audience to the Vice-Chamberlain, all alone, under the garden wall."

Protest as you will, Mr. Pope, treading the moonlight with Molly Lepell, I say I'll not believe you. That was an enchanted night with a periwigged king under the garden wall giving audience to his vice-chamberlain; such a night as only you can conjure with your cunning verse, so softly marching in double file; such a night as when we hear the beckoning syrinx of a discreet Pan in the ordered garden or from the depths of the maze where satyrs lurk in lace for petulant lovesick maids. Your own Zephyretta, Brillante, and

Momentilla are abroad while you unmoor the skiff on the silky
Thames by the wrought-iron gates:

> *He summons straight his denizens of air;*
> *The lucid squadrons round the sails repair:*
> *Soft o'er the shrouds the aerial whispers breathe,*
> *That seemed but zephyrs to the train beneath.*
> *Some to the sun their insect-wings unfold,*
> *Waft on the breeze, or sink in clouds of gold;*
> *Transparent forms, too fine for mortal sight,*
> *Their fluid bodies half dissolved in light.*
> *Loose to the wind their airy garments flew,*
> *Thin glitt'ring textures of the filmy dew,*
> *Dipped in the richest tincture of the skies,*
> *Where light disports in ever-mingling dyes;*
> *While ev'ry beam new transient colours flings,*
> *Colours that change whene'er they wave their wings.*

Let Pope himself, in prose, insist that " our gallantry and gaiety
have been great sufferers by the rupture of the two courts here;
scarce any ball, assembly, basset-table, or any place where two or
three are gathered. No lone house in Wales, with a rookery, is more
contemplative than Hampton Court. I walked there the other day
by the moon, and met no creature of quality but the King, who was
giving audience all alone in the garden to the birds under the wall,"
and thus betray the over generous heart of a poet who presents to
different correspondents similar words that they be not wasted on
one. This time, however, he tosses aside the vice-chamberlain and,
more appropriately, gives the king birds for companions. Such
metamorphoses took place at Hampton Court when warlocks like
Pope, that little crippled genius, tiptoed in daylight under the moon.
A gibbering gibbous moon it must have been, unloosing its solid
wraiths in silks and satins, its Molly Lepells and Mary Bellendens—
fit company, indeed, for such a poet.

These ladies who, with their worshippers the poets, give now such
delicate brilliance to our palace were the two acknowledged beauties,
and men quarrelled about which was the lovelier, Molly or Mary.
Mary was passionately in love with penniless Colonel John Campbell,
one of the grooms of the bedchamber, whom she was later to marry,
and therefore she was safe from the guile of poets or the bluster of

princes. Yet the prince—let us call him George Augustus to avoid confusion with his father, George Lewis—was a persistent dog at her high heels, pursuing her with Germanic subtlety. She tells how she used to cross her arms over her breasts at sight of him to stop him touching her "and told him I was not cold, but I liked to stand so." Not taking this crude hint, the prince set cunningly to work by, one evening, opening his purse while he sat at her side. Slowly he began to count the coins: slowly coin after coin clinked in his hands, wheedling her virtue with clear tinkling, while all the while he peeked at her. " Sir," cried she desperately at last, " I can bear it no longer; if you count your money any more I shall go out of the room." That charming tattler, Horace Walpole, reports another story which might, in truth, be the same tale embroidered, for he says that the royal George yet pursued her, ceaselessly clinking coin on coin until she knocked them from his hand and fled the room, leaving him to grovel for his money on the floor.

> *What pranks she played behind the scenes,*
> *And who at court the belle;*
> *Some swear it is the Bellenden,*
> *And others say Molly Lepell.*

Molly was the more reserved of the two and she married that mincing gossiping ape, Lord Hervey—of whom Lady Mary Wortley Montagu observed: " God created men, women—and Herveys "— and I feel angry with her for it. Although worshipped by Pope and a hundred others, she turned to this creature with a painted face and effeminate manner, fit only for a lady's drawing-room; yet young Voltaire had once sung to her in English:

> *In my silence see the lover,*
> *True love is by silence known;*
> *In my eyes you'll best discover,*
> *All the power of your own.*

Lord Chesterfield—that " dwarf baboon," George II was to call him despite his affectations and gentlemanly frivolity—swore that Molly was a most finely polished and high-bred woman of fashion, yet, I repeat, she married the best-hated man in court. No wonder her friends despaired ! But it must be remembered that at this date, Hervey was only twenty-four and it was thirteen years later that Pope revealed him as pretty-pretty vindictive Sporus.

Nor were Molly and Mary the only goddesses to be worshipped in our Court. There was also Mrs. Howard, for whom Swift bought a plaid nightgown, then damned her for ingratitude because, when she found he expected her to pay for it, she was not enthusiastic in her thanks. She was married to that " wrong-headed, ill-tempered, obstinate, drunken, extravagant " Earl of Suffolk, and therefore cannot morally be blamed for becoming the prince's mistress, however we may argue with her æsthetically about such a choice, for the prince was a crude creature, as the episode with Mary Bellenden has shown. And Howard was a charming woman, Pope's " *rara avis*, a reasonable woman," and although Gay and Bolingbroke later turned against her, they showed merely their own ill manners and their spitting does not really spatter Mrs. Howard.

> *O wonderful creature! a woman of reason!*
> *Never gay out of pride, never gay out of season;*
> *When so easy to guess who this angel may be*
> *Would one think Mrs. Howard ne'er dreamt it was she?*

as sang Lord Peterborough, great general and friend of Pope, who shocked Bath by wearing boots—for no gentleman would wear boots except for travelling—and being seen " with his blue ribbon and star, and a cabbage under each arm, or a chicken in his hand, which, after he himself has purchased at market, he carries home for his dinner."

Whatever spite might be spat at Mrs. Howard, such as the insinuation, immortalised by Pope, that you could expect from her either slander or poison because she was alleged to have driven to her death a young girl of whom she was jealous, she remains a charming lady. Pope's imputation becomes base coin when placed on the gold of her heart, for king's mistress though she had been from Hanoverian days, she rarely presumed on her position—there was, however, one scene to be recorded later—never boasted of her conquest, got little money from him or favours for her friends, and was in fact often publicly snubbed by him; her main reward appears to have been her escape from a brute of a husband and payment for the building of her house at Twickenham. Every evening, George Augustus spent three or four hours in her apartment. Courtiers would grin to see him striding up and down, watch in hand, until nine o'clock struck, when he would hurry off for his nightly *tête-à-tête*. The idea that Mrs. Howard loved the fellow can be dismissed. She was merely a lonely impecunious lady. As bedchamber woman her salary was a mere £300 a year and although the prince was by no means princely in his payments, she managed—according to Lord Hervey on Caroline's authority—to get about £2,300 a year from him; and since she was sufficiently disillusioned about love she was content to relax as the royal whore with a good grace, her emotions being unstirred.

Princess Caroline accepted Mrs. Howard's position gladly, for, knowing that a mistress was inevitable, she was glad that her rival was no ambitious woman and therefore she could smile, if a trifle wryly, on her husband's smug conceit, his round-eyed pride in possessing a lover. He would repeat to her in detail his affair and she would smile as on a silly boy—as, indeed, he was in love—while moralists snapped at her for being her husband's bawd as well as cuckold. Only girls or fools, she once cried, moped at conjugal infidelity; but can one not detect a certain defiant anger in that cry? She left hatred of Mrs. Howard to her friends, like Charlotte Clayton. We must not forget Charlotte in this list of Hampton Court ladies for she was Caroline's favourite. Walpole called her a pompous simpleton and, more briefly, the bitch; while Hervey, ever on Caroline's side, said that she had an excellent understanding and a good heart. But perhaps she is a trifle vinegarish for this gay company and might be left indoors with that blatantly virtuous Miss Meadows of whom Pope rimed when singing of Mary Howe:

> *What is prudery?*
> *'Tis a beldam*
> *Seen with wit and beauty seldom,*
> *'Tis a fear that starts at shadows;*
> *'Tis (no 'tisn't) like Miss Meadows;*
> *Old and void of all good nature,*
> *Lean and fretful; would seem wise*
> *Yet plays the fool before she dies.*
> *'Tis an ugly envious shrew*
> *That rails at dear Lepell and you.*

Besides Mary, there was also a Sophy Howe in our palace, grand-daughter of Rupert of the Rhine. A delightful girl she seems, ever pouting for flirtations, ever laughing and carefree and so quick in her moods that herself rarely knew why she did this or that, or why she laughed, or why, poor child, she tumbled from kissing to perilous love.

Perhaps Miss Howe came there by chance,
Nor knows with whom, nor why she came along,

as Pope sang, for she committed the unconcealable *faux pas* with
" Nunty " Lowther who refused to marry her.

But seduced by the moonlight over Hampton Court, this evening I
have been as careless with words as was sweet Miss Howe with her
virtue, for we have run far ahead in time. Yet if you would see the
palace in the days of the first Georges you must people it with these
ladies; you must imagine them with their powdered hair drawn back
from the forehead and over the ears, tight over the head, to a bun at
the back; and for more formal occasions, see the hair unloosed and
ringlets falling to the shoulder or curling down the nape of the neck.
Tight-bodices pushing up the breasts, the stomach flattened with a
busked stomacher, often of wood, and the skirt, gathered full on the
hoops, opening down the front to reveal the bright petticoat, they
seem to float, rather than walk, along the halls of Hampton Court,
quick feet glimpsed as the hoops swing, heads back to show white
throats and bosoms. You have seen them often in porcelain, delicately
tinted, but these, in life, were no porcelain wenches as many a lover
found under the trees with a passionate Miss Howe in his arms.

It is the age of sanity and sentiment. Gone the luxurious flesh of
Charles II's court, gone the primness of Mary's and the boredom of
Anne's: these women come nearer to us, are more clearly seen and
understood. You must never place them in the Tudor palace, impossible to imagine them in the Great Hall or vast kitchens or draughty
courts; you must see them in the gardens towards the river, chattering
while they stroll down that long alley of wych-elm called Queen Mary's
Bower, or seated in the sunlight outside the Orangery, or on the
terrace near the black figures of Mars and Hercules; or at the west of
the terrace strolling down the steps to the walk by the little gardens
there.

We are far from the dark Tudor world lit by torches, a world of
threats and lechery and treachery; we are with Watteau and Pope and
the ladies are innocently sophisticated with such an air that it would
baffle all the satyrs lurking in the Wilderness. So self-assured they
seem in their frames when we look on them that we wonder how men
had courage enough to find whether blood flowed under the marble
skin, whether hoops could be unlaced to reveal a white body inside
the frame; so superciliously, so complacently they look at us that we
retire, baffled but reverent.

It is impossible to like our first George any more than he liked England which he hated almost as much as he hated his eldest son. This second hatred was probably transferred from the boy's mother whom he had married for political reasons. On discovering him to be unfaithful, she too proved unfaithful, only to find that adultery was a male prerogative. George had her lover murdered, then divorced her and locked her into a castle where she remained till death. It was, therefore, understandable, if not forgivable, that George Lewis should hate her son. As Mr. Griffith Davies writes in his *A King in Toils:*

" There was no bond of sympathy between George Augustus and his father. On the contrary, George Lewis positively hated his son, and did all he could to suppress him. The explanation of this parental aversion is not easy to find. No doubt George Augustus's small, slender figure, the delicate cut of his features, the lack of self-control demonstrated by blushes and tears, reminded George Lewis of the woman who lay imprisoned at Ahlden, the woman whom he wished for ever to put out of his mind. No doubt, too, George Lewis found it difficult to tolerate his son's exuberance and garrulity; while his habit of putting his father in the wrong was unbearable. George Augustus also had his grievances. Why should his father keep him so abominably short of money ? He could not remain deaf to the criticism of enemies: that his father was ' a mean little beast,' who liked money. And he suspected that the parental refusal to allow him to become more than a parade-ground soldier was due to an insane desire to avoid rivalry."

Inexplicable because pathological as this hatred of father for son might appear, it became almost traditional. When George Augustus became king, he, too, quarrelled with his son, and when his son became king, he too, quarrelled with his son. Whether the blame be on father or son in each case cannot be decided, but as in most quarrels it probably was weighed between the two and each must take his share.

Shortly after his arrival in England, George I had the good sense to move to Hampton Court, thinking it a refuge from the English, where he could live in comfort with his German mistresses. Models of two huge seahorses and two large tritons were raised to welcome him, being built to spout water into a great basin; but what George thought of them we do not know. What he thought of the English we do know by his shutting himself up and refusing even the time-honoured ritual of being dressed and undressed, for he was a man who, being fussy himself, hated fuss.

"We are ruined by trulls," wailed the people, "and what is worse, by ugly ones!" for these German women were grasping, miserly, and horrible to look upon.

Although George lived here for so long, his associations with the palace are slight; the promenade of his mistresses, however, is alleged to have inspired the name of frog walk for the walk under the tilt yard, near the palace gate, *frog* being a corruption of *frau*. Mr. Law, however, and it seems rightly, believed "that the Fraus, who gave this name to the walk, were those in attendance on the Stadtholder of Holland, who, when driven from his native land by the French Revolution in 1795, found . . . an asylum for himself and his family in this palace."

The king was rarely seen by his people for he continually lurked indoors behind the wide skirts of his fraus; and when he did appear, it was only to be hurried, hidden in a sedan chair, to the river, six footmen striding before him with six yeomen of the guard behind him; in similar chairs, his awful mistresses would follow, being borne by servants in royal livery and surrounded by attendants. Then aboard the state barges that were bright with coloured cloths, they would be rowed to the city, another boat being cheerfully noisy with the king's musicians playing them down the river.

There is little to relate of George's first sojourn here, but when he left for his beloved Hanover in 1716, the Prince and Princess of

Wales established themselves in semi-regal state in the apartments used by Queen Anne, now known as the Queen's State Rooms. The ceiling had recently been painted by Mr., later Sir, James Thornhill, teacher and father-in-law of mighty Hogarth, for which he had been paid £3. 11s. a yard: should we dare to compare it to the work of blind Verrio, it is a vast improvement. Thornhill was no genius but he was a conscientious and pleasing painter, and this ceiling of Aurora in her golden chariot drawn by four white horses, cherubim about her, with night and sleep drowsing below, is excellent decoration and well proportioned and coloured for this room with its tall four-poster bed—Queen Anne's bed and undoubtedly slept in by prince and princess on this occasion—and its cunningly moulded silver chandelier dropping with glass balls like a cluster of glittering stalactites. You will see crowned George I's portrait over the bed, Caroline's above the fireplace, her husband's opposite, and that of their son, Frederick, at the age of nine, above the window.

The anniversary of the king's accession being August 1st, soon after the prince and princess's arrival at Hampton Court, they celebrated it with filial gusto, dining in public and entertaining enthusiastic crowds, including Surrey's grand jury which hurried from Kingston to swear loyalty. These public dinners must often have been embarrassing and they continued for hours, long into the afternoons, while the public gaped at every mouthful. It was a pageant in which prince and princess, ladies and gentlemen, ate and drank and whispered together with an aloof pretence that they were private, while dishes were brought them by servants in bright livery.

After dinner, the prince would collapse into bed while the princess, following a brief siesta, would rise to receive company and to hear the latest political moves, for she was the more intelligent of the pair. Then she would retire to write letters until the prince, having slept off his indigestion, would get up, get dressed, and escort her for an hour or two through the gardens, the maids of honour with their beaux and the ladies and gentlemen of the court following, flirting, teasing, and quizzing one another. The men pranced along with powdered wigs on their shaven skulls; their tight-waisted coats, with buckramed skirts fanning out to rival the ladies' hoops, were open on the embroidered waistcoats falling as far as the coat's hem; they were powdered and patched and some of them painted, but all were witty in a languid fashion. Witty, too, were their companions in their tossing hoops luring one with a peep of ankles and the thought of legs in empty space. Behind the prince and princess they walked, no matter how weary they felt; and the walk over, there would follow unexhausting exercise in the bowling green while in the four pavilions, one each corner of the green, the ladies and their beaux would talk of love and scandal, one feels, in Popish couplets. Some would play cards or drink tea or coffee to music from one of the maids at the softly tinkling spinet. Sightseers would row or sail along the river, mooring near the palace until late at night " to hear the Prince's music which sounded much sweeter than from the shore," or to glimpse a lovely lady stroll on the pebbled paths in moonlight, listening to the lies of her gallant.

Such was the daily round and, bored though the ladies insisted that they were, in later years they were to lament their passing as though sighing at their own vanished youth and the threat of wrinkles on their throats. For those young days and evenings were all romance and laughter, the prince and princess being determined to make themselves loved in contrast to the surly king.

" I wish we were all in the *Swiss Cantons* again," sighed Miss Bellenden, now Mrs. Campbell, writing in 1721; and Molly Lepell, now Lady Hervey, lamented in 1728 when writing to Mrs. Howard that the address on her letter recalled a thousand agreeable things, for, she wrote, " I really believe a frizelation [flirtation] would be a surer means of restoring my spirits, than the exercise and hartshorn I now make use of. I do not suppose the name still subsists; but pray let me know if the thing itself does, or if they meet in the same cheerful manner to sup as formerly. Are ballads and epigrams the consequence of those meetings? Is good sense in the morning, and wit in the evening, the subject, or rather the foundation of the conversation? That is an unnecessary question; I can answer it myself, since I know you are of the party, but, in short, do you want poor *Tom* [herself] and *Bellenden* as much as I want *Swiss* in the first place, and them? "

One is reminded of Pope's:

> *Still round and round the ghosts of beauty glide,*
> *And haunt the places where their honour dy'd,*

although only poor Sophy's honour can be said technically to have died, Mrs. Howard's having perished—if it ever existed—with the alleged loss of her hair to pay for a dinner in Hanover. Yet again the same swan, Molly Lepell, sings: " My spirits, which you know were once very good, are so much impaired, that I question if even Hampton Court breakfasts could recover them, or revive the *Schatz* [herself, meaning *treasure*], who is extinguished in a fatigued nurse, a grieved sister, and a melancholy wife."

Useless, of course, for Mrs. Howard to retort that " Hampton is very different from the place you knew; and we say we wished *Tom Lepell, Schatz*, and *Bella-dine* at the tea-table, is too interested to be doubted. *Frizelation, flirtation* and *dangleation* [to dangle after or to court] are now no more, and nothing less than a Lepell can restore them to life; but to tell you my opinion freely, the people you now converse with [books, which Lepell had lamented were dead] are much more alive than any of your old acquaintances." They were mourning their own youth and we mourn with them. Not only must it have been glorious then to have been alive, trebly glorious must it have been to have laughed and danced and frizelated with Bellenden, Lepell, and Howard when they were young.

That reference, by the by, to the Swiss Cantons was a private jest and referred to Mrs. Howard's apartments, a retreat of neutrality from the quarrels of court-life. We must accept Mr. Law's authority for stating that their position in the palace " cannot, unfortunately, be exactly determined. But we may be pretty sure that they were in the eastern range of the new palace, and not improbably in the Round Window, or Queen's ' Half-Storey,' over the Queen's apartments, at this time, as we have said, occupied by the Princess. A direct communication with the Queen's State Bedchamber existed by means of a curious old staircase in an ante-room, which could itself be approached from the Queen's back stairs. In the Queen's half-storey, at any rate, we may presume, lived the maids of honour, and up and down the Queen's back stairs they must often have gone, recalling the lines in the ' Excellent New Ballad '—

> *But Bellenden we needs must praise,*
> *Who, as downstairs she jumps,*
> *Sings o'er the hills and far away,*
> *Despising doleful dumps !* "

Here Mrs. Howard and her chosen friends would meet to sip tea and gossip, and the circle was as select as a court circular. Fortunate were those invited to this Dianic refuge.

In the mornings, either the prince went stag-hunting or was rowed with his princess in a crimson-hung barge, while there was one September day when he gathered the local lasses for a race: a smock, a quilted petticoat, or a sarsanet hood being for the winners, and pairs of scarlet stockings for consolation prizes, free biscuits and wine following the sports. Not only did prince and princess attempt to win the affections of countryfolk but they tried also to poise themselves in politics between whig and tory, although their hearts were tory—perhaps because the king was a whig—and offered hospitality to either party. Yet they could not hide their predilections and the continual coming and going of the Duke of Argyll woke such whig suspicions that Walpole despaired, remarking that Argyll went " constantly to Court, appears in public, and has his private audiences, and not without influence." But Argyll's continual visits to Hampton Court were not purely for political purposes. He was ogling one of Caroline's maids, simple Jenny Warburton, an innocent country lass fresh to the seductions of a court who was soundly quizzed for her continual *faux pas* and the duke's passion.

The whig Townshend followed his suspicions in person but he so misunderstood the court that he paid attention to the mistress, Mrs. Howard, instead of to the wife, Caroline, to whom he showed " all the contempt in the world." Caroline's natural reaction was to consider him " the sneeringest, fawningest knave that ever was." But soon friends pointed out his error to Townshend and he played such subtle court to Caroline that he soon brought her to " perfect Tranquillity " and became quite a favourite. The moment was politically a dangerous one, for George Lewis was striving to drag England into war for his Hanover's sake and it was decided to send his friend Lord Sunderland to him to explain the risks of such a policy.

Naturally, Sunderland, true courtier, reflected his master's moods and therefore when he visited Hampton Court before leaving for Hanover he treated the princess with small courtesy. She received him in the Queen's Gallery with its seven tall windows opening on to the Great Fountain Court. She and her husband had had this gallery decorated—it could not have been completed before the accession of George I—and had hung tapestries from tenterhooks along the walls. You can see them there to-day: they are seven pieces woven by Charles le Brun illustrating the life of Alexander the Great.

Fountain
Court.

Here in this long gallery—eighty-one feet long by twenty-five feet broad—the princess greeted supercilious Sunderland smug in the king's affections, and she wished him God-speed to Hanover. We do not know what or who started the argument, what small or large discourtesy from Sunderland stung Caroline into raising her voice, but rise both their voices did, shrill princess and shouting lord, while courtiers winked and shrugged aside, pretending not to hear as they listened from the garden below. Speak lower! hissed Caroline: for those in the garden could hear, she said. Sunderland roared: " Let them hear ! " " Well, if you have a mind, let 'em," said the princess graciously, " but you shall walk next the windows, for in the humour we both are, one of us must certainly jump out of the window, and I am resolved it shan't be me."

Such, even in a quarrel, was this lady's humour that one cannot help but love her.

She is queen of this fairyland and her nymphs are about her, but there are also ogres present: Hans Caspar, Count von Bothmar, for example, the Hanoverian envoy to St. James's, the king's spy, who was to watch and report on the prince's doings while his father was away; and the whigs, all likely devils because they were the king's government; and for ogresses there were the fat and lean Hanoverian mistresses of the king who detested English women. One of them, the Countess of Buckenburgh, almost comically fat, slipped and twisted her ankle one evening while returning to the palace after a game of cards in one of the pavilions. Until this accident, the princess, following her evening walk, would play in the dusk by candlelight with her ladies and courtiers while the prince ogled Bellenden; and in these golden-lit pavilions, dusk purpling beyond the sword-blades of light, merry were the evenings until the fat German had this tumble. After that the princess refused to stay out late but would play in the Queen's Gallery from nine until about ten-thirty, or with her friends she would sup in Buckenburgh's chamber.

This accident brought no tears in the Swiss Cantons, for Buckenburgh was disliked for her ill manners. There had been that occasion, for example, when during supper she had had the audacity, this monstrous " Hanoverian rat," to say before many ladies that " English women do not look like women of quality, they make themselves look as pitiful and sneaking as they can; they hold their heads down and look always in a fright, whereas foreigners hold up their heads and hold out their breasts, and make themselves look as great and stately as they can, and more noble and more like quality than you English." Upon which, Lady Mary Deloraine had retorted: " We show our quality by our birth and titles, madam, and not by sticking out our bosoms."

Yet this Lady Mary, known as the Fly, was not so scornful of Hanoverian rats when they clinked gold in their hands, for later she was to become the next king's mistress. Herself denied it, although the truth was plain in George II's gloating eyes and predatory fingers, while she would pout and say that old men and kings should pay well for their pleasures. Surely, whatever her protests, those pleasures went beyond the " little bawdy " which George Augustus was wont to whisper to her at night? She was a charming creature who at thirty-five, when the king petted her, boasted that the bloom on her face was such "that not one woman in ten thousand has at fifteen. . . ."

But we are running, again, ahead. . . . Such is the wizardry of this age that the bare mention of a lady's name will set us gossiping like any of the beaux and belles at Hampton Court who fluttered the candle-flame with whispers. George Augustus is yet Prince of Wales, his father who hates him is returning soon from Hanover, and now he and his princess are leaving our palace. Late in October, they set out for St. James's, being rowed in the royal scarlet-draped barges. " The day was wonderfully fine," sighed Lady Cowper, " and nothing in the world could be pleasanter than the passage, nor give one a better idea of the riches and happiness of the kingdom. . . ."

> *But now secure the painted vessel glides,*
> *The sun-beams trembling on the floating tides;*
> *While melting music steals upon the sky,*
> *And softened sounds along the waters die.*
> *Smooth flow the waves, the zephyrs gently play,*
> *Belinda smiled, and all the world was gay.*

But the ogre was returning, that tremendous periwigged ogre who shivered the paradise of prince and princess: His Royal Majesty King George I was coming back from Hanover and no longer would

> *. . . the heroes and the nymphs resort*
> *To taste awhile the pleasures of a court;*
> *In various talk the instructive hours they passed,*
> *Who gave the ball, or paid the visit last;*
> *One speaks the glory of the British Queen,*
> *And one describes a charming Indian screen;*
> *A third interprets motions, looks, and eyes;*
> *At every word a reputation dies.*
> *Snuff or the fan supply each pause of chat,*
> *With singing, laughing, ogling, and all that.*

I am perfectly aware that the British Queen referred to in these rimes was Queen Anne, but as already remarked, I cannot disassociate *The Rape of the Lock* from this brief reign of prince and princess at our palace. Its gossamer reality does not fit that fat queen, but it does—most definitely it does—seem the rightful world for Lepell and Bellenden and Howard and the other lovely frizelating ladies under Princess Caroline.

George I rumbles back to Hampton Court and dullness reigns. Yet this is the date when should be placed Pope's already quoted letter and his vision of the king giving audience to the birds under the garden wall; but even such a moonlit scene cannot lighten our palace at this time. Soon king and prince were openly quarrelling and the prince fled to St. James's while his father inserted in the *Gazette* an announcement that he would not receive at his court anyone who visited his son.

There is one good mark now to be scored for George I, and all the more pleasant to score because it is a surprising act for one who knew so little English: he built a theatre at Hampton Court. Building is perhaps too definite a word; what he did was to convert the Great Hall into a playhouse, after the fashion James had used for his masks. On September 23rd, 1718, the first play was acted here, and the choice was also surprising, being probably the greatest masterpiece ever written for the English stage, *Hamlet;* and it was followed by *Henry VIII* on October 1st. Piquancy must have been given to this production by having it performed within the very walls which remained a monument to Henry's and Wolsey's love of building. Here, periwigged, patched and powdered, an actor re-enacted the tragedy of the cardinal's fall under the hammer-beamed roof of which much of Wolsey's must have remained even after Henry's rebuilding.

The Royal Company of Actors, commonly called the Drury Lane Company, were led by Colley Cibber and Mrs. Oldfield; Cibber's father, Gabriel, by the way, had worked on the palace decorations, carving the tympanum over the East Front. Colley tells us: " This throwing open a Theatre in a Royal Palace, seem'd to be reviving the Old *English* hospitable Grandeur, where the lowest Rank of neighbouring Subjects might make merry at Court, without being laugh'd at themselves. . . . A Play presented at Court, or acted on a publick Stage, seem to their different Auditors a different Entertainment. . . . At Court, where the Prince gives the Treat, and honours the Table with his own Presence, the Audience is under the Restraint of a Circle, where Laughter or Applause rais'd higher than a Whisper would be star'd at. . . . But this Coldness or Decency of Attention at Court I observ'd had but a melancholy Effect upon the impatient Vanity of some of our Actors, who seem'd inconsolable when their flashy Endeavours to please had pass'd unheeded: Their not considering where they were quite disconcerted them; nor could they recover their Spirits 'till from the lowest Rank of the Audience some gaping *John* or *Joan*, in the fullness of their Hearts, roar'd out their Approbation."

Particularly did the king enjoy *Henry VIII* for he liked to smile at the passage (Act I, Scene II) when Henry orders the cardinal to write circular letters of indemnity to every county where the payment of certain taxes were objected to, and Wolsey whispers to Cromwell:

> *A word with you.*
> *Let there be letters writ to every shire,*
> *Of the king's grace and pardon. The grieved commons*
> *Hardly conceive of me; let it be noised*
> *That through our intercession this revokement*
> *And pardon comes: I shall anon advise you*
> *Further in the proceeding. . . .*

for he saw in this situation his own, ministers often assuming the merit of his generosity. Acting the cardinal, Colley would always be careful to stand close to the king's box when loudly he whispered these lines, and always, he tells us, the king was overjoyed.

So overjoyed was he indeed that Steele, who had written the prologue and who with another held the patent of the company, answered a solemn nobleman who asked how the king had liked the performance: " So terribly well, my Lord, that I was afraid I should have lost all my Actors ! For I was not sure the King would not keep them to fill the Posts at Court that he saw them so fit for in the play." We possess the warrant for the payment for the performance, dated November 15th, 1718, and the expenses were heavy. Apart from the cost of transforming the Hall into a theatre, there was the carriage of the actors to be paid, and the royal purse had to produce £374. 1s. 8d., while the king gave as a personal gift to Cibber £200, the total therefore reaching £574. 1s. 8d.

Although the king might appreciate one art, his treatment of that genius, Sir Christopher Wren, was abominable. Having received his patent as surveyor-general under Charles II, Wren had retained it nobly during five successive reigns, only to be now abruptly dismissed at the age of eighty-six. That scrawny mistress of the king's, Schulenburg, must be blamed for this ignoble act, Wren having refused to permit her to deform Hampton Court with her bad taste, and in revenge she had the king dismiss him while in his place she put an unknown nincompoop called William Benson.

Wren, however, remained associated with the palace, for in 1708 he had leased from the crown a house on the Green at a rental of £10 a year for fifty years. The low rental can be explained by the house being in a state almost of collapse, which was all to Wren's taste, for

Sir Christopher Wren lived here 1706 1723

then he could rebuild it to his liking. You can still see it beyond its wall, shaded by trees in summer, near the Lion Gates. Its garden reached to the Thames beside which he raised a terrace and an arbour. Here, content, he remained until his death, reading his Bible and entertaining friends. Once a year only would he leave his loved Hampton, to be carried to London that he might meditate in the majestic shadows of his own St. Paul's: and what deeper joy could an artist know in painless old age than to sit under the splendid dome himself had raised, within the walls that he knew would be both his tomb and his memorial?

It was at his home at Hampton that he died, on the afternoon of February 25th, 1723, peacefully in his sleep after dinner, seated in his chair. The panelled room in which he died is on the ground floor, on the left-hand side as you approach from the Green. Only once in these latter years was his peace disturbed, when the upstart Benson, not content with stealing his position, accused him—or rather, the late clerk of the works—of jobbery, having the charges preferred through his brother as he did not wish too openly to reveal his jealousy. The mud he stirred, however, stuck only to himself. His own jobbery, his own incompetence, were so clear against Wren's honesty and genius that investigations soon sent him running off less than a year after his appointment. Being a royal favourite, he was, of course, given other work, and was excellently if absurdly paid with £1,200 a year; but Sir Christopher could sit back well content in his delightful home on the Green, relaxing from his scientific investigations—for that busy brain could not be stilled save by death—to smile at the pismire who had dared try to foul his name.

Of this first George's reign there is little else to tell save that eventually king and prince were reconciled, probably urged by Caroline, as the king had taken charge of his grandchildren and she was a loving mother. In public, father had kissed son, but in private they continued to detest each other while Hampton Court figures rarely in the records. We hear of little but the smallest backchat, although it might be of interest to note that the performance of *Henry VIII* was by no means the only play acted here. Little though he knew of English, the king liked the stage. In the *London Journal* for October 2nd, 1731, for example, we find this advertisement: "Wednesday a Messenger came from Hampton-Court, to Mr. Wilk's in Bowstreet, to signify, that the Theatre in the Palace there was entirely fitted up; and that 'twas their Majesties Pleasure to have Plays acted there very speedily: And this morning Mr. Cibber, by Command, is to attend at Court with a List of such Plays as the Company have in Readiness to perform."

But even such entertainments lapsed as the years passed. Sadly, however, we might mention that Molly Lepell now married Hervey, Pope's Lord Fanny,

> . . . *that thing of silk,*
> *Sporus, that mere white curd of asses milk,*
> *Who at the ear of Eve, familiar toad,*
> *Half froth, half venom, spits himself abroad;*

and that Miss Bellenden married her Colonel Campbell who, in time, long time, was to become the Duke of Argyle. These weddings tolled farewell to the Swiss Cantons and we might cry like Giles Earle, groom of the prince's bedchamber, in 1717: "Would to God I was at Hampton Court; I stupify myself by eternally thinking of that place. . . ."

CHAPTER XIV
KING GEORGE THE SECOND

DULLNESS remained, a formal cloud, on Hampton Court. The charm of those days when George II had been Prince of Wales was gone with his princeship, and Mrs. Howard, royal mistress though she was, laments the change in the already quoted letter to her friend Molly. Poor Mrs. Howard had cause to lament, for she soon became involved in an embarrassing argument on etiquette. Caroline was a gentle person but one can sympathise with her grain of malice in this quarrel. She desired that her bedchamber woman in waiting should bring the basin and ewer for washing and present them kneeling; and as Mrs. Howard had this appointment, her dignity could not permit her thus to debase herself to her wittol. "With her little fierce eyes," the queen wrote to Hervey, "and cheeks as red as your coat," Mrs. Howard said "that positively she would not do it: to which I made her no answer then in anger, but calmly, as I would have said to a naughty child, 'Yes, my dear Howard, I am sure you will; indeed you will. Go, go! fie for shame! Go, my good Howard; we will talk of this another time'."

Before such calm malevolence, Mrs. Howard could but turn scarlet and scribble a note to a friend, asking him to inquire of Lady Masham, one-time bedchamber woman to Queene Anne, whether she or the queen were in the right. Lady Masham's reply could have given Mrs. Howard small satisfaction but it is of interest to us for it shows the intricate ritual of court etiquette.

"The Bedchamber-*Woman*," wrote Lady Masham, "came into waiting before the Queen's prayers, which was before her Majesty was dressed. The Queen often shifted in a morning: if her Majesty shifted at noon, the Bedchamber-*Lady* being by, the Bedchamber-*Woman* gave the shift to the Lady without any ceremony, and the *Lady* put it on. Sometimes, likewise, the Bedchamber-Woman gave the fan to the *Lady* in the same manner; and this was all that the Bedchamber-*Lady* did about the Queen at her dressing. When the Queen washed her hands, the Page of the Backstairs brought and set down upon a side-table the basin and ewer; then the Bedchamber-Woman set it before the Queen, and knelt on the other

Hampton Court from the River—Rowlandson

side of the table over-against the Queen, the Bedchamber-Lady only looking on. The Bedchamber-Woman poured the water out of the ewer upon the Queen's hands. The Bedchamber-Woman pulled on the Queen's gloves, when she could not do it herself [this refers to gouty Anne]. The Page of the Back-stairs was called in to put on the Queen's shoes. When the Queen dined in public, the Page reached the glass to the Bedchamber-Woman, and she to the Lady-in-Waiting. The Bedchamber-Woman brought the chocolate, and gave it without kneeling. In general the Bedchamber-Woman had no dependence on the Lady of the Bedchamber."

In short, the queen was in the right of it and, after a tormented week, Mrs. Howard had to give way and kneel with the basin. Many a time must she have longed to throw it into Caroline's plump smiling face. That the queen later wished to be agreeable is shown by her remarks to that ubiquitous Hervey: " About a week after, when upon maturer deliberation, she [Mrs. Howard] had done everything about the basin that I would have her, I told her I knew we should be good friends again; but could not help adding, in a little more serious voice, that I owned of all my servants I had least expected, as I had least deserved it, such treatment from her, when she knew I had held her up at a time when it was in my power, if I had pleased, any hour of the day, to let her drop through my fingers—thus—"

You can see to-day at Hampton Court the room in which this petty quarrel took place almost as it was in Caroline's time and, what is of peculiar interest, still stands the marble bath in which Caroline washed. It is in the oak-panelled dressing-room with the lofty marble-lined recess with basin and tap. Near the bath opens a door leading into her Private Chapel which had been especially arranged for her; therefore while she dressed the queen could listen to prayers as she gossiped with her ladies and visitors. Dr. Madox, later Bishop of Worcester, was her chaplain, and he appears to have had no serious objections to having an undercurrent of feminine chatter beneath the words of God. On one occasion, indeed, when bade to begin the service, he nodded at a painting of a nude Venus over the mantelshelf and remarked: " And a very proper altar piece is here, madam ! "

Lord Hervey, priding himself as a wit, exposed his lack of it by writing a trifle called: *The Death of Lord Hervey; or, a Morning at*

Court. The scene is laid in this dressing-room or bathing-closet and the queen is " discovered at her toilet cleaning her teeth, with Mrs. Purcell dressing her Majesty's head, and the princesses, and ladies and women of the bedchamber standing around her. The Litany is being said in the next room:—

" *First Parson* (behind the scenes): ' From pride, vain-glory, and hypocrisy, from envy, hatred, and malice, and all uncharitableness. . . .'

" *Second Parson:* ' Good Lord, deliver us ! '

" *The Queen:* ' I pray, my good Lady Sundon, shut a little that door; these creatures pray so loud, one cannot hear oneself speak. (Lady Sundon goes to shut the door.) So, so, not quite so much; leave it open enough for those parsons to think we may hear, and enough shut that we may not hear quite so much.' "

There is a tale—it is sometimes attached to Queen Anne, but as she was most devout it is unlikely to refer to her—that on one of these mornings Caroline ordered the door into the chapel to be closed for a minute or two, then not hearing the usual accompaniment of prayers, demanded to know why the parson defaulted. The parson's furious retort was that he refused to whistle the word of God through the keyhole. Yet for all this casualness about morning prayers interrupting the sacrament of the looking-glass, the queen was fascinated by theology: she read deeply of it and enjoyed arguing with divines.

Rarely did the king intrude on this morning toilet, for he disliked large gatherings and bedroom-salons were the fashion. In Hogarth's *Marriage à la Mode* you can see the lady's morning levee in Print IV where she chats with the parson while her hair is being curled and gentlemen read and play on instruments about her. Such were Caroline's mornings, only on a more splendid scale. Although the king usually kept away on these occasions, there was one time when he wandered in and noticed that Caroline had a kerchief over her chest. Furiously he snatched it off and turned on Mrs. Howard, crying: " Is it because you have an ugly neck yourself that you love to hide the queen's ? " which was scarcely nice treatment for the mistress, however consoling to the wife.

But soon Mrs. Howard was to escape this vexing court. Her brother-in-law died in 1731 and, becoming the Countess of Suffolk, she could no longer retain her lowly position, as she wrote to the poet Gay: " To prevent all future quarrels, I shall let you know that

I have kissed hands for the place of mistress of the robes. Her Majesty did me the honour to give me the choice of lady of the bedchamber, or that, which I find so much more agreeable to me, that I did not take one moment to consider of it. The Duchess of Dorset resigned it for me; and everything as yet promises more happiness for the latter part of my life than I have yet had a prospect of. Seven nights' quiet sleep, and seven easy days have almost worked a miracle upon me."

She resided in chambers in the south-east corner of the palace, on the ground floor, and here at eight o'clock, as already recorded, the king would punctually visit her.

The court was exhaustingly dull, enlivened only by hunting. " We hunt with great noise and violence," moaned Mrs. Howard, " and have every day a tolerable chance of having a neck broken." On one occasion, Princess Amelia was nearly killed when chasing a stag in the Park, for she was thrown, but luckily not hurt. Although she did not care for the sport, Caroline, to please the king, would follow him in her chaise, usually with her vice-chamberlain, that inevitable Hervey, for he " loved hunting as little as she did, so that he might ride constantly by the side of her chaise, and entertain her whilst other people were entertaining themselves by hearing dogs bark and seeing crowds gallop." The king hunted only the stag, for he despised fox hunters. " It was a pretty occupation for a man of quality," he once said to the Duke of Grafton, " and at his age to be spending all his time in tormenting a poor fox, that was generally a much better beast than any of those that pursued him; for the fox hurts no other animal but for his subsistence, while those brutes who hurt him did it only for the pleasure they took in hurting." When the duke attempted to apologise for his bloodthirsty pleasure by explaining that he only did it for his health, the king asked why then did he not ride post for his health ?

Every Wednesday and Saturday George would hunt for four or five hours in the parks and afterwards would often dine in public with his court in the public dining-room which had been originally intended for a music-room. Cards were for the evenings, ombre being his favourite game, while the queen preferred basset; piquet and quadrille were also popular card games of the time, while those who had money to lose tossed it on dice at hazard. Some evenings, while watching the clock for his visit to Mrs. Howard, the king would discuss politics and other important matters with his few favourites.

Up and down the room he would walk, for he talked better walking than seated, asking Mr. Hervey this or that, muttering aside to his queen in German—that being their intimate language—or talking with those unfortunate Huguenot refugees, Lord Lufford and his sister, Lady de Roucy, about soldiers or genealogies—both pet subjects—for he " never forgot their goodness, but never remembered their poverty," George being somewhat of a miser.

He loved money and he hated his son, as his father had hated him. He grudged a penny spent and it was the queen's cleverness in instituting public dinners that kept him popular with a public that loved display and thought kings should spend the money they were given. Crowds would lean on the barriers, watching each mouthful vanish into royal gobs, while George himself must have been groaning to think of the expense. With his ministers he would contest the slightest cost for the slightest thing and he would keep court places open for as long as possible so that he need not pay the salaries. When he gave the queen a present it was usually something he wanted himself, such as houses or horses, which he would use far more than she. On the question of his children's incomes he made his greatest blunder, for he alienated both their and his people's love.

The traditional hatred of father for son was again to bring unhappiness, George treating Prince Frederick—or Fitz, as he was known—with calculated lack of generosity, and Fitz, being a conceited pop-eyed young fool, retorted by favouring always the opposition party in the House. For all the queen's intelligence and efforts to keep the peace, it was no happy family. Even the daughters were unhappy, dreaming of power. Anne, Princess Royal, spiteful and clever, would, as Fitz probably realised to his chagrin, have made a far more successful Prince of Wales than he.* Always she would rise early in the morning to paint or read or use her needle. She played the harpsichord, Fitz the fiddle or 'cello, and her taste was superior to his, for there were squabbles about her love for Handel and his for the Italian opera. A shrewd lass with few illusions, she once remarked of her father that when important matters went wrong, he would fret, but when he was in his worst humour and the devil

---

* Lovers of Hampton Court, however, should not be too harsh to the memory of Frederick. Inferior to his sister's may have been his judgment of music, but he had some love of the arts and was a discriminating dilettante, helping and encouraging many artists. George Vertue tells in his *Notebooks* how Frederick wished to have the royal collections at Hampton Court and Windsor thoroughly catalogued and cared for; and this interest was no pose, for he was able to recite almost a complete catalogue from memory. When his memory failed he would race to Hampton Court, sometimes with Vertue, to refresh it. For this, at least, we must respect him.

to everybody it was because one of his pages had powdered his periwig ill or a housemaid had set down a chair where it was not usually set.

This is the last royal family to inhabit Hampton Court and with the glory of the palace fading, echoes of Tudor and Stuart dying before the guttural voices, it is well that so dull a group should conclude its history. Dull, indeed they were; forgotten now the days when happy maids had laughed in the garden and Pope had watched, bewitched, bewitching them in rime: gone with all the beauty and terror of its past, the warriors, the poets, the merry wenches. . . . Boredom reigns in our palace.

This is a miserable back-biting family with only genial Caroline to give some human light, but we must meet them all in a last farewell. Nor must we forget the Huguenots mentioned above: Lord Lifford and Charlotte de Roucy, "two miserable court drudges," as Hervey calls them, "who were in a more constant waiting than any of the pages of the backstairs"; they "were very simple and very quiet, did nobody any hurt, nor anybody but His Majesty any pleasure, who paid them so ill for all their assiduity and slavery that they were not only not in affluence, but laboured under the disagreeable burdens of small debts, which £1,000 would have paid, and had not an allowance from the Court, that enabled them to appear there even in the common decency of clean clothes. The King nevertheless was always saying how well he loved them, and calling them the best people in the world. . . ."

Amongst other foreigners the Hanoverian, Schutz, must not be forgotten, if only to quote Hervey's couplet:

> *Charlotte and Schutz like angry monkeys chatter,*
> *None guessing what's the language or the matter;*

but we have passed over Princess Amelia, a discourtesy to one who neither deserves nor would tolerate such treatment. She was a shrewd, cruel, spiteful girl, although more attractive in appearance than Anne, for she could inspire Lady Pomfret to enthusiasm. She was, wrote Lady Pomfret, "the oddest, or at least one of the oddest princesses that ever was known; she has her ears shut to flattery and her heart open to honesty. She has honour, justice, good-nature, sense, wit, resolution, and more good qualities than I have time to tell you, so mixed that (if one is not a *devil*) it is impossible to say she has too much or too little of any; yet all these do not in anything (without exception) make her forget the King of England's daughter, which dignity she keeps up with such an obliging behaviour that she charms everybody. Do not believe her complaisance to me makes me say one *silible* more than the rigid truth; though I confess she has gained my heart and has added one more to the number of those few whose *desert* forces one's affections."

Although she loved flattery and men's company sufficiently to cause many a titter behind fans, Amelia also loved the open life, hunting particularly, and on one occasion she horrified all Hampton Court by striding to church in a riding-habit with a dog tucked under each arm. This habit was of a masculine cut with a laced scarlet coat and a round hunting-cap; and she was not adverse to combining that other dangerous sport, the usually indoor sport of love, with hard riding. Her name became entangled with that of the Duke of Grafton, a conceited bad-mannered hunting-man—we have already recorded the king's remark to him about fox-hunting—who, being the grandson of Charles II, behaved like a prince, talking to the queen as though to an equal and quizzing her about her love for her husband; when she declared that she truly loved George, the duke smirked. " By God, ma'am," said he, " I do not know, but if I were King of France I would soon find out whether you did or not." Instead, however, of testing Caroline's virtue, he tested her daughter's and, apparently, found it engagingly frail, for once when out hunting with her near Windsor, they galloped ahead of their attendants and did not return to the castle until long after dark, airily explaining that they had stopped at a private house.

Lastly, the pathetic Caroline the younger, tormented with love for mincing Lord Hervey which he swiftly sensed and had the bad taste and cruelty to mention in the already quoted playlet. She alone at court he made shocked at the news of his death; hiding her sorrow, she yet could not stop her hands from writhing until her mother cried: " My God, Caroline, you will twist off the thumbs of your glove ! " Such was her reward for her melancholy worship of that she-knave.

On one occasion, the king was smugly tabulating the weaknesses of his royal predecessors. Charles I, said he, was governed by his wife; Charles II by his whores; James II by his priests; William by his men, and Anne by her women favourites; his own father by anyone who could get hold of him; and himself? Well, said he: who do you say governs now? The summing up was shrewd but not quite shrewd enough, for although George II was governed not by whores, priests, men or women favourites, he was assuredly ruled by his wife, if not so blatantly as had been Charles I by Henrietta Maria. Caroline was too clever a woman to reveal her power; she let the king think himself master and thereby, with the aid of gossiping Hervey, ruled the nation so far as royalty then could rule. And she had Robert Walpole for friend, and we see both her good sense and good humour in this friendship; Walpole would jocularly call her the Bitch and Caroline, hearing of it, instead of losing her temper, sent him a message, saying: "Tell him that Fat Bitch . . ." They were firm friends after that.

Every morning, Hervey in all his paint and powder would breakfast with her in her gallery adjoining the Queen's State Bedchamber to discuss affairs and personalities. "It is well I am so old," said Caroline, "or I should be talked of for this creature." At about nine o'clock, her eldest children would join this breakfast of fruit and sour cream with chocolate to drink, and sometimes the king, who was usually ill-tempered in the morning, would arrive and take his queen, should the weather prove fine, for a trot in the gardens. But in later life, having lost his beloved Hanover with its Hanoverian mistresses, he was growing querulous and—although this happened at Kensington Palace, not Hampton Court—would snub Caroline for always stuffing, Emily for not listening to him, Princess Caroline for growing fat, and his son William for standing awkwardly; then off into the garden would he carry the queen to be snubbed again.

What he needed was another mistress, Lady Suffolk having at last departed, and Caroline, weary of insults and contradictions of every word she said, resigned herself to the bleak necessity. As the princess royal, Anne, complained to Hervey: she could not bear her father "giving himself airs of gallantry; the impossibility of being easy with him; his affectation of heroism; his unreasonable, simple, uncertain, disagreeable, and often shocking behaviour to the Queen; the difficulty of entertaining him; his insisting upon people's conversation who were to entertain him being always new, and his own being always the same over and over again." Sadly, the queen realised that she must find someone to take Howard's place; but who? Walpole added his advice, pointing out that you could scarcely expect George to spend his evenings with his own daughters "after having tasted the sweets of passing them with other people's wives." Princess Caroline agreed, wishing, she said, with all her heart that he would find some woman so "that mamma might be a little relieved from the *ennui* of seeing him for ever in her room."

It is now that the already mentioned Lady Deloraine, the Fly, flutters to Hampton Court, although Walpole was against using her: she had, said he, " a weak head, a pretty face, a lying tongue, and a false heart." But Walpole's protests were flicked aside and Lady Deloraine achieved the not too coveted post, the king visiting her every night as he had visited Mrs. Howard, and having her always sit beside him and taking her for walks in the garden. She was a lovely woman, but, as Walpole had remarked, her head was weak and she must be continually boasting of her royal conquest, saying once to Hervey: " Do you know the king has been in love with me for two years ? " Hervey, that curdish Lord Fanny, was no man to listen to a woman's trills. He but smiled and shrugged and said: " Who is not in love with you ? " and thus clamped down the soul's conversation. Walpole still feared her talk might cause trouble, but Hervey reassured him. " If she got the ear of anybody in power," he said, " it might be of very bad consequence, but since 'tis only the king I think it is of no great significance."

In speaking so long of the court-life, peopling those chambers to the south and east, I fear we have neglected the fabric which housed

The Tennis Court & Herbaceous Border

these ghosts, for even now alterations and additions continued, although on a small scale, being little compared to Wren's destruction. William Kent took a hand at the work, for he was just emerging into fashion, and brilliant architect though he became, he did only wicked harm to Hampton Court, for like most of his intelligent contemporaries, he was in the first whirl of fake gothick—and I feel the *k* is essential if we would differentiate this eighteenth century parody from genuine gothic. Probably Horace Walpole had much to do with the craze, but his was a serious antiquarian interest. Others actually built gothick bookcases and summer-houses, gothick farms and mantelpieces. A tragic, if sometimes comic, revival was this, with gables and turrets and ruins and battlements and what Scott called curly-whirls, all placed anywhere without design or reason, in a nightmare medley of a medieval craftsman's dream of hell, to culminate in a frenzy towards the end of the century in Walpole's Strawberry Hill and Beckford's Fonthill which was eventually half to tumble down, to the owner's satisfaction, for then it made a delightfully genuine ruin.

Architects had returned from Greece and Italy in a flare of love for ruins that were beautiful only because they had not been intended to become ruins, and now arose imitation parthenons on the green fields of England, while Kent even planted dead trees because they looked picturesque. It was, perhaps, a reaction from the classicism of Wren that made architects build asymmetrically: therefore the love of ruins, destroying order. Broken columns were placed on lawns and hermitages were built with live hermits paid to live in them and bridges were raised to break the view, although you could not walk on them—there is one to be seen at Ken Wood, a most deceptive one when noticed from the house. England fell in love with ruins. It was a rebellion against discipline, a passion for decay because decay was free, weeds were free, ivy and brambles, all were free, and now they were artificially cultivated to give an artificial air of freedom to nature. Again we find this revolt against classicism in the glorification of the perpendicular in contrast to the horizontal, for although classic architecture is often perpendicular, the columns lead somewhere and are finished with an architrave or a pediment and thereby become horizontal, as on Wren's east front. This new gothick was all perpendicular, except when columns were tossed down to lie in the grass. And now Kent, in a young lover's rage, thought to bring this fashion to poor Hampton Court.

He was unloosed on the east range of the Clock Court and managed to raise a monstrosity only equalled by Wren's colonnade slicing that same court—a barrier holding back the Tudor beauty, grotesquely out of place. He tore down the old bay windows, blinded those perfectly proportioned Tudor eyes, and in their places built a pointed window, a gothick doorway, and two new turrets. Even inside the palace he penetrated, violating further Tudor work, dividing two exquisite rooms into six boxes.

But enough. . . . Let us, to escape the suffocating despair of seeing this vandalism, contemplate instead the gardens, for Queen Caroline, as one would expect with so gracious a lady, loved flowers. Unfortunately, however, she called in the aid of this wretched Kent, for however fine an architect he may have become when the madness left him, we can have little but contempt for him at this period. The old garden of the Great Fountain Court, so refreshingly friendly with its patterned beds and curving parterres, was pulled up, flattened, demolished, and buried under grass. Even the fountains were uprooted for the sake of grass, as though he would turn the palace to a cowshed. Plain lawns now unrolled where flowers had lived and all was laid out in stiff geometrical designs, curiously ungothick, but equally as maddening when we realise what we have lost.

In this melancholy mood, contemplating the modish madness of Kent, I think it would be as well to take up Hervey's pen for a time and record that, within the palace, all remained as dull as one would expect when it was inhabited with the souls of those who could approve such barbarism.

With his usual self-conscious wit, he writes on July 31st, 1733: " I will not trouble you with any account of our occupations at Hampton Court. No mill-horse ever went in a more constant track, or a more unchanging circle, so that by the assistance of an almanack for the day of the week, and a watch for the hour of the day, you may inform yourself fully, without any other intelligence but your memory, of every transaction within the verge of the Court. Walking, chaises, levees and audiences fill the morning; at night the King plays at commerce and backgammon, and the Queen at quadrille, where poor Charlotte [de Roucy] runs her usual nightly gauntlet— the Queen pulling her hood, Mr. Schutz sputtering in her face, and the Princess Royal rapping her knuckles. It was in vain she fled from persecution for her religion: she suffers for her pride what she escaped for her faith; undergoes in a drawing room what she dreaded from the Inquisition, and will die a martyr to a Court, though not to a church. The Duke of Grafton takes his nightly opiate of lottery, and sleeps as usual between the Princesses Amelia and Carolina; Lord Grantham strolls from one room to another (as Dryden says), 'like some discontented ghost that oft appears and is forbid to speak,' and stirs himself about, as people stir a fire, not with any design, but in hopes to make it burn brisker, which his lordship constantly does, to no purpose, and yet tries as constantly as if it had ever once succeeded. At last the King comes up; the pool finishes, and everybody has their dismission: their Majesties retire to Lady Charlotte and my Lord Lifford; the Princesses, to Bilderbec and Lony; my lord Grantham to Lady Frances and Mr. Clark; some to supper, and some to bed; and thus (to speak in the scripture phrase) the evening and the morning make a day."

We come now to the inevitable father and son quarrel and I fear we must return to Lord Hervey's *Memoirs* in which he recounts what happened one night at Hampton Court when the queen idly mentioned some fellow who had misbehaved at the playhouse and the king remarked that he supposed nobody knew such a scoundrel. The queen said that his name was Bray and that the king knew his father, which prompted George to roar: "His father might be a very worthy man, though his son is a puppy. One very often sees fathers and sons very little alike; a wise father has very often a fool for his son. One sees a father a very brave man, and his son a scoundrel; a father very honest, and his son a great knave; a father a man of truth, and his son a great liar; in short, a father that has all sorts of good qualities, and a son that is good for nothing."

There was no mistaking the point of this outburst, as Hervey remarks, for "his Majesty drew this picture of a father and a son with so much eagerness, complimenting the one so strongly and inveighing against the other so vehemently, that the Queen (though a good mistress of her countenance), looking towards Lord Hervey [himself], betrayed that she took the parallel as it was meant, and the King himself, feeling he had pushed too far, turned off the ridicule he thought he had incurred, with quickness enough, by saying that sometimes it was just the reverse, and that disagreeable fathers had very agreeable men for their sons. I suppose in this case he thought of his own father, as in the other he did of his own son."

However, there was no open quarrel until after the king's last visit to Hanover and his return in 1737. He always had preferred Hanover to England; on one occasion he had wailed that neither English nor French could cook, no English player could act, no English coachman drive or jockey ride, nor were English horses fit to be ridden, while no Englishman knew how to enter a room, nor did Englishwomen know how to dress. Therefore on this final visit it was long before he could be cajoled from German food and fat women, while Caroline had not only to manage state affairs but to suffer the boredom of her eldest son's company.

Frederick was now married to Princess Augusta of Saxe-Gotha, and purely to make his mother feel uncomfortable he discovered that his wife had a conscience. Being a strict Lutheran, he said, she could not receive the sacrament according to the rites of the Church of England. Caroline quickly stopped that nonsense by threatening to pack Augusta back to Germany, for which country she apparently had less love than her father-in-law, as she quickly dried her tears and with the rest of the family entered the Chapel at Hampton Court. But she was always late. She and Frederick would linger until the last moment so that Augusta had to push past the queen to her seat in the pew, and the pew—as you can see on your next visit—being narrow and Caroline fat, such proceedings were both painful and embarrassing. So constant was this ill-mannered behaviour, the service always being interrupted, that Caroline sent word that if Augusta with her numerous suite were late again, she must come in by another entrance. As Augusta ignored this decree, Caroline posted a servant at the main entrance to stop her coming in until the service had ended, so that either Augusta had to stay away or enter by another door. Fitz thereupon commanded her to stay away unless she could use the main door; and thus the silly squabble held fire.

Caroline was determined to keep her temper and to give her son no opportunity for rudeness. She had prince and princess to dine with her at Hampton Court once or twice a week and in the evening she invited them to cards and music in the gallery. The prince could not wriggle from these dinner invitations, but in the evenings Augusta usually came on her own; and the poor queen was sunk in intolerable ennui when in their company. "The silly gaiety," she wailed, "and rude railleries of her son, joined to the flat stupidity of her daughter-in-law, has oppressed her to that degree that she felt ready to cry with the fatigue of their company, and felt herself more tired than she believed she should have done if she had carried them round the garden on her back."

But soon boredom went in rage. The prince was meddling—almost treasonably it seemed to his parents—in politics and, what from George's point of view was even worse, he was attempting to get the House of Commons to increase his allowance, appealing above the king to the king's subjects. According to Hervey, a hundred times a day, George—now at last back from Hanover—and Caroline prayed that Fitz might drop down dead of apoplexy, Caroline cursing the hour of his birth and calling him a " nauseous beast " who cared " for nobody but his nauseous self."

Fitz's demand for money, however, was frustrated by the king's ministers and in an explosive state he arrived at Hampton Court in the summer of 1737. His revenge on his parents now was to tighten his lips about his wife's pregnancy which was becoming rather obvious: whenever the worried queen questioned him about it he would obstinately mutter: " I don't know." He had admitted, he could scarcely do anything else, that Augusta was with child, but he would not give even a hint of the expected date of birth until the queen began to wonder whether he were not lying, whether his wife's stomach were not padded so that somebody's bastard could be palmed off as her grandchild, or whether Fitz were not impotent; and she even questioned Hervey, as they had shared the same mistress. Hervey assured her that, although inexperienced, his mistress had told him that Fitz was potent. Caroline's suspicions were largely hope, for she shared the general misconception that Augusta could not bear a child and her desire was for the crown to descend to her younger boy, William, whom she adored.

In every way wishing to frustrate his miserly parents, Fritz decided that his child would be born in St. James's Palace while his mother was too suspicious of trickery to agree. She was determined that the birth should take place at Hampton Court, under her eyes, so that no bastard should be smuggled in. When Hervey said that Fitz would not obey her, she retorted: " Well, if it is to be so, I cannot help it; but at her labour I positively will be, let her lie-in where she will; for she cannot be brought to bed as quick as one can blow one's nose, and I will be sure it is her child. For my part, I do not see that she is big; you all say you see it, and therefore I suppose it is so, and that I am blind."

Blind she was, for on the last Sunday of July, after dining in public with the king and queen, Augusta retired to her rooms to join the prince—he had not spoken to his parents since the failure of his parliamentary application—and very soon her labour pains began. Their apartment stands to the north of the Public Dining Room, and the floor would have been practically empty at this hour while downstairs, all unaware of the excitement above, Caroline played quadrille with Princess Amelia; the king, with his Deloraine and the maids of honour, played commerce; Hervey and his adoring Princess Caroline played cribbage. Thus did the royal family and their attendants fiddle with cards while prince and princess upstairs waited for night with terrible impatience. At ten o'clock the games broke up and by eleven all had retired to bed.

The prince had ordered his coach to be ready for a rush to London. By now, Augusta was in such agony that she cared no longer about any plots to exasperate the king and queen, for the first writhings of imminent gestation were painfully apparent. A dancing-master and one of the prince's equerries, ignoring her yelping protests, bundled her down the stairs and along the passages, the prince following and refusing to heed the remonstrances of attendants while his wife was " begging, for God's sake, the Prince would let her stay in quiet where she was, for the pains were so great she could not set one foot before the other, and was upon the rack when they moved her."

" But the Prince," we are told, " with an obstinacy equal to his folly, and a folly equal to his barbarity, insisted on her going, crying, ' Courage ! courage ! *ah, quelle sottise* ! ' and telling her, with the encouragement of a tooth-drawer, or the consolatory tenderness of an executioner, that it would be over in a minute. With these incitations, and in this manner, after enjoining all his servants not to say one word what was the matter, for fear the news of the Princess's circumstances should reach the other part of the house, and their going should be prevented, he got her into the coach."

I call again on the assistance of Mr. Law to follow in the track of this lunatic and his wretched wife, for his knowledge of the palace was so profound that it would be foolish arrogance to attempt my own reconstruction when his appears so plainly to be correct. " The stairs down which the Princess was dragged," he wrote, " we presume to have been the Prince of Wales's Stairs, which are situated at the back of their apartments, and lead into the cloister of the Fountain Court. Having reached the cloister, she must have been either hurried through the courtyards to the great western gate, or more likely through the Tudor cloisters, past the chapel, to one of the side-doors in the Tennis Court Lane, whence they could have started with less danger of detection."

Many hours later, about half-past one the following morning, a courier from St. James's Palace galloped to Hampton Court with tidings that the Princess of Wales was in labour. Startled, uncomprehending, the queen sat up in bed crying was the palace on fire? but her dresser, Mrs. Tichburne, explained that not the palace but her daughter-in-law was in danger. " My God! my nightgown," cried the queen, " I'll go to her this moment." " Your nightgown, madame," said Tichburne, " ay, and your coaches, too; the princess is at St. James's." " Are you mad ? " wailed the queen, " or are you asleep, my good Tichburne ? you dream."

But Mrs. Tichburne soon proved it was no dream and, when he heard, the king raved. Husband-like, he turned on the queen and roared at her in German: " You, see, now, with all your wisdom, how they have outwitted you. This is all your fault. There will be a false child put upon you, and how will you answer for it to all your children ? This has been fine care and fine management for your son, William; he is mightily obliged to you ; and as for Anne, I hope she will come over and scold you yourself; I am sure you deserve anything she can say to you."

The queen knew better than to answer. She wasted no time in argument but quickly dressed and sped to London in her coach, the Princesses Amelia and Caroline going with her with some lords in waiting. At about four o'clock she reached St. James's and, at top of the palace stairs, met the prince triumphant in his nightgown. He kissed her hand and cheek and told her that she was too late, that the princess had borne a daughter. It was " a little rat of a girl, about the bigness of a good large toothpick case." " The good God bless you, poor little creature," said the queen, taking up the baby which was wrapped in an old red mantle and some napkins; " you have come into a troublesome world," she sighed.

Reassured at sight of " this poor little bit of a thing " instead of the " brave fat jolly boy " she had feared to see, the queen realised that the child actually was her son's. That did not, however, dissipate her wrath, nor the king's. He called his son a "scoundrel and puppy, knave and fool, liar and coward." When they had cooled a little, later that morning, with Walpole's help, they composed a letter to Fitz, reprimanding him strongly. George's intention had been to take almost violent action but the wise Walpole restrained him, pointing out that when the truth was discovered all sympathy would go to him and the queen. And he was right. The friends who had spurred and supported Fitz in his rebellion, now shyed from him, particularly when it was learned that the fool had confessed that twice during the previous week he had driven Augusta to London when the pains had appeared to be starting, and twice had he driven the unfortunate woman back to Hampton Court on finding they had been premature.

Realising that this time he had gone too far, Fitz announced that he would go to Hampton Court to pay his respects to his parents, but when George heard he forbade him to approach. Then followed a wearisome correspondence in which Fitz attempted to throw all blame on to his mother: she, he insisted, had caused the quarrel between him and his father ; and this was the key which his followers did not shirk using. They dared not insult the king, but the mud intended for him they threw at the queen, for she was Walpole's friend and his political opponents, the tories, naturally stabbed at him and his party through her. Fitz, when he wrote to her, refused to title her queen; but Caroline was too sensible a woman to become annoyed by such silly insolence. She laughed while she told Hervey that Fitz had once argued that he was superior in rank to her. " Since, believe me, my dear Fitz," she had said to the fool, " let your quality be ever so great, the king, if I was to die, would never marry you."

Caroline was soon in bed with gout and in her pain and boredom so far forgot court etiquette as to have Hervey in to chat with her while she lay in bed. Not only had gout dragged her low, but twice lately she " had been seized with vomiting and purging, which had lasted in the most violent manner for three or four hours, and then left her so easy and well, that she had played the same night in the drawing-room as usual, and talked with the utmost cheerfulness." But gout, as any who has suffered this excruciating affliction, this hot coal under the skin, should know, is not something to be borne with cheerfulness. Yet this " delicate Hermaphrodite, such a pretty little Master-Miss," Hervey, could always make Caroline smile and now he amused her with impromptu verses which he carefully preserved in his memoirs.

She had not long to live, but only herself knew the truth of her illness. The king was one of those testy people with no patience for others' suffering and therefore the queen, although often in agony,

would smile and play cards and even walk with him. Once when she
had gout and the king wanted her to walk, she plunged her tortured
legs into ice-cold water; and such extreme treatment could scarcely
have helped. But gout was only a minor ailment. For years, the
news-sheets had been describing her various ills, her gout, her ague,
her rash, her pleurisy, her colic, but never the true and dangerous
one which was eventually to kill her. At the birth of her youngest
child in 1724, she had suffered a serious umbilical rupture, but

Banqueting
House.

fearing to lose her spiritual hold on her husband by releasing the physical one, she would not mention it to George and preferred pain to the risk of losing him. When he noticed the swelling, she laughed his fears away; even when he besought her to consult a doctor, she would not listen, protesting that it was not serious, while she became quite angry, accusing him—for that was her secret fear—of using the swelling as a pretext for neglecting her. After that, of course, the king had to hold his tongue. If this was foolish of her, it was criminal to maintain the same pretence to the doctors; even when she had to be wheeled in a chair into her presence chamber, she told no one the truth.

She was not to die in Hampton Court. On October 28th, 1737, she left it for St. James's Palace and there, on November 20th, she died, only at the last sending Fitz a message of forgiveness, although she did not see him.

With the passing of Caroline, Hampton Court begins to die as a royal residence. Perhaps memories of the dead queen were sufficient to darken the palace, to turn shadows to mourning and dim even sunlight, for memories can often be more real than reality and ghosts can seem more lovely than the living. On her death-bed, George had sworn to Caroline when she counselled him to remarry: " No, I will have mistresses ! " and he kept his word. It was usually with Lady Yarmouth—a married German whom he had bought, according to Hervey, for a thousand ducats—that he was now to be seen at Hampton Court. And even then, but rarely. The people, as usual, protested at a foreign mistress while ministers were cynically advised to court her as " she certainly can give good or bad impressions in the many hours of conversation she has; for even the wisest man, like the cameleon, takes without knowing it more or less of the hue of what he is often *upon*."

George no longer resided at Hampton Court, as though the ghost of Caroline haunted him in those echoing chambers where that footpad of memory, sentiment, might strike him with a sudden pang at the sight of some small thing which had been hers—her hair tangled in a comb or brush, her slipper forgotten to be thrown away, her embroidery put aside never to be finished, her powder still spilt upon the edges of the closet floor. Occasionally, hurriedly, he would visit the palace on a summer afternoon with his mistresses for bodyguard against memory, and a few ladies and gentlemen of the household. " They went," according to Walpole, " in coaches

Entrance to Hampton Court—Rowlandson

and six in the middle of the day, with horse-guards kicking up the dust before them—dined, walked an hour in the garden, returned in the same dusty parade, and his Majesty fancied himself the most gallant and lively prince in Europe."

He would dine well during such a visit—or as well as despised English cooks could dine him—then take off his clothes for an hour's nap in bed; after which he would dress completely again and spend the evening at cards with Lady Yarmouth and a few friends. If important matters pressed during his siesta, Mr. Pitt, then secretary for state, would kneel on a cushion at his bedside while he talked with the drowsy king. This bedroom is still to be seen much as it was when George lay there, while in a nearby room stands a bed of crimson silk, his portmanteau at its foot, where last he slept.

There is little to report during these last years, the demise of a royal palace. Now that royalty was usually absent, many visitors rode out to examine the treasures, and once when the famous beauties, the Misses Gunnings, arrived they became most angry— according to Horace Walpole who often visited the palace from his nearby Strawberry Hill, that gothick horror—for there was one room labelled the Beauty Room—now called the Oak Room, in the south range on the ground floor, under the King's Guard Chamber— and when " the housekeeper said, ' This way, ladies; here are the Beauties,' " the Gunnings " flew into a passion, and asked her what she meant; that they came to see the Palace, not to be shown as sights themselves."

But there is one episode that must be recounted, as from this small matter arose the royal dislike of Hampton Court which doomed it for a palace. As he grew older, George II grew more ill-tempered and he would roar loudly and jump on his wig when annoyed, and one day in the state apartments he boxed the ears of his grandson, the future George III. We have the word of the Duke of Sussex, the son of this boxed George, that because of this insult, his father could never bear the palace, so that when he became king, he took most of the furniture away and granted rooms to private persons. Perhaps we should be grateful for it, however we regret the loss of the furniture, for he might have been stung like so many of his predecessors with a passion to rebuild and, as gothick was all the rage, with *chinoiserie*—in 1753 some justly unknown creature threw a Chinese bridge across the Thames at Hampton Court, which was shortly afterwards demolished: we have Canaletto's sketch of its switchback ups and downs between pagodas, and we must be profoundly grateful to whomever swept it away—we can imagine, should we dare, what monstrosity might have arisen, another Brighton Pavilion perhaps, like some blind cyclops over treasure trove.

Already, before George's death, the palace had become a museum. Horace Walpole would come from Strawberry Hill, that barbaric temple of an æsthete, but, no matter how his taste might frighten us, he was an enthusiastic, if rather ignorant, antiquary and archæologist. We may laugh at these old antiquarians, at Sir Walter Scott in fake Abbotsford, but we cannot despise their enthusiasm, their gusto for the past, as when young Scott discovered an old horn with " the original chain, hoop, and mouth-piece of steel," and in his delight slung it about his neck and blew on it as he rode from Liddesdale to Jedburgh. Meyrick was gathering his vast collection of plate and mail and old weapons and was compiling his dictionary of armour. That his dictionary is out of date, that his armoury harboured numerous worthless pieces, does not detract from his achievement. Scott in that mighty novel, *The Antiquary*, can make gentle fun of Monkburn, as a man may jest with tenderness at those he loves, but he does not make him a butt of foolery as Dickens did with his antiquarian Pickwick Club. To such had the noble lust of archæologists fallen: it had become a matter of laughter for gaitered gentlemen to dig their beloved country for relics of the past.

The late eighteenth and early nineteenth century revival has all my love; even in Strawberry Hill and Fonthill, even in Batty Langley's designs, even in Pope's queer grotto with its flints, its marbles, its crystal, where he could lurk like a crippled satyr, can I find beauty. It was a rush back into the past from which they attempted to create an eighteenth century order in disorder, to a past made magical, darkly shadowed with drawn swords behind the arras, by books like Mrs. Radcliffe's fascinating romances of melancholy youths and lovesick maids of sensibility.

On the death of George II this gothick passion began to blossom fruitily, to die for a time under the belching factories and dragon furnaces, the satanic mills of Blake, the dark horrors seen by Little Nell in her wanderings, only to be revived in the æsthetic drawing-rooms of the late nineteenth century. Because of George III's dislike of—or indifference to—Hampton Court, the palace was saved this final desecration. And we should applaud to see the builders more or less restrained and chiefly gardeners permitted to alter and beautify. The palace was becoming safe at least.

No restorers to-day can mutilate it and the work being done is supervised by antiquarians who love the past. Already one of the medallions of Roman emperors has been painted, many ceilings have been cleaned so that the paintings shine as fresh as from the artists' brushes, and the palace can remain content, knowing that never again may enthusiasts restore, rebuild, destroy. Here England's past from Tudor to Georgian can be seen, can be touched and loved; for this palace is, indeed, our history.

CHAPTER XV
UNTIL TO-DAY

IT is now our melancholy task to seal the ghosts for ever in their sanctuary. No longer a royal palace, Hampton Court became under George III substantially what it is to-day, a home for private families given apartments by grace and favour of the king. Unfortunately, restoration did not entirely cease. The Great Gatehouse of the West Front being found unsafe was partly taken down and rebuilt. From old prints we can see how noble must have been this front compared to what remains, for degenerate bricks were used, the two upper-stories were sliced off, thereby destroying the proportions, so that it became dwarf-like as it is now, while all the delightful Tudor vanes and crockets and pinnacles were thrown down. And it is at this date that we must record that Vine which, for some peculiar reason, is more famous to-day even than the palace and attracts so many greedy visitors. I have actually seen people, gaping at its swollen girth, by a natural association of ideas declare that Henry VIII had planted the monster; but I would suggest that when next you approach this vine house to stroll a little up that passage to your right beside the Lower Orangery where you will find yourself in a Tudor nook with twisting Tudor chimneys friendlily close.

This vine was planted in 1769, a slip having been taken from a huge vine at Valentine House, near Ilford, in Essex, of the "black Hamburgh sort." From our Hampton Court vine another slip was cut and planted at Cumberland Lodge, Windsor Castle. These are the three most famous vines in England, although elsewhere in the kingdom there are vines equally as large, if not larger. Once it was believed that its yield of grapes was because it fed on the sewerage from a nearby cesspool, but actually the roots reach the Thames and it is Thames water we must thank for the plump fruit.

At one time this vine yielded over 2,200 pounds of grapes in a year but to-day it gives roughly 500 which are sold every August in baskets woven by the blind heroes of St. Dunstan's. Its stem is seventy-two inches in girth and its main branch one hundred and fourteen feet long. Had the glasshouse been enlarged, the vine would, of course, have grown yet greater, but enlargement is impossible as it stands in a corner between two walls.

Although royalty had deserted the palace, great people yet lived there by grace and favour, and Horace Walpole would ride over often to listen to the music* or to visit friends, and on one such occasion he had a nasty fall. Writing to the Countess of Upper Ossory on September 13th, 1789, he tells how on " the night before last, going into a stone hall at Hampton Court, a very low step, that I did not perceive in the dusk, tripped me up, and gave me a worse fall than I had when your Ladyship did me the honour of dining here this summer. I fell headlong at once on the stones, and against the legs of a table, bruised one of my fingers, both knees and an elbow, and battered my hip so much that it has a patch as large as the crown of a hat, and as black; there again my featherhood saved me, and I did not break one of my straw-bones."

Yet his straw-bones were sufficiently jarred for him to lament a week later to Mary Berry that " I went to sit with my cousins, the three Phillips's, on Hampton Court Green; it was dusk; there was a very low step at the door, I did not see it; it tripped me up. I fell headlong on the stones, and against the frame of a table at the door, and battered myself so much, that my whole hip is as black as my shoe for above half a yard long and a quarter wide, besides bruising one hand, both knees, and my left elbow, into which it brought the gout next day. Now, pray admire my lightness: if I had weighed a straw, what mischief might not have happened to me ? "

But greater mischief than a bruise and shaken bones was caused in the palace in 1793, for Walpole writes to a friend on November 7th of that year to say that Richard Tickell, a commissioner of the stamp office and a very minor poet, had committed suicide. His " death," he writes, " was a determined measure, and more shocking than the usual mode by a pistol. He threw himself from one of the uppermost windows of the palace at Hampton Court into the garden—an immense height ! Some attribute his despair to debts; some to a breach with his political friends. . . ."

Walpole was not our only visitor, for in 1797 cattish Fanny Burney visited Mrs. Garrick in her house nearby, then with friends strolled to the palace where, she writes, " I dined and spent a very laughing and agreeable day on Thursday, hearing the band of the 11th regiment

---

* Of one such night he wrote: " It was moonlight and late, and very hot, and the lofty façade of the palace, and the untrimmed yews and canal, made me fancy myself of a party in Gramont's time—so you don't wonder that by the help of imagination I never passed an evening more deliciously. When by the aid of some historic vision or local circumstance I can romance myself into pleasure, I know nothing transports me so much."

play in the gardens to the Prince and Princess of Orange during their *lonchon*—then saw the palace. . . ."

But these were visitors. Of the distinguished gathering that has lived in the grace and favour apartments it is unnecessary for us to talk in any detail, for this book would then become a tedious *Who's Who* of the recent past. It is of greater interest to mention one who did not live there: Dr. Samuel Johnson; for in 1776 the doctor wrote to the lord chamberlain: "Being wholly unknown to your lordship, I have only this apology to make for presuming to trouble you with a request—that a stranger's petition, if it cannot be easily granted, can be easily refused. Some of the apartments at Hampton Court are now vacant, in which I am encouraged to hope that, by application to your lordship, I may obtain a residence. Such a grant would be considered by me as a great favour; and I hope, to a man who has had the honour of vindicating his Majesty's government, a retreat in one of his houses may be not improperly or unworthily allowed. I therefore request that your lordship will be pleased to grant such rooms in Hampton Court as shall seem proper to " Sam Johnson.

Alas, the request was refused, otherwise a new and splendidly garrulous life would have come to the palace and Boswell's bright eye would have brought living before us the ladies and gentlemen who are now merely names in the list of occupants. But the request being refused, the mighty doctor was left in Bolt Court with his cats and dependants and we have no shy Goldsmith, no wise Joshua Reynolds, no chattering Mrs. Traill, no posturing Garrick—who had a villa at Hampton—to light these autumn days and nights for us with wit and thunderous common sense.

Yet one famous figure does step in his perfect breeches, his well-creased coat and semi-starched cravat for a moment into Hampton Court; for in one of the apartments here, Beau Brummell wooed and failed to win Julia Storer, daughter of a maid of honour and the niece of Lord Carysfort. With exquisite plump arms and hands which she well knew how to make appear even more exquisite by playing the harp in dim-lit rooms, Julia bewitched Beau—then merely Buck—Brummell, for he was young; nor did his affection for her fade in years, not even after she fell passionately in love with her Hampton Court host, Colonel Cotton, and bore five of his children without the preliminary of marriage, the colonel being already married and the father of nine.

Harriette Wilson tells us that Brummell jealously remarked that no man in England stank like him, but it was an odour delectable to Julia. Again according to Harriette: " Julia received part of her education in France, and finished it at the palace of Hampton Court, where her mother sent her on a visit to the wife of Colonel Cotton, who was an officer in the 10th Dragoons. Mrs. Cotton had a family of nine children, and very little fortune to support them. Julia had been, from her earliest youth, encouraging the most romantic passions which ever fired a youthful breast. With all this, her heart, unlike mine, was as cold as her imagination was warm. What were parents, what were friends to her ? What was anything on earth, to love ? The first night Colonel Cotton danced with her, she was mad ! In four months more, she was pregnant. In nine months more, having concealed her situation, she was seized with the pangs of labour, while in the act of paying her respects to her Majesty ! and all was consternation in the *beau château de Hampton!* Mrs. Cotton, instead of sending for the accoucheur, with extreme propriety, though somewhat *mal-apropos*, loaded poor Julia with abuse ! ' Have yet a little mercy,' said Julia, ' and send for assistance.'—' Never, never, you monster ! you wretch ! will I so disgrace your family,' exclaimed Mrs. Cotton. Poor Julia's sufferings were short; but dreadfully severe. In about five hours, unassisted, she became the mother of a fine boy.

" Julia could not attempt to describe the rage and fury either of her mother or brother. It was harsh, it was shocking, even as applied to the most hardened sinner, in such a state of mental and bodily suffering. Julia was, with her infant, by her noble relatives, hurried into the country, almost at the risk of her life, and Colonel Cotton was called out by young Storer, Julia's brother, and, I believe, wounded."

Eight years after his meeting with her at the palace, Brummell still remembered Julia with affection when he met her again at the lodgings of that malicious whore, Harriette Wilson. Harriette tells us that " it appeared plain to me and evident that his attention to Julia was no longer the effect of love. Piqued at the idea of having been refused marriage by a woman with whom Cotton had so easily succeeded *sans ceremonie*, he determined in his own mind soon to be even with his late brother officer." Here, however, Harriette is interpreting Brummell's feelings by the red light of her own vindictive heart, for there was nothing petty in the Beau, and it is probable—a thing impossible for Harriette to understand—that he still loved Julia. When she had borne her first child by Cotton he sent her some trite verses that yet have feeling in them, beginning:

> *Unhappy child of indiscretion,*
> *Poor slumberer on a breast forlorn !*
> *Pledge and proof of past transgression,*
> *Dear, though unwelcome to be born.* . . .

Julia's own description of the adventure, as reported by Harriette, has none of the sentiment Brummell squeezes poetically from her heart and is interesting as showing the difficulty of lovers meeting in such a place as Hampton Court. Cotton first succeeded with her, Julia told Harriette, " ' on a stone staircase. . . . I can scarcely describe to you the difficulty,' " she added, " ' which existed in the palace of securing a *tête-à-tête:* with all joint inventions on the stretch, and all our hopes of happiness depending on it, we did not accomplish more than three private interviews in a month.' " Her bedroom was next to her mother's and her sister slept with her mother but " ' used my room as her dressing-room, wherein was deposited the whole of her wardrobe.' " " Suppose," said Cotton one day to me, " suppose I were to conceal myself under your bed ? " " But then my mamma always comes into my room before she sleeps, to kiss me, and wish me good-night." " I will wait patiently till all are retired to rest." " How will you endure to be under a bed for three or four hours ? " " What would I not endure ? " " But then this is my sister's dressing-room, and here she always undresses." " I will be silent as the grave," said Cotton. . . .

" ' Fancy him then,' Julia went on, ' safely concealed under my bed. Fancy myself and sister about to undress together. Fancy the contrast ! while I was studying my attitudes, as I folded my hair gracefully round my head, and bathed my hands and face with rose-water, just as might be expected by any woman who believed herself watched by an adoring, romantic lover; my sister was carelessly washing, splashing, and rattling, and talking to me of her sensations, her pimples, her wants, and her wishes, etc. I really thought I should have fainted with terror and dismay'. "

Although royalty had gone with its hordes of watchful servants, love was still a stealthy kiss on the stairs in Hampton Court, as it had been when Katherine Howard had stolen to Culpeper. The walls had grown old, had been torn down, rebuilt and patched, but those who lived within them acted no differently, it seems, from those who had lived there when the bricks were fresh-baked and the ceilings shone with paint and gilding: still lovers sneaked tiptoe to meet and hid under beds, as Elizabeth's maids had probably done—risking in her days not merely the exposure of their sin and consequent shame, but imprisonment. . . .

When Julia read Harriette's malicious indiscretions, quickly she seized her pen to answer in 1825, but she could scarcely deny, having abundent proof in progeny, that she had loved and been loved by the colonel. Her defence was to accuse his wife of having a bad temper and " repulsive manner " while she justified herself by arguing that the woman would not go to parties: naturally therefore she usurped her place at the theatre and dances, as well as in bed. " Fate thus," she cried like a novelist's heroine, " threw me into the arms of the

Lady
Morningtons
Garden

Junction of Wren • Tudor

Colonel, who was a very gallant man. He lived on the worst possible terms with his wife, and on that account saw but little company at home. At the early age of sixteen I fell a victim to my own inexperience, and the impassioned solicitations of a man, one of the handsomest and most accomplished of the age." Naturally she did not long remain at Hampton Court, for when she discovered herself to be in "a peculiar situation," the colonel set her up in a cottage near Primrose Hill.

Of other later inhabitants of the palace we cannot ignore the Countess of Mornington, mother of those mighty brothers, the Marquess Wellesley and the Duke of Wellington. To the palace would travel these great warriors to visit their old mother and they would chat with her in the little enclosed garden that is still known as Lady Mornington's Garden. But the chief memory of the Iron Duke in the palace is his having named the nook in the east front— on the right of the gate as you enter from the cloister into the garden— Purr Corner, because here the old ladies loved to sit snoozing or chattering in the sunlight.

Of royalty after George II, only William IV has any associations with the palace, for being Ranger of Bushey Park when Duke of Clarence, he was often here, making merry at sport and singing at dinners and, of course, drinking doughtily like a true British tar. He was president of the Toy Club which met in that now vanished tavern to drink and sing and play whist; and when king, often William would recall those days wistfully, declaring that no dinner now equalled the dinners he had eaten at the Toy, where marrow pudding had been his delight. After visiting the palace—which he nicknamed the Poor House because of the grace and favour residents—far into the night would he booze at the tavern with sailor oaths and sailor jollity.

But of greater importance than a king, Sir Walter Scott arrives to visit his son, Walter, now stationed at the Palace. On April 20th, 1828, Scott noted in his diary: "We went to Walter's quarters in a body, and saw Hampton Court, with which I was more struck than when I saw it for the first time about 1806. The pictures are not very excellent, but they are curious, which is as interesting to connoisseurs." On May 25th, he came again, this time with "the following lions and lionesses—Samuel Rogers, Tom Moore, Wordsworth, with wife and daughter." Of this visit, Tom Moore remarked in his journal: "On our arrival at Hampton (where we found the Wordsworths) walked about, the whole party in the gay walk, where the band plays, to the infinite delight of the Hampton blues, who were all *eyes* after Scott, the other scribblers not coming in for a glance."

That was a day I sigh to think of, to have walked in this palace, in those gardens, by the side of Sir Walter Scott, to have heard his great laughter, to have seen his endearing smile and to have listened to that voice which charmed all who heard discoursing on the antiquities, damning the pictures, and jesting with Tom Moore, while smug Wordsworth drooped his lower-lip in scorn of bluestockings who could be so short-sighted as to peep at Scott when he stalked by. For vanity was strong under Wordsworth's selfish guise of hermit, as Southey acutely noted when he wrote: " Wordsworth flourishes in London, he powders and goes with a cocked hat under his arm to all the great routs. No man is more flattered by the attentions of the great, and no man would be more offended to be told so." I can see him now with his sheep's head bleating after Scott who is shouting with glee at finding some detail of Wolsey's palace and laughing with Moore, while Wordsworth is probably calculating who will pay for dinner and why weren't the bluestockings ogling him instead of this noisy limping giant.

Not only the great but also unknown multitudes visited the palace after Queen Victoria opened it to the people. Up the river they came in launches and yachts with gaily coloured sails ; from the railway-station they crowded in merry mobs, or were rattled to the palace on coaches, in cabs or dog-carts or carriages. Moralists protested in newsprint and from pulpit at this continental Sabbath when people enjoyed themselves in the open, in the parks, in the palace, or dancing to the band. It was a hell upon earth, wailed the Rev. D. Wilson in *The Times*, November 5th, 1852, " the people come intoxicated, and the scenes in these gardens on the Lord's day are beyond description." From the fetters of work, from the terrible poverty in which most of them lived, Londoners, for one gay day, could remember that they were human and lovers could steal to Bushey and seek the shade on a grassy bed.

That professional humorist, Theodore Hook, on a murderously hot day in mid-July, when staggering through the crowds along the Chestnut Avenue in Bushey Park, threw up his arms and hurled himself to the dust. The kindly Cockneys tore a door from the gatekeeper's lodge and laid the stiff apparent corpse upon it, then gallantly carried the scoundrel, stopping now and then to rest, all the long way. " At length their wearisome pilgrimage came to an end. The iron gates leading to the Wilderness were reached, and, as the gardener in charge proceeded to open them, Hook slowly rolled himself off the improvised 'shutter,' and taking off his hat, thanked his bearers, and wished them a very good morning." The rascal would have been justifiably murdered had not someone recognised him and, such being his journalistic reputation, the people let him go unharmed.

On other days more noisy mobs were carried to Hampton Court, for there were races at Hurst Park, while Kempton and Sandown Parks are each roughly two miles from the palace. Writing in 1872, Blanchard Jerrold in his *London: A Pilgrimage*, that work so superbly illustrated by Gustave Doré, tells us how a " few carts loaded with holiday-makers travelling from the East End to Hampton Court races, or returning thence, afford a good illustration of the way in which the lower class of London work-folk love to amuse themselves. To them play means coarse jests, practical joking of a very brutal kind—all copiously covered with beer and tobacco. Observe this cartload of hawkers, who are fixed between an omnibus and a carriage. It is a golden opportunity, dear to the heart of the Whitechapel rough. He falls upon the gentleman who wears a white hat, and tells him to take care of the lady. He exhausts his humour upon the groom— criticising every item of his livery. Everybody is 'governor.' He calls upon each passer-by whom he detects with bottle or pocket pistol, to give him a drink; recommends every horseman to get up inside; asks a gentleman of particularly dignified air whether the 'missus' is quite well, and generally conducts himself with a levity, the spirit of which is closely akin to that of undergraduates on their great holiday. Now what should these poor, ignorant fellows do at the National Gallery, or poring over Mr. Layard's Assyrian stones ? Listen to their songs, and you will soon know what kind of people society has made them."

But others had not the sanity and tolerance of Jerrold. To them these poor devils were devils indeed and they looked with envious sorrow on the palace walls that people now should walk where kings and gentlemen, such as they thought themselves, alone were once privileged to walk.

Our history nears its close, for the records now are meagre, but we must not neglect the famous royal stud which, under George IV, was increased and improved, for a stud had existed here from, at the least, the time of Queen Anne. When Prince of Wales, George had been very fond of his Hampton Court horses in the paddocks on either side of the road dividing Bushey Park and the House or Home Park, and had bred riding horses of pure blood, attempting to breed them of a uniform grey. From these endeavours grew the royal stud, many of the horses being descendants of those brought by George I from Hanover.

We have now only to tell of a murder, a fire, and some bombs, and then these records must close.

The murder took place on Thursday, June 21st, 1838, when John Rickey, a private in the 12th Lancers, then quartered at Hampton Court, shot Sergeant Hamilton of the same regiment. It appears, from newspaper reports, to have been a meaningless affair, but anyone who has studied the histories of murderers knows that the impulse to kill springs often from some act, some gesture, so paltry that we ordinary folk refuse to accept it and persist in burrowing for subtler motives. What we do is to confuse act and motive, for the act itself can often be its own motive, sufficient in itself, an orgasm of the spirit as shattering when repressed as any other violent urge. There have been cases—there was one recently when a soldier slew a woman he had never seen before—that had no reason beyond the act, as in love. We do not often question why Henry loves Harriet, and often with no more reason should we inquire why Henry murders Harriet. Such things just happen, and many a wretched murderer has been hard put to it to find a convincing explanation for a crime that was but a sadistic impulse burgeoning suddenly from long germination in the unconscious. Very rarely does the motive satisfactorily explain a murder and often the most trivial thing, a snub, an imagined slight, so unimportant that a normal person would barely notice it, is sufficient to justify to the murderer his most bloody act.

So with this Hampton Court affair. Rickey returned drunk to the barracks from Hampton races and at about seven o'clock in the evening, being ordered under arrest, he seized a pair of loaded pistols and, running from the barracks, posted himself at the gate of the First Court. On being attacked here, he ran towards the apartments on the south side of the West Front and, standing in an angle of the passage, fired both pistols at his pursuers, hitting Sergeant Hamilton who lingered a few days before dying.

Surprisingly, Rickey was not hanged. Condemned at the Old Bailey on July 11th, he was later reprieved and his sentence commuted.

Of the two fires, the first in 1882 and the second in 1886, full accounts are given in contemporary newspapers and neither, I am glad to record, did serious damage. Mr. Law remarks that of the first fire " only three out of the thousand rooms which the Palace contains having been burnt; not more than five or six rooms touched by fire or smoke; not one two-thousandth part of the structure of the Palace destroyed, and no permanent injury whatever done to any work of art." About the second fire, Mr. Law is almost jubilant as he tells us that it " occurred in a portion of the Palace, of all others, where least mischief could have been done to anything of historical or archæological interest . . . it afforded an opportunity, which could not otherwise have occurred, of re-erecting the whole of the inside in a solid and substantial manner, and also of thoroughly restoring the Tudor aspect of this part of the Palace."

More threatening than fire were German bombers in the recent war. They cared naught for beauty; indeed, as we know too well, they hated it; and Hampton Court was not ignored while search-lights fumbled the sky, silvering the devils momentarily, and the bombs came down. But as with St. Paul's and the Tower, history, it seems, protected the palace and often the damage caused by firemen with that monster, that subtle destroyer, water, did more harm than the incendiaries which shuttled from the sky. Bombs fell in the Home Park, sliding over the palace, and their blast rattled and broke many windows. That was all.

Hampton Court which has stood through revolutions and once had its brief day as a fortress has survived. Reluctantly now I move from its walls, happy only in the thought that, when I wish, I can return; but here are the final words that I can write of it. And as a lover cannot move from his beloved but dangles her hand and grins and shuffles, unable to say good-bye, so do I sit before my typewriter, unable to write *finis*, for there are so many other things I wished to say, so many beauties I have not had the space to examine. Were I to express my love in full, twenty volumes, at least, would be required, for there is no palace which means so much to me as this. Under the archway you walk into the past and it is not difficult to feel King Henry close or to hear in the echoes down the galleries the laughter of ladies, Charles's or Caroline's; Nell Gwyn or Molly Lepell, hand in hand, sisters in the past, are waiting here to greet you. No record can recreate history as a building can, no words have the reality of stone and brick. Therefore, I ask you when next you visit the palace do not gape at it as though it were a museum, do not scamper through it as though it were just any house, but pause and listen—if in these modern days people have time to pause—and you will sense, as nowhere else, the living ghosts around you, almost physically near, so that you feel that, should you suddenly move, you will catch sight of Anne Boleyn or Queen Caroline before she fades in beauty through the wall.

APPENDIX I
OF THE GHOSTS IN HAMPTON COURT

WE tread on dangerous ground, we pass into a world where suddenly a shadowed corner takes on form and an ebon ghost steps out, where sunlight is moulded to human shape and where pale faces press against the window-pane, where shrieks are heard in empty rooms and hands appear from arras only to fade while you watch. . . . Already I have stated my belief in ghosts, not as living creatures but as projections from the past, a trick of time snapped by the lens of light. It is therefore with reluctance I confess that I can accept none of the ghosts in Hampton Court; but in this excursus, that you may decide yourself, I give all the evidence I have been able to collect on both sides, for and against; and I must thank the editors of the *Sunday Times* and the *Surrey Comet* for opening their columns to me and sending on the many letters they received.

These letters are too many to quote and mostly they repeat one another, but a few correspondents proved of great value. Particularly I mention Miss Evelyn Hutchinson who, having been born in the palace and still resident there, has a knowledge of the subject beyond that of any outsider. Again, too, I must thank Mr. Gordon Roe for his help, and the editor of the *Connoisseur* for being allowed to quote from his article. The two others to whom I owe the deepest debt are Mrs. Catherine M. Tucker and Field-Marshal the Earl of Birdwood who to-day resides in the alleged haunted chamber. For full " evidence " of Mrs. Penn I refer the reader to Mr. Law's book and Mr. Roe's article.

There has long been doubt about these ghosts and I have been assured, on good authority, that Mr. Law himself was more than suspicious of them, while Mr. Yates, in his excellent book on the palace, writes most sceptically that " in recent years a venerable resident was asked if she had seen a ghost or heard screams in the gallery and her reply was that she had heard the screams and seen—the tradesmen's boy responsible for them."

Amongst the numerous letters I received on this question there were, unfortunately, none with evidence that could stand any scientific test, none authentic enough, I fear, to tempt the curiosity of Mr. Harry Price, for not one of the correspondents could swear to having seen a ghost. Lady Joan Kennedy, for example, was kind enought to inform me that her relative, the late Lady Georgina Peel, had apartments at the palace and had seen Anne Boleyn " with her head under her arms at times. The apparition was seen round the gallery." But Lady Joan herself did not see it and to-day, and rightly so, the ghost hunter must be a combination of scientist and magistrate. He must sift evidence and, however regretfully, suspect any that is unsupported by more than one unbiased witness.

Hearsay evidence is ruled out and, therefore, much as I would like to accept it as authentic, we must discard such a statement as the following from Miss Lilian D. Irwin, published in the *Sunday Times* on May 27th, 1945: " I have often heard my late father describe how he saw a female form in curious old-world dress walking in the grounds at Hampton Court. He remarked to his companion about her odd appearance and was amazed that his friend saw no one and could not understand what my father was talking about. This occurred at noon, and during lunch my father asked the waiter, who replied that it would be Katherine Howard he had seen as she had been ' walking a good deal lately.' A man at an adjacent table overheard the talk and related that he was an artist working in one of the galleries, and on several occasions a hand had come between him and his work. On this hand was a remarkable ring, of which he had made a drawing, and identified it with a ring known to have been worn by Katherine."

This has the authentic frightening touch of a Montague James' story: the hand coming between the artist and his sketch, as if a vain woman would display her ring. But the artist remains anonymous, he did not come forward to verify the tale, and therefore we must discard it. Besides, Miss Hutchinson writes to say that she remembers this incident " of the artist who saw a hand (no mention then of a ring) waving near some tapestry in the Great Watching Chamber. He either did not know or failed to mention that that tapestry concealed a door leading to a room where the warders on duty kept their uniforms, etc. The hand was probably one of theirs rearranging the tapestry after closing the door unobserved by the artist; or if there really were a ring it was the work perhaps of a practical joker—I have never heard of any ghosts seen in the Palace or Gardens by day, except the above story. Among the many visitors it would be difficult to identify anyone, however oddly dressed. There are several entrances into private apartments and doors unopened to the public through which a resident could 'disappear.' When I was young the ghosts were considered rather a joke and noises were called 'rats' and shrieks 'cats'."

Although Miss Hutchinson has heard of no ghosts at the palace being seen by day, that is no unusual time for them to appear; as Mr. de la Mare has noted, they can walk at noon as well as midnight, although dusk seems to be their favourite hour, the light being then diffused and able to cheat one with trickeries of shadow. Fear of darkness, that old primitive terror, usually populates the night with spectres and sees them moulded by the moon, but they will walk at any time, and poltergeists will rap on your walls at breakfast as defiantly as they will at supper. The poltergeist, however, is not a ghost, is not an emanation of the once living, but seems rather an unconscious act of creation, as though an artist painted with sound on air instead of with colour on canvas, for they are, most probably, projections from ourselves. But these airy ghosts, trapped so rarely in atmospheric prisms, are glimpsed as if from the corners of a mental eye and are often lost as quickly as they are seen, for their vanishing is your own doing, caused by some movement, even a blink.

Many have been the attempted explanations of ghosts, and one of the most interesting, and most probable, was given by Mr. Chapman Pincher in the *Daily Express* for January 4th, 1946. He argued that they are visual projections. " Suppose," he wrote, " that the one-way valves in the optic nerve fibres suddenly became inefficient in preventing the forward surge of nervous impulses back to the retina. It would then be possible to think up a picture and transmit it forwards. In the retina (since all chemical actions are reversible) these impulses would become an image of the thought picture. And the backward surge, taking this image to the brain again, would produce a picture as vivid and 'real' as would an image formed on the retina in the normal way. This is the important point to grasp. *An image produced on the retina by this reverse process would seem as real as any object seen by the eye.*" This is a most convincing theory and well worth discussion, if I could spare the space, particularly as no less an authority than Mr. Harry Price endorses it; but we must not wander too far from our palace.

Because she does deal with our palace I feel safer, therefore, in quoting from that delightful book of anecdotes *Life's Mosaic*.

Memories: Canny and Uncanny by A. M. W. Stirling, where she also has her theory to explain these tantalising phenomena. " As is well known," she writes, " the haunted gallery at Hampton Court is said still to echo with the shrieks of the unhappy Katherine Howard as she raved in her despair on the occasion when she tried to reach Henry VIII and was dragged back by her jailors. A friend of mine asked a lady who had rooms in the Palace if she or her daughter had ever heard the sounds alleged, and the reply was that they personally had never heard anything, but that numbers of people said they had, and swore also that they could distinguish not only the voice of the unhappy woman but the actual words she uttered.

" My friend was relating this to an Indian once and he gave her his explanation of the phenomenon. ' There are certain places,' he said, ' which retain sound like the music shut up in a record, or the murmur of the sea in a shell. It is as though the voice of the speaker were corked up in a bottle, and it depends on the construction of the bottle whether this is retained or dissipated . . . Moreover, it can only be reproduced under certain atmospheric conditions. We have a building in India which is just the same. When the wind is in a certain quarter the voices of long-dead inhabitants are reproduced. So it is at Hampton Court. You will find that it is only when the wind is in a certain quarter that the sounds are heard, and the actual voice of the unhappy lady reproduced. If the authorities ever tamper with the conditions of that gallery, the record will be lost for ever.'

" Now the gallery has been opened to the public, and in the words of the Indian, the ' bottle has been uncorked ' so that the sounds may be heard no more. The theory is at least suggestive ! "

Of greater interest than this discussion about poor Kate's screaming is Mrs. Stirling's details about another and, this time, more authentic ghost given in the same valuable book. It is, I feel, legitimate for us to leave the palace walls for a stroll over the green, as we have visited this house before. Mrs. Stirling writes : " Mr. Norman Lamplugh and his sister own the beautiful Old Court House at Hampton Court, built by, and once the home of, Sir Christopher Wren, who died in the dining-room there. In this house and the pretty garden reaching to the water's edge, the present owners give parties to which all London flocks; and it was on the occasion of one of these parties, given on a Friday in June, 1929, that the following incident occurred.

" About 3-30, when the house was at its fullest, Mr. Norman Lamplugh's brother and a friend, standing on the landing, suddenly noticed among the crowd of guests a small boy about eight years of age, with a pretty face and long, fair hair, making his way through the crush. The boy arrested the attention of both men for two reasons; first, because no children had been invited to the party, and secondly, because he was wearing what they thought to be fancy dress. He was clad in the costume of a page of the period of Charles II, and his clothes were all black-and-white; his breeches and doublet were of black velvet, a short black-and-white cape hung from his shoulders, he had white silk stockings and black shoes with large silver buckles. The boy, indeed, passed so close to the two men that they had to step back to make way for him; but he took no notice of them and walked on. Outside the drawing-room door Miss Lamplugh espied him, and likewise felt considerable astonishment, as, apart from the fact that no children had been invited, she naturally could not understand why any child should come to a garden party dressed in this strange old-world costume. Again, however, the boy took no notice of her nor of any of the guests, but made his way with considerable speed upstairs to the top floor, and was never seen again.

" Afterwards, comparing notes about their strange visitor, Mr. Lamplugh and his sister realised that there had been something inexplicable about the occurrence. They therefore questioned the servants closely, and ascertained beyond a doubt that no child answering to their description had ever entered the house, and none had been seen to leave it. They next made exhaustive inquiries from a number of the guests who had been present, but none had brought a child with them, and certainly not a child so strangely dressed. Moreover, the boy had been seen to go up to the top floor whence there was no exit, save by returning the way he went, which he had obviously never done, but the very peculiarity of his clothes made it impossible for him to pass unnoticed. In short, the mystery could not be explained.

" A sequel to the story is that the man, Mr. Lamplugh's friend, who first saw the supposed apparition, died less than six months later. He had always been passionately fond of children, had loved to surround himself with them, and had a great attraction for them; so that it was suggested that this ghostly boy, clad in mourning, had come as a warning of his decease. Such a conclusion, however, is most fantastic; but the facts which are indisputable are that this strange visitant appeared suddenly in the midst of the guests at the party, and disappeared as suddenly, that he was seen by three people separately, who all took special notice of him on account of the peculiarity of his clothes, and that for the same reason it was impossible for him to have entered or left the house without attracting attention; finally, that no explanation of his presence was ever forthcoming.

" The house where this occurred is not haunted, but on the anniversary of the night in February upon which Sir Christopher Wren died, the sound of footsteps hurrying to and fro upon the stairs can be heard, and there seems an air of suppressed commotion throughout the beautiful building."

Naturally, on reading the above, I wrote to Mr. Lamplugh and he kindly gave me all further information he could. To my regret, for I had hoped to be able to explore the house, he no longer lives at Hampton Court and it was in his Kensington home that we met and there, over a glass of sherry, I heard again the details, with unimportant corrections, as given by Mrs. Stirling. That there was any association between the " visitor " and the death of his friend, a painter, and his brother, who died of an attack of angina shortly afterwards, he could not accept, although it is curious to note that his sister was afterwards ill for two years. Such are plainly coincidences. Of other experiences he had little to tell, except once hearing a man's footsteps in the gallery room opening on to the staircase, only, on opening the door, to find no one there.

If this ghost be authentic—and there is certainly no reason to doubt the good faith of those who vouch for it—Mr. Pincher's theory fails. But his is a theory I will not willingly surrender, although I confess to being unable to explain this boy out of the past, seen by three different people, walking in his seventeenth-century garments through a gathering of modern folk.

But to return to Hampton Court. The stoutest defender I have met of the ghosts there is Mrs. Tucker. She tells how, when she was resident there, her servants left her on one occasion because they had seen a " tall lady, dressed all in black, with a long train and a shining light on her face, come through the queen's gate, but the doors neither opened nor shut after her. She held a taper in her hand and seemed to glide down the stairs.

" One night," she writes, " I woke suddenly, feeling that someone was in the room with me, that someone was bending over me. The pillow was pulled from under my head and the mattress seemed pressed down. I was too frightened to light a candle by my bedside: it was quite dark. I could not account for it in any way. My apartment was situated near the Haunted Gallery and I have distinctly heard loud screams at dead of night which are supposed to be uttered by the ghost of Queen Katherine Howard, whose restless spirit still haunts the Long Gallery. A tall figure [Kate was tiny], dressed all in white, has been seen going towards the royal pew and, on approaching the door, has rushed hastily back again, her garments disordered and a look of utter misery and despair on her face as she utters a succession of unearthly shrieks till she passes through a doorway to the queen's staircase. These shrieks are constantly heard to this day, especially when there is no moon, and in the autumn [Katherine was indicted in November] when these shades appear to be particularly restless.

" The great gates of the palace were ordered to be closed and secured at midnight; after that, no one could go in or out. When the resident ladies went to any evening social event at Surbiton, they had to walk back through the great park and would sometimes ask the door-keeper to delay closing up for a short time. One cold clear night with some moonlight, the door-keeper was looking out down the Broad Walk and thought: Here come my ladies. Six figures, three ladies and three gentlemen, were approaching and he said that the ladies were in evening dress, the dresses cut low at the neck, as in Tudor times. They were gesticulating in an excited manner but there was no sound. They advanced closer, then turned to the right and went through the gate by the side of the palace. The gate-keeper followed them and looked through the gate. They were standing in the old Dutch Garden, still gesticulating, when suddenly they vanished. The man said he had felt no terror until then, but at that moment he grew terrified. This is exactly as he told it.

" The Haunted Gallery was only opened about twenty-seven years ago and was in a terrible state, having been used only for lumber. The residents in the nearest rooms were frequently disturbed by a loud scream. The old stones of the quadrangle had to be taken up once for repairs and just outside the ladies' private gate the workmen found two bodies of men in soldier's dress of Cromwell's time. It was thought they were surprised by royalist men and killed and buried secretly."

Mr. Law mentions this discovery of the skeletons in the Fountain Court and tells of the argument about their identity; but who they were was never decided.

While giving the ghosts' defence it might be as well to quote here from Henry Ripley's *History and Topography of Hampton-on-Thames*, 1885, to which Miss Audrey Cozen kindly drew my attention.

After the removal of Mistress Penn's monument, he tells us that "the Rev. Merewether, curate of Hampton, together with one of the churchwardens, arranged to have a private investigation of the contents of the receptacle beneath, to effect which the foreman of the works and a trustworthy workman were ordered to be in readiness on a certain night at eleven o'clock. An hour or so before the time appointed, the two latter proceeded to the church to get everything in readiness, lit a lantern and marched through the rood screen into the chancel. On getting near the tomb, which they were about to desecrate, they were staggered to hear low moaning sobs proceeding from its vicinity. They gaped, their knees trembled, the lantern dropped from the hands of the foreman and was extinguished and then, to their horror, they saw that a strange unearthly glow was diffused over the monument, and that the previously recumbent effigy of Mistress Penn had left the position it had retained for two hundred and sixty-eight years, and was sitting up, with hands over its eyes, sobbing piteously.

" This settled matters, they rushed from the church in great agitation, and although they met their employers at the church gate, nothing could induce either of them to return, or in any way assist in the molestation of the tomb. There had been great local prejudice against the contemplated removal of this tomb, it having been in the past always regarded with a sort of superstitious reverence; in fact, local tradition foretold decay and misfortune to the village in the event of the contents ever being molested. Popular rumour asserted that, undaunted by their first failure, Dr. Merewether and his colleague made another and more successful attempt, that they really found a coffin and removed it to the crypt under the church; that they then reclosed the vault, which, when it was opened by the workmen in due course, was declared to have been found empty. In Catacomb No. 14 is a portion of an old leaden coffin, which Mr. F. J. Kent, senior, informs us was generally believed to have once held the body of Mistress Penn. If so she was buried in a woollen shroud, remnants still remaining."

Again, all is hearsay, rumour, country gossip, and most unconvincing. Mr. Gordon Roe has dealt so thoroughly in his already mentioned article about Mistress Penn's ghost that there is little for me to add. Mr. Roe, however, suggests that as the tale coincides with the gothick revival, the truth of it may be found in the romantic aspirations of those determined to have a ghost and to make of Hampton Court a Castle of Otranto. It is certainly a fascinating and probable theory, for there seems to be no real authority for the tale, while the sketch of the spirit which Mr. Law reproduces in his work is so plainly a drawing of Mistress Penn's monumental effigy that I am surprised he troubled to print it.

Of the spinning-wheel and Mistress Penn's busy ghost, Miss Hutchinson writes most plausibly that " this wheel was really found years afterwards in a small room till then unknown, having a window overgrown with ivy, the draught through which in certain winds caused the wheel to revolve, making a queer whirling noise." This apartment is now occupied by Field-Marshal Lord Birdwood, and perhaps a soldier's courage has scared the creature away, for he tells me that " alas ! although some of my family have anxiously looked out for Mrs. Penn she has so far refused to appear."

Further valuable information comes from Miss Hutchinson that Mr. Law's " allusion to a recent arrival seeing Mrs. Penn's ghost was the late Princess Frederica of Hanover who, with her husband, Baron von Powel Rammingen occupied the rooms from 1880 till she resigned them about 1897. Her baby was born in March, 1881. The story I remember was that H.R.H. went into the nursery and saw an old woman leaning over the child's cradle, instead of the usual nurse. Annoyed at the nurse allowing, as she supposed, a stranger in the nursery, H.R.H. questioned her only to discover that no one had been admitted. Another version of this tale is that the nurse, not H.R.H., discovered the old woman and reported it to the baron. Whenever he afterwards alluded to the incident, he would say: ' No doubt the good woman had had beer with her supper ! ' Personally, I rather prefer the first version and that it was in fact a friend of the nurse taking a look at the baby who, surprised by the princess's arrival, ' vanished ' as quickly as possible. The infant died soon afterwards being, it would appear, unable to survive visits from, firstly, Mrs. Penn, and a few days afterwards, Queen Victoria.

" The tale of the sentry's alarm I remember—although not the date or his regiment. It happened before the moat was reopened.

He walked up and down on flat ground which, in Mrs. Penn's time, had been a moat, although not filled with water. The really rather curious thing is that when the moat was restored, an old staircase was discovered in the turret close to where the sentry had stood which led into the moat. This might account for his story of a phantom walking into the wall, should it be true and not again the result of beer.

" The late Lady Maude when she first came to the ' haunted ' apartments scorned the idea of ghosts, but later she told me that she had felt strange cold draughts in the ante-room, and a visitor had seen something—unfortunately she did not say what. I have never heard of any ghosts being heard or seen in the Wren part of the Palace. There was a lot of trouble some years ago with death-watch beetles in the Tudor beams and I wonder if the dangerously rotting wood caused many of the creakings and strange noises said to have been heard at times. The residents rather discourage any talk on the subject as, even before the present shortage of servants, it was difficult to get maids to ' live in'. "

Mr. Law recounts the story of Lady Hildyard—although he does not give her name—who was so disturbed by rappings that she called on the lord chamberlain for help. Of these alleged hauntings Miss Hutchinson writes : " From the discovery and removal of the skeletons [of Cromwellian soldiers, already referred to] the lady was no longer troubled till her death in 1878. Those apartments were then occupied till 1906 by Mrs. Goodenough who never complained of any disturbances; from that date till 1913 by Mrs. Burges Watson, widow of my mother's brother, and she never, I know, saw or heard anything strange or unaccountable. In 1914 the late Mrs. Fegan was granted these rooms and from time to time strange things happened. She was a catholic and got a priest to exorcise the ghost, which she herself assured me was successful. Since her death in 1940 the apartment has been vacant."

All the tales, so lovingly repeated with a shiver, of ghosts fade when we dig for facts. It is always somebody else who has seen them, felt them, apart from Mrs. Tucker's evidence. The hunt has been a disappointment. The ghosts in Hampton Court, it seems to me, are those one conjures for oneself when one walks the galleries and peers into little chambers. Then one can vividly imagine the cardinal, the kings and queens, the courtiers and royal mistresses and ladies in waiting. There is no need for them to step from a past of shadows to

take on solidity. Indeed, that would most likely bring disillusion-
ment, for reality can rarely reckon up to imagination and we might find
our cardinal a blotch-faced ordinary fellow and even King Henry
merely a small-eyed bully with a squeaky voice. Therefore am I glad
that the ghosts have never been seen—or rather, that they have not
been proved to have materialised—for I would prefer to people the
palace from my own mind with the splendid men and lovely ladies
that once lived there and who, I am certain, were all beautiful, all
vital, although alas ! now all dead.

APPENDIX II
ON KENT'S DESIGN OF "HAMPTON COURT"

This is an imaginary landscape illustrating part of the course of the River Mole and its confluence with the Thames at Hampton Court. To the left, at a little distance, a more or less fanciful version of the gate-house and banqueting hall of Hampton Court Palace. From it, a wide road stretching across the foreground, where, in the centre, a lady and gentleman are seen engaged in conversation. To the right the Thames on which rides Neptune in a chariot drawn by sea-horses preceded by Tritons and Nereids. On the opposite bank of the river, a partly wooded hill surmounted by a domed temple. At the foot of the hill, right, the River Mole which flows into the Thames at this point.

In the distance, Esher Place.

Pen and Sepia Wash, 7⅛in. × 12¼in. Ref. 1927—7—21—5.

Inscribed with verses from Michael Drayton's *Polyolbion* Song XVII.

Hampton Court. He meets the soft and Gentle Mole. (1. 26).
Homesdale raised hills. (1. 56).
Mole digs her self a path. (1. 59).
Tames understood what pains the Mole did take. (1. 65).

The Ocean doth return, and thrusteth in the Tide up tow'ards the place, where first his much lov'd Mole was seen He ever since doth flow, beyond delightful Sheen.

Esher Place, which included the gate tower of Wolsey's former palace on the banks of the Mole, was purchased by the Rt. Hon. Henry Pelham in 1729. He converted the gate tower into a dwelling-house by the addition of wings after Kent's designs in the Gothic taste (which were the subject of severe criticism from Horace Walpole), and improved the grounds also under Kent's direction. The temple on the hill has not been identified. It may be intended for a building in the grounds of Esher Place or perhaps in those of the neighbouring Claremont, which were also laid out by Kent for Pelham's elder brother, Thomas Pelham Holles, first Duke of Newcastle. Another possible suggestion for it is Pain's Hill, also on the Mole, an early example of landscape gardening which, however, is not specifically recorded as being Kent's work.

Reproduced by courtesy of the Trustees of the British Museum.

BIBLIOGRAPHY

When I began compiling this book I kept a careful note of almost every work consulted, but the list became absurdly bulky and might have served for a history of the kings of England from Henry VIII to George II. After all, this is a history of the palace written, not for experts, but for the ordinary reader; therefore I grew ashamed of my huge bibliography and eventually discarded it, deciding to refer in the text or in footnotes to modern works quoted—contemporary ones I fear the reader must take on trust, for the footnotes are numerous enough as it is—and to list here only books I found of value, whether for text or illustrations, dealing with the palace itself.

An Inventory of the Historical Monuments in Middlesex. Report of the Royal Commission on Historical Monuments, England (H.M. Stationery Office), 1937.

Archæologia. See Peers, C. R.

Chettle, G. H. *Hampton Court Palace* (H.M. Office of Works), 1943.

Cole, Sir Henry. *A Hand-Book to Hampton Court* (Bell & Sons), 1884.

Connoisseur, The. See Roe, F. Gordon.

Fletcher, Major Benton. *Royal Homes Near London* (John Lane), 1930.

Jesse, Edward. *A Summer's Day at Hampton Court* (John Murray), 1841.

Law, Ernest. *The History of Hampton Court Palace* (George Bell and Sons), 1885–91.
> Mr. Law also wrote many small books on the palace, but as these were either absorbed into the above three volumes or were chapters taken from them, I have thought it best to ignore them.

Peers, C. R. *On the Stone Bridge at Hampton Court. Archæologia*, 2nd series, Vol. XII (Society of Antiquaries), 1910.

Pyne, W. H. *History of the Royal Residences*, 1899.

Ripley, Henry. *History and Topography of Hampton-on-Thames* (Wyman & Son), 1884.

Roe, F. Gordon. *Portrait of a Ghost: Mrs. Penn, Edward VI's Foster Mother. The Connoisseur.* Vol. CXII, December, 1943.

Wren Society, The. Vol. IV. *Hampton Court Palace*, 1689–1702 (Oxford University Press), 1927.

Yates, Edward. *Hampton Court* (Duckworth), 1935.